VOLUME 2: WHISKEY, DRUGGIST, MEDICINES

THE
BOTTLES
BREWERIANA
AND
ADVERTISING JUGS
OF
MINNESOTA
1850-1920

A COMPANION PRICE GUIDE IS AVAILABLE --- COPIES OF VOLUME 1:
BEER, SODA, HOUSEHOLD ARE STILL AVAILABLE

BY

RON FELDHAUS

AND THE MEMBERS OF

MINNESOTA'S FIRST ANTIQUE BOTTLE CLUB

AND

NORTH STAR HISTORICAL BOTTLE ASSOCIATION

ORDER
ADDITIONAL COPIES FROM
RON FELDHAUS
6724 XERXES AVE S
EDINA, MINN 55423

ISBN 0-9617664-3-3 (HARDCOVER)

ISBN 0-9617664-4-1 (SOFTCOVER)

CONTENTS

INTRODUCTION

Back in 1975, at the November meeting of the Minnesota's 1st Antique Bottle Club, a club member made the innocent suggestion, "Why don't we publish a book about Minneapolis and St. Paul bottles?" A lively discussion followed as to the feasibility of such a project. Would the book be hardbound, softbound, or simply mimeographed pages stapled together? Would the book feature only rare bottles, or all hand finished bottles, or all bottles including machine made and silk screened bottles? Opinion was divided over whether or not the project would be a short easy project or if it was an overly ambitious project. Discussion was tabled until the next meeting where it was agreed to proceed with the project and start by accumulating rubbings and research material. Doug Shilson and other members of the North Star Historical Bottle Association had also long dreamed of such a book. They too had been doing research for years. Therefore, the North Star Club quickly threw it's support behind the project. The project expanded to include dating lists for all breweries and bottling companies in Minnesota, as well as photographs of outstanding Minnesota bottles and photographs of related collectibles and breweriana. Finally, after ten years, thousands of hours researching, writing, and drawing, a couple of hundred afternoons spent at the Minneapolis Public Library and Minnesota Historical Society staring at city directories and newspaper microfilms until back muscles cramped up like pretzels and bloodshot eyeballs resembled the results of a three day binge photographing trips to collectors homes all the way from Burnsville to Silver Bay, Volume 1 of Minnesota Bottles was finished. Now a year later Volume 2 is finished. These two books are the results of the efforts of at least two dozen members of the bottle clubs, and they can truly be proud.

RESEARCH BACKGROUND

Research for the book started in 1967, when the first Minnesota's 1st ABC newsletter research article was written. Articles from eighteen years of club newsletters, by both clubs, provided many of the stories in this book. Because these stories were originally only intended to be light reading, and because the research was conducted with less than scientific methods, it is probable that mistakes have been made. For these mistakes we apologize. These newsletter stories also suffered from a lack of footnoting and liberal doses of plagiarism. It is now impossible to go back and add footnoting and give due credit to copied material. For this we also apologize. It was never our intention to cheat anyone of the credit they deserved.

Resources included:

1. The city directories for Minneapolis, St. Paul and Minnesota from 1857-1910. Unfortunately, dating information obtained from the directories is suspect because it is not known if a company name was no longer listed because the company went out of business or simply stopped paying to have their name included in the directory.

2. Microfilms of Minneapolis and St. Paul newspapers on file at the Minneapolis Public Library and Minnesota Historical Society.

3. Books about Minnesota history at the Minneapolis Public Library and the Minnesota Historical Society.

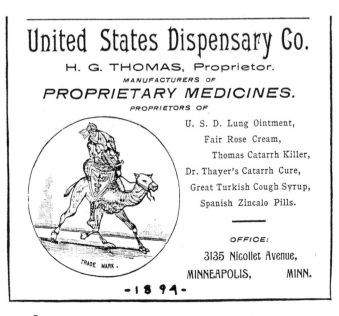

HOW TO USE THIS BOOK

Information in this book is intended to aid the bottle collector in dating his Minnesota bottles. Also included are stories and biographical material about the companies behind these bottles. The following material will be found in this book:

1. Dating Guides: The dating guides list all the known addresses for a company and years during which a company was at an address between 1856 and 1910. 1910 was picked as a cut-off date because after that date most bottles were machine made. Many companies listed as being in business in 1910 continued on for years afterwards.

2. Photographs: The book includes photographs of hundreds of bottle related collectables such as shot glasses, beer glasses, signs, trays, trade cards and liquor jugs. Also included are pictures of breweries and bottling companies and of rare bottles.

3. Bottle Embossings: The book includes drawings of the embossing of every known Minneapolis and St. Paul bottle (excluding machine made bottles). In addition to the drawings, all variations in size, color, or glass manufacturer are listed. A coding system gives information about the bottle which displays the embossing shown. The following are examples of how this coding system works:

Example:
825. BROWN, J.F.
825A . Style F5Q, clear; half pint, pint
825A2. Style F5C; clear; half pint, pint
825B.. Picnic flask with spiderweb pattern - style K8K; clear; half pint

825 Each company listed in the book has been given a number, for example, J. F. Brown is #825. When a company's status changed such as by adding "and Son" or "and Company" the resultant company has been treated as a new company and was assigned a new number.

825A This code number identifies the first variant of bottles displaying the embossing identified as "825A." Variations in color, style, or glass manufacture but with the identical embossing will have numbers "825A2", "825A3", etc. For a variation in the embossing the number "825B " is assigned to the bottle.

Style F5Q This code identifies the bottle's closure or shape as illustrated by the shape identification guide at the beginning of each section of the book. In the druggist sections, the double asterisk (i.e. "A **") indicates a clear bottle in one of the many common druggist bottle styles.

Clear This code identifies the color of the bottle's glass.

825 Each company listed in the book has been given a number, for example, J. F. Brown is #825. When a company's status changed such as by adding "and Son" or "and Company" the resultant company has been treated as a new company and was assigned a new number.

825A This code number identifies the first variant of bottles displaying the embossing identified as "825A." Variations in color, style, or glass manufacture but with the identical embossing will have numbers "825A2", "825A3", etc. For a variation in the embossing the number "825B " is assigned to the bottle.

Style F5Q This code identifies the bottle's closure or shape as illustrated by the shape identification guide at the beginning of each section of the book. In the druggist sections, the double asterisk (i.e. "A **") indicates a clear bottle in one of the many common druggist bottle styles.

Clear This code identifies the color of the bottle's glass.

Half pint, pint This code identifies the various sizes in which the bottle is known to exist. Rectangular shaped bottles are specified by height (H), length (L), and width (W).

SB & G Co. This code identifies the company that manufactured the bottle. In this case, Streator Bottle & Glass Co., as indicated by initials on the base or the side of the bottle. The following is a listing of the company initials used, the companies they represent, and the year the glass companies were in business.

A B Co. -	American Bottle Co., Chicago, ILL. 1905-1916; Toledo, Ohio 1916-1929.
A&DHC -	Alexander & David H. Chambers, Pittsburg, Pa. 1843-1886.
BFG Co. -	Maker unknown.
C.B. Co. -	Maker unknown.
C.C.G. Co. -	Cream City Glass Co., Milwaukee, Wis. 1888-1894.
C.&Co.Lim. -	Cunningham & Co., Pittsburgh, Pa. 1879-1907.
C.G. Co. -	Crystal Glass Co., Pittsburgh, Pa. 1868-1882; Bridgeport, Ohio 1882-1907.

C.&.I. - Cunningham & Ihmsen, Pittsburgh, Pa., 1865-1879.

C.V.G. Co. - Chase Valley Glass Co., Milwaukee, Wis. 1880-1881.

C.V. No. 1 Same as above. The No. 1 stands for the furnace in which the glass was made. Chase Valley had two furnaces.

C.V. No. 2 - Same as above. The No. 2 tells the bottle was made at the second furnace.

D.F.&D. - Manufacturer unknown. Possibly Dean, Foster & Co. 1870's-1890's.

D.O.C. - D.O. Cunningham Glass Co., Pittsburgh, Pa. 1882-1937

D.S.G. Co. - De Steiger Glass Co., La Salle, Ill. 1879-1896.

Karl Hutter - Karl Hutter of New York, purchased the patent for the Lightning Stopper about 1878 and invented the porcelain stopper in 1893.

I.G. Co. Illinois Glass Co., Alton, Ill. 1873-1929; or in a few cases Ihmsen Glass Co., Pittsburgh, 1870-1895.

McC.- Wm. McCully & Co., Pittsburgh, Pa. 1841-1886.

N.B.B.G. - North Baltimore Glass Co., North Baltimore, Ohio, 1885-1895; Albany, Ind., 1895-1904; Terre Haute, Inc., 1900-1930.

N.B.G. - Maker unknown.

O.B.C.- Ohio Bottle Co., Newark, Ohio 1904-1905.

Root - Root Glass Co., Terre Haute, Ind. 1901-1932.

S.B.&G. Co. - Streator Bottle & Glass Co., Streator, Ill. 1881-1905.

W.F.&S. - William Franzen & Son, Milwaukee, Wis. 1895-1926.

Wis. Glass Co. - Wisconsin Glass Co., Milwaukee, Wis. 1881-1886.

Footnote:

The Minneapolis business directories listed the following two companies as bottle manufacturers:

MINNEAPOLIS BOTTLE MFG. CO.	
24th & Corner 34 Ave. So.	1886
27th between 28th & 29th. Ave.	1887
MINNEAPOLIS GLASS CO.	
Fort Ave. between 35th & 36th	1886-1889

Bottle Makers and Their Marks by Julian Toulouse talks briefly about these companies. He says that in the September 1886 National Bottlers Gazette the Minneapolis Bottle Mfg. Co. advertised "green, amber and blue bottles, flasks, fruit jars and packers, with beer bottles 'a specialty'." They also made Apollinaris bottles in 'German green'.

Bottle collectors will probably have a hard time proving that a bottle was made by either of these companies. Possibly they may be embossed with the initials MMBC or MGC on the base.

ACKNOWLEDGMENTS

This book is the result of many people working long hard hours. They all deserve a hearty "Thank You." However, I would like to single out a few people for special thanks. First, my wife Vernie, my children, and the spouses and families of all the researchers for their understanding and patience when we abandoned them for hundreds of evenings and weekends to work on the book. Second, Fred Wolter who spent hundreds of hours preparing over half of the drawings in this book, and Ron Feldhaus for preparing the remaining drawings. Third, Bill Travers for collecting the drawings of the St. Paul druggists and researching the St. Paul druggists listings. Fourth, Linda Glass for typing the text and Steve Ketcham for editing the text. Fifth, Doug Shilson, Ron Baker, and Paul Neuburger for their layout work. Sixth, Wayne Laswell for preparing the index. And, finally, all of the following researchers for their biographical material as noted and for the fellow collectors who allowed us to photograph their collections.

BOYDE BECCUE
    Alfred Andresen
    Chas Cirkler
    Minnesota's 10 Best Bottles
    Dr Ward's Liniment Story

JIM CARLSON
    J.L. Linker
    Sam Alexander

EARL DEAN
    Jordan Brewery

JEAN DONOVAN
    D.A. Edwards
    W.L. Perkins
    Dr. Partridge P.Q. Medicines

BEV EHRNREITER
    Dr. Partridge P.Q. Medicines
    W.L. Perkins

RON FELDHAUS
    Minneapolis Saloon & Liquor Dealers Listing
    C.H.A. Richter
    Minneapolis Druggist Listing
    Issac Weil
    J.R. Watkins
    Nicollet Drug Store
    Nicollet House Drug Store
    Jonas F. Brown
    Minneapolis Bottle Manufacturers
    All of Photography in Book
    Guide to Minnesota Bitters
    Whiskey Bottle Shape Identification Guide
    Patent Medicine Bottle Shape Indent. Guide

VERNIE FELDHAUS
    T.K. Gray
    J.O. Peterson
    J.C. Oswald

JIM HAASE
    Dr. Gregory's

J & E ANTIQUES
    Photographs of Collection

STEVE KETCHAM
    Photographs of Collection
    J.M. Davis
    B. Heller

JOHN & KENDRA LOUKS
    Koehler & Hinrichs

FRANCES MILLER
    P.J. Bowlin

PAUL NEUBURGER
    Jacob Barge
    Adolph Wolff

JIM NORINE
    Photographs of Collection

LARRY PETERSON
    Photographs of Collection

BARB ROBERTUS
    George Benz
    Hoff's German Liniment
    A.H. Persall
    Mathew Wittich

FRAN RUTHERFORD
    Issac Weil
    J.E. Rogers (Toozes)
    A.M. Smith

DOUG SHILSON
    Aberle-Westheimer
    Dr. Belding - International Stock Food Co.
    J.P. Allen
    Great Mormon Remedy Co
    Anderson & Sandberg
    Photographs of Collection

BILL TRAVERS
    St. Paul Druggist List
    Dr. Partridge P.Q. Medicines

FRED WOLTER
    Austin's Antiseptic Dandruff Destroyer
    John Danek
    Dr. E.B. Halliday's Blood Purifier
        (Samuel Blackford)
    Wallace Nye
    Herbert Mengelkoch
    Sapphine
    Edward LaPenotiere
    F.W. Ames

TIM WOLTER
    Sapphine
    United States Dispensary Co.
    Norgren Frisco Cough Syrup
    Sixth St. Bodega
    Hygenol
    Dr. Gregory's Scotch Bitters
    J.P. Davison
    Herbert Mengelkoch
    Post Office Pharmacy
    Swan Drug Store
    W.K. Hicks
    Introduction to Pharmacy Section
    Introduction to Patent Medicines Section
    Introduction to Liquor Bottles Section
    A.M. Smith
    J.R. Hofflin's Liebig's Corn Cure
    John Danek
    R.D. Eaton
    Matt J. Johnson
    Melendy & Lyman
    Napa Valley Wine Co.
    The California Wine House

1

MINNEAPOLIS

WHISKEYS

Hard liquor, although thought by many to be a great curse of civilization actually was instrumental in establishing the metropolis of Minneapolis/St Paul. For it was in 1838 that a certain Pierre "Pigs Eye" Parrant was thrown off the Fort Snelling military reservation for bootlegging and contributing to the delinquency of the soldiers. Undaunted, Pigs Eye loaded his goods on a raft, floated downstream a few miles and became the first resident of what would become Saint Paul.

Now, old Pigs Eye moved on a few years later, but his fellow saloon keepers found Saint Paul and Minneapolis very fine places indeed to peddle their wares throughout the 19th century. In fact, by 1900 Minneapolis had no fewer than 332 licensed saloons, 16 liquor wholesalers and an undetermined number of illegal tippling houses known as "blind pigs," (a term whose origins are obscure, but possible a reference to the aforementioned Mr. Parrant). Many saloons had fascinating names such as The Beehive, The Casino, The Dog's Head Bodega and so forth. The story of these establishments is less well known than we would like; written records are few as liquor was considered a distasteful industry, and most of the saloon fixtures, signs and so forth seem to have been discarded during Prohibition.

THREE TYPES OF WHISKEY BOTTLES. THE "GLADER" AT LEFT (STYLE H7N), THE "BILLY" IN CENTER (STYLE V4G), & THE "ANDERSON" AT RIGHT (STYLE D3E).

Fortunately for collectors, embossed liquor bottles have survived in large numbers. Quite a number of different bottle types were employed, and a few words should be said about each type.

The earliest liquor dealers probably sold their stuff by the drink, in unembossed bottles, or by filling the "historical flasks" carried by tipplers of the day. The first embossed liquor bottles in our area were probably amber strap sided flasks, which made their appearance in the early 1870's. While the Jacob Barge flask is the only known bottle of this type from the Twin Cities, others exist from Winona and Red Wing. These bottles are highly collectible. Strap sides continued in use until about 1910, but later versions were invariably of clear glass.

Cylinder shaped bottles of various styles seem to have been used from the 1860's up to the present day. These were usually about one fifth quart in capacity and were generally unembossed. The few exceptions, such as the 1870's Montfort whiskeys and the later J.F. Brown cylinders, are highly prized.

Another early bottle type was the "pumpkinseed." These bottles came in a variety of sizes and were specially designed to fit unobtrusively into a gentleman's pocket, being somewhat unstable if set on a flat surface. They were in use from about 1875 to 1895. Three embossed pumpkinseeds are known from Minneapolis, none from Saint Paul. These bottles are fragile and seldom dug intact.

Various types of "straight-sided" whiskeys were used from about 1890 until Prohibition. Even when embossed these bottles are considered slightly less desirable than other styles, as they differ little from liquor bottles still in use today.

But it is the "coffin" or "shoefly" whiskey that is most typical of our area. Depending on how you view things, these are either very rare or very common bottles. On the one hand, there are a great many different coffins from the Twin Cities, close to one hundred with new ones popping up every digging season. Most of these, however, are very scarce bottles with only a few known specimens, or perhaps only broken pieces. So many diggers can point with pride to a "one of a kind" coffin on their shelves.

TWO RARE FLASKS, THE "RICHTER FLASK" AT LEFT & THE
"CUMMINS FLASK" AT RIGHT, COLLECTORS CALL BOTH
"PUMPKINSEEDS".

In our area coffin whiskeys are always clear and with few exceptions come in half pint, pint or quart sizes. For unknown reasons, there are many more coffins from Minneapolis than from Saint Paul. Embossed coffins date from about 1890 to 1908, although unembossed ones were in use since about 1880. While all coffins are desirable bottles, those with embossed pictures such as the Five of Hearts or saloon names such as the Valhalla are the most valuable.

Beginning collectors should have little difficulty acquiring a small collection of interesting liquor bottles, especially straight sides. These bottles are fairly commonly dug or can be purchased at reasonable prices. Pumpkinseeds, nicer coffins, and any of the amber whiskeys, are generally found only on the shelves of collectors with large pocketbooks or lucky shovels.

The Story "Noah's Ark"

"At Twelfth Avenue and Second Street, there was a three story building covering an entire half square block from Second Street to Washington Avenue and halfway down the block toward Thirteenth Avenue. This building was Beard's Block, in popular parlance "Noah's Ark".....cannot be passed up in this story, not because I happened to have my home there during my first seven years in the city, (1882-89) but because it is doubtful if anywhere in America so many Norwegian families have lived under one roof. There were about sixty apartments in the half square block. A large archway led into the courtyard, which was the playground for the children, besides giving space to sixty water closets (!!!) and sixty woodsheds.....In the center of it all was a subterranean garbage repository with a very tall chimney to carry the odors as far skyward as possible.

"Rushing the growler" was a common practice. The nearby saloons were quite liberal in pouring five cents worth of the amber fluid into the tin dinner-pail. Only a few places the quart would be carefully measured out. Most children knew just where to go for real good measure. Some people who felt a bit conspicuous carrying a dinnerpail to a saloon would place it in a baby carriage, covering

it up carefully in case someone came along who wanted to have a look at the baby. Often on summer evenings the families would sit on those outside stairways or porches and enjoy life, made just a little more cheerful by a sip of beer now and then. The housewife made no serious objection, knowing that in this way hubby would stay home in place of patronizing the saloon. Occasionally a whole keg would be brought home. Then "Sjung Ballerd" would resound late into the night; but it never occurred during my years in "Noah's Ark" that any situation called for police interference."

Taken from My Minneapolis, By Carl G.O. Hansen. Privately published, Minneapolis, 1956.

MINNEAPOLIS SALOONS & LIQUOR DEALERS

800 ACME   ?
  44 S. 6th
800A . Coffin; Clear; Pint

801 ALEXANDER, SAM & CO
  38 S. 6th 1890-1891
  34-38 S. 6th   1892-1903
Samuel Alexander first appeared in the city directory in 1888 at the age of 22. He operated the S. Alexander & Co. saloon at 38 South 6th St. From 1888 to 1903 he operated this saloon with Albert Mikolas as his manager. In 1893 Alexander was listed as the proprietor of the Great Northern Bottling Company. It is not known why he quit the saloon business, but in 1904 he started the S. Alexander & Company Real Estate at 622 Andrus Bldg. with Albert Mikolas. He returned to the liquor business in 1912 when he ran the Samuel Alexander Buffet & Bottled Goods at 16-18 North 5th St. until 1919, when it was called Alexander & Dryer for one year. Prohibition again forced the saloon keeper into the soft drink business, known as Alexander Soft Drinks at 10 North 5th St. In 1925 he operated the Check Cashing Bureau with "soft drinks" until about 1930. Sam Alexander died April 5, 1940, at the age of 84, while living at the Nicollet Hotel.
801A . Style D3B; Clear; Pint
801B . Coffin; Clear; Half Pint
801C . Shot Glass
801D . Match Safe

(801A)

(800A)   (801B)

8

(801D-VIEW OF LID)

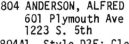

804 ANDERSON, ALFRED
    601 Plymouth Ave   1903-1910
    1223 S. 5th   1904
804A1. Style D3E; Clear; Half Pint, Pint
804A2. Style D3L; Clear
804B . Perpetual Match

(801C)

(801D)

(804A)

(804B)

GUIDE TO WHISKEY BOTTLE STYLES

Unlike beer or soda bottles that have only about ten different body, closure, and base styles, liquor bottles have many variations in slug plates, necks, bodies, and bases. This guide has been prepared to describe the more common styles of whiskey flasks found in Minnesota. Thruout this section of the book the whiskey bottles will be described by style number as follows:

BODY SHAPE + BASE SHAPE + NECK STYLE

For example, a bottle described as STYLE A2A would have a type A body shape, a type 2 base shape, and a type A neck style. The photos on the preceeding pages show C.H.A. RICHTER (style K8P), P.M. GLADER (style H7N), MORRIS FINK (style D4G), etc. Coffin flasks (style A2A) are the exception and are simply called COFFIN FLASK. The guide may not be perfect but it provides a starting point for describing a bottle shape. At the end of the guide is a list of bottle styles and the associated name that various bottle manufacturers assigned that bottle style. In some cases the authors have invented names for a particular style.

BODY SHAPES

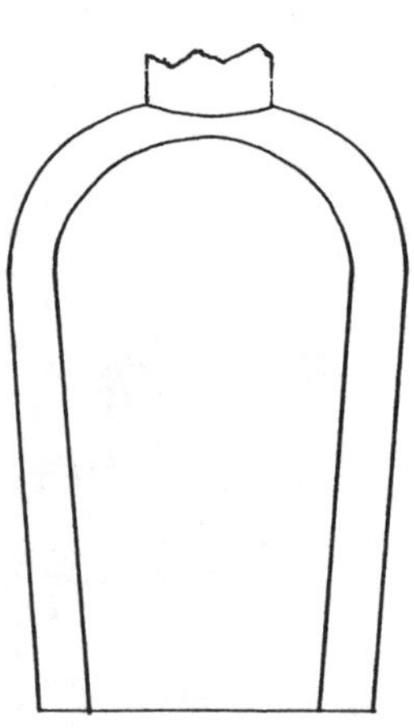

A

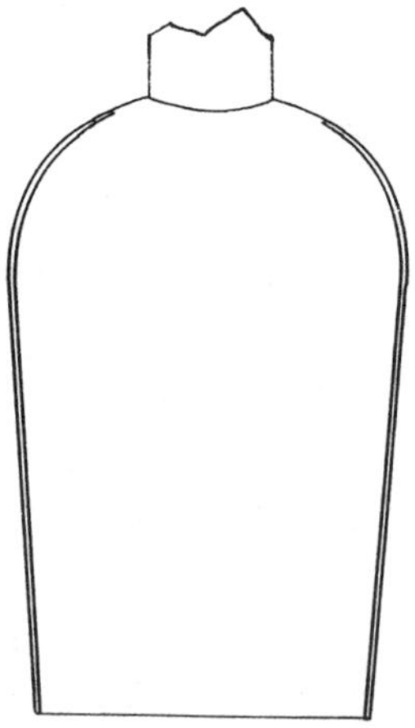

B-STRAP SIDED

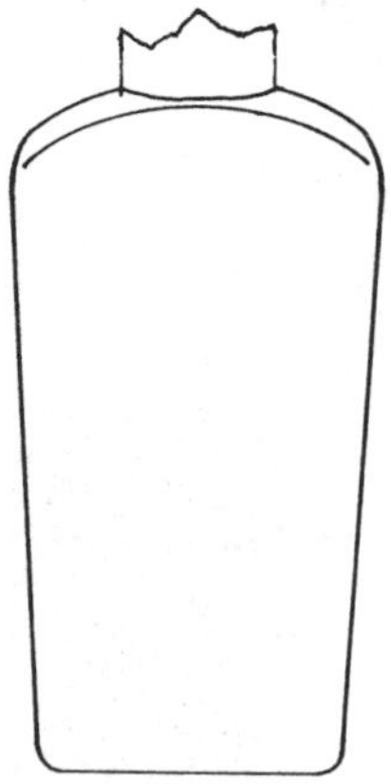

C

D

E

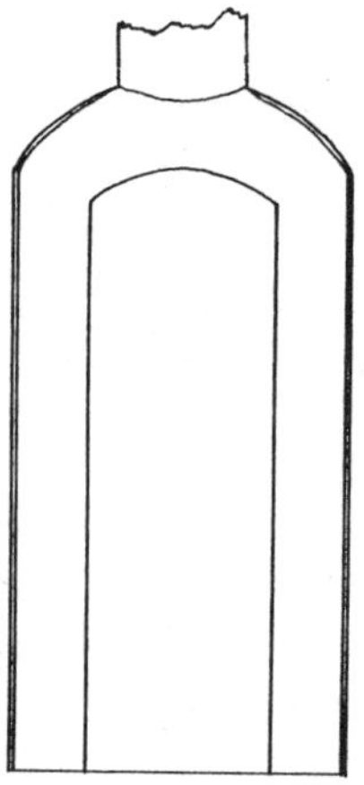

F-STRAP SIDED

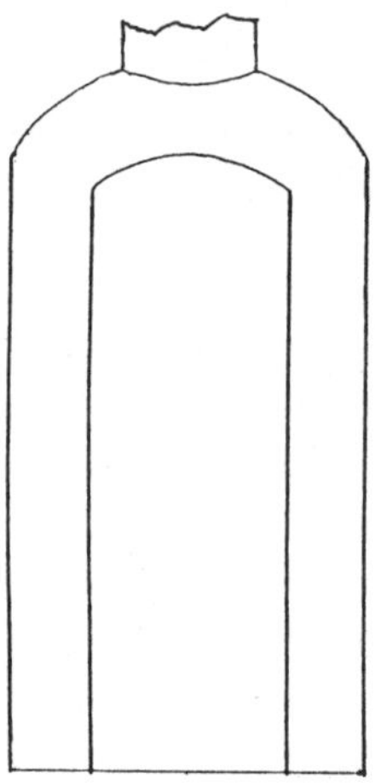

G

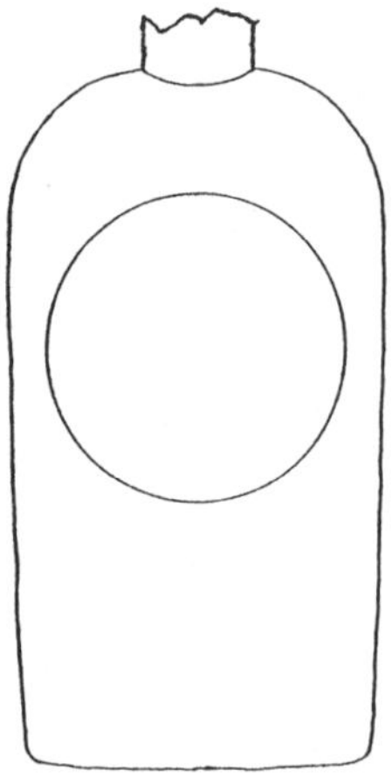

H

I

J

K

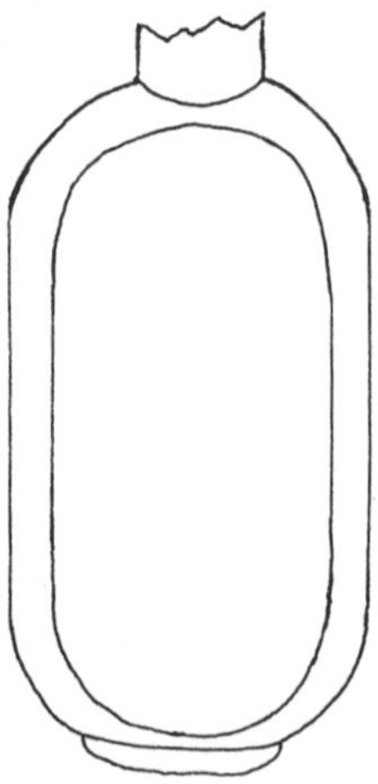

L

BASE SHAPES

1	2	3
4	5	6
7	8	9
10	11	12

A

B

C

D

E

F

G

H

I

J

K

L

M

N

P

Q

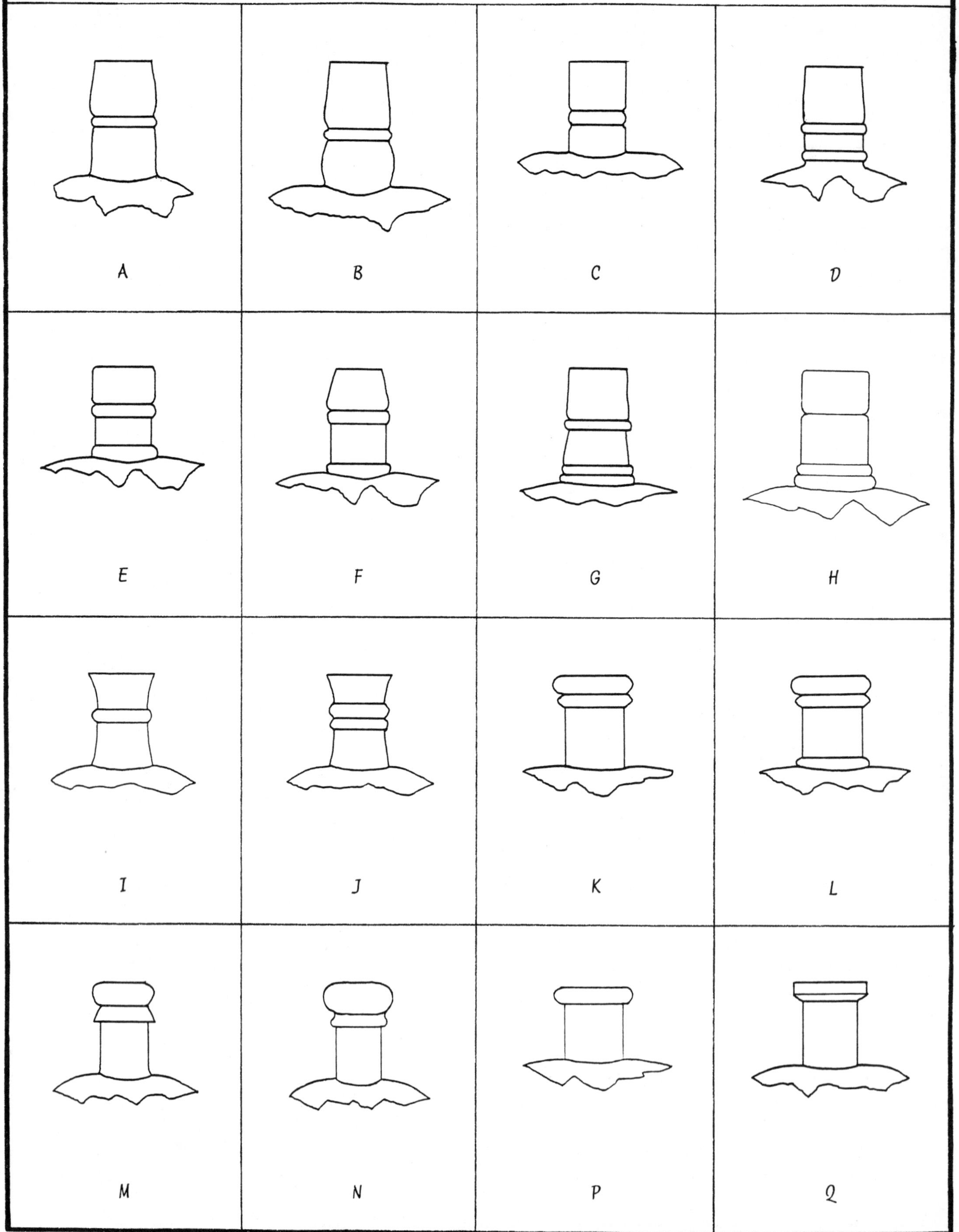

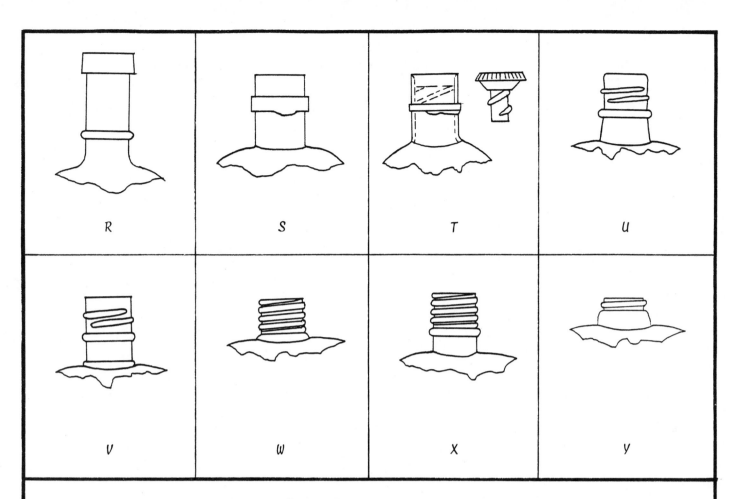

R   S   T   U

V   W   X   Y

BODY STYLE NAMES

A1A-SHOO-FLY
A2A-COFFIN

B6K-UNION OVAL DOUBLE RING FINISH
B6S-UNION OVAL LAID ON RING FINISH
B6T-UNION OVAL INSIDE THREAD

D3A-MADISON
D3B-BULB NECKED DANDY
D3E-ANDERSON
D3F-PHOENIX OR RING DANDY
D3H-KLONDYKE
D3L-ALTON
D3U-BI-METALLIC SCREW CAP
D3W-FLINT DANDY SCREW CAP OR
    COLUMBIA SCREW CAP
D3X-ILLINIOS OVAL SCREW CAP OR
    DANDY LONG CAP SCREW CAP
D4A-BRANDY FINISH DANDY
D4D-EAGLE
D4G-BILLY
D4J-O'HEARN

E10J-KELLY
E10Q-GOLDEN GATE OVAL

F5A-BALTIMORE OVAL BRANDY FINISH
F5U-BALTIMORE OVAL SCREW CAP

H7N-GLADER

I10A-WHEELING OVAL

J3A-EXCELSIOR OVAL OR
    PHILADELPHIA OVAL BRANDY FINISH
J3U-PHILADELPHIA OVAL SCREW CAP
J9J-FORD
J10A-ST LOUIS OVAL
J10U-ST LOUIS OVAL SCREW CAP
J10W-CHICAGO SCREW CAP

K8A-CUMMINS PICNIC FLASK OR
    PUMPKINSEED
K8K-PICNIC OR PUMPKINSEED
K8P-RICHTER FLASK OR PUMPKINSEED
K8U-CUMMINS SCREW CAP OR PUMPKINSEED

L8K-JO JO FLASK

(805A)

(807A)

(810A)

(810B)

(813A)

805 ANDERSON, A. M.
    2010 Cedar Ave   1883
    1328 2nd Ave S.   1888-1899
805A . Coffin; Clear; Pint

807 ANDERSON, GUSTAV
    2 N.E. Main   1896-1900
    1203 Wash. Ave S.   1901
    1219 Wash. Ave S.   1905
    1107 Wash. Ave S.   1908-1910
807A . Style A1J; Clear; Pint

810 ANDERSON, LUDWIG & SANDBERG, ANDREW -
    (White Star Saloon)
    227 Nicollet   1897-1901
    47 Wash. Ave S.   1902-1908
810A . Style D3E; Clear; Half Pint
810B . Style Unknown; Clear; Half Pint;Pint
810C . Toothpick & Token

811 ANDERSON & SANDBERG, JOHN
    1419 Wash. Ave. S.   1900
813 ARCADE WINE DEPOT (possibly Arcade Hotel 1892 &
    1902 or Arcade Bar 1914-1915)
813A . Coffin; Clear; Quart

814 BAKKEN & PALMER
    221 Cedar Ave   1896-1901
814A . Style A1J; Clear; Half Pint

(816A)

816 BARGE, JACOB
    49 Wash. Ave S.   1875-1887
    49 Wash. Ave. & 25 S. 4th 1894-1896
    18 S. 5th   1897-1901
    12 N. 3rd   1902
    8 Wash. Ave S.   1901-1906
Jacob Barge was born in Treves, Germany, in 1836.
He immigrated to the United States, fought in the
Civil War, and finally settled in Minneapolis.
During the forty plus years that he resided in
Minneapolis, Barge was a prominent restaurant and
saloon owner.

The first directory listing for Mr. Barge was in
1867, when he was listed as a confectioner at
Bridge near High. There was also a Barge & Henry
Saloon at First near Kansas. This is surely the
same Barge as there were no others listed. From
1869 to 1872 Barge was in the fruit and confec-
tionary business on Washington Avenue and Oregon.
(Most Minneapolis street names were changed around
1880 to the way we know them today; Washington
Avenue was one of the few old names that was kept.)

Liquor first became a part of Barge's business in
1873, when he is listed as the sole proprietor of
the Baltimore Oyster Depot and Restaurant where he
specialized in "wines, liquors, and cigars of best
quality."

From 1875 to 1887 Barge remained in the saloon
business.

During the period 1888-93 Jacob Barge apparently
did not operate a saloon. Instead, he owned
Medicine Lake Park, which had its office at 47-49
Washington Avenue.

In 1890 he was also the secretary and treasurer of
the Germania Brewing Co. Barge was the president
and general manager of the Continental Catering Co.
at 25-27 So. 4th Street in 1893.

Then, suddenly in 1894, Barge was back in the
Restaurant, wines, liquors and cigars trade. He
continued in that line of work through 1906,
operating out of several different addresses.

In 1909 he is listed as being a farmer.

Jacob Barge's habit of moving his place of business
often can be difficult to follow, but it is
understandable because he was a heavy investor in
real estate. While in Minneapolis he lived at no
fewer than 12 different addresses.

(814A)

Jacob Barge
Minneapolis
(816B)

On June 24, 1909 Jacob Barge was "taken by apoplexy" while on a business trip in Brownsville, Texas. He was 73, outliving his wife by 15 years. Supposedly he had lived in San Antonio for 3 years.

Only three specimens of Jacob Barge bottles are known. They are believed to have been made by the Frankstown Glass Works between 1872-1874.

816A . Amber Strap Side Flask; Inside Screw Glass Stopper (Style B6T)
816A2. Same as 816A except Style B6K with Inside Threads
816B . Private Mold Flask; Clear

819 BIRD, H. P. & WARK
  323 S. 3rd   1891-1892
  18 S. 3rd   1893
819A1. Style E11Q; Clear;

822 BRACKET, C. S.
  215-217 Nic. Ave   1885
822A . Glass Packer Jug
822B . Shot Glass
822C . Clear; Cylinder; Quart; Shard only
822D . Shot Glass

825 BROWN, JONAS F.
  216 Nic. Ave   1866-1907
Jonas F. Brown was born near Worcester, Massachusetts in 1830. As a young man he worked for the Providence and Worcester Railway. He left New England about 1860 and came to Minneapolis for his health. Soon after, he married Emma (last name unknown), and they lived at Sixth St. and Fourth Ave. for 40 years.

Brown had a scrape with the law in 1875 when he was arrested for failing to pay a $1,200.00 rectifier's tax (rectifier here meaning one who blends or purifies liquors). The case was covered well by the press, but no record of a verdict can be found. The fact that he continued in business, however, may be indicative of the outcome. Had he been found guilty, Brown would have lost his stock, paid a fine, and gone to prison.

In February, 1908 Jonas died in Los Angeles, California. Emma died in September of that same year. The March 1, 1908 Minneapolis Journal obituary said he was one of the city's most widely known men. It continued by saying Brown "was the last survivor of the old school of liquor dealers. In the days when card and wine rooms, slot machines, music and free lunches were recognized as the requisite adjunct of the saloon, Mr. Brown continued himself strictly to the business of selling liquor as an ordinary commercial proposition." After Brown's death, the Jonas F. Brown Co. continued its listing in the directories. By this time the firm had moved from its original address, at 216 Nicollet, to 19 Washington Ave. No. The last directory listing was 1915.

A 1903 book of Minneapolis resources and industries gives this description of Mr. Brown's Business place:

"There are a number of palatial resorts in our city, and pre-eminently among them is that of the above named (J.F. Brown), established in 1866 by the present proprietor. He is located in a three-story brick building, where he occupies the

(819A)

FROM BIRD & WARK
323 THIRD STREET So.
MINNEAPOLIS MINN

1890 VIEW OF C.S. BRACKETT'S STORE

(822B)

(822D)

(822C)

(822A)

entire building, with basement for storage, which gives him a combined floor space of 11,000 square feet, situated at No. 216 Nicollet Avenue. The interior is very handsomely fitted up with bar and fixtures composed of black walnut, the shelving behind being resplendent with fine large mirrors and cut glass. Mr. Brown prides himself upon keeping the finest and choicest brands and qualities of imported and domestic wines, liquors, brandies, sherries, mineral waters, all the leading brands of whiskies and bottled beers, making specialties of "Old Crow," "Old Taylor Bourbon," "Green Brier," "Old Monogram Rye," "Golden Wedding Rye," whiskies, "Finest in America," made in 1876, and a full line of cognacs, champagne, etc.

Mr. Jonas F. Brown is the sole proprietor, and hails from Massachusetts; he is an old resident of Minneapolis, coming here thirty-seven years ago, and has always been prominent in any movement inaugurated for the welfare and betterment of the city.

825A . Style F5Q; Clear; Half Pint, Pint
825A2. Style F5C; Clear; Half Pint, Pint
825B . Picnic Flask with Spiderweb pattern - Style K8K; Clear; Half Pint
825C . Standard Brandy (Cylinder); Amber; Quart
825C2. Standard Brandy (Cylinder); Clear; Quart
825D . Jug
825E . Jug
825F . Same as 825A2 except wording reads "Half Pint" instead of "1/2 Pint"
825G . Style D5J; Clear; Half Pint

828 BROWN, JONAS F. & CO.
    216 Nic. Ave   1884-1907
    19 Wash. Ave N.   1907-1915
828A . Style F5C; Clear; Half Pint, Pint, Quart
828B . Style F5C; Clear; Half Pint, Pint, Quart
828C . Short Brandy (Cylinder); amber; Fifth
828D . Shot Glass
828E . Jug
828F . Jug
828G . Jug
828H . Jug
828I . Jug
828J . Metal Needle Case
828K . Shot Glass
828L . Shot Glass

(825A)

(825G)

(825F)

(825C)

(828A)

(828C)

(828B)

16

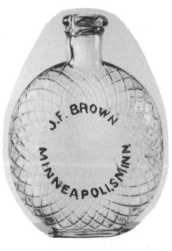

(825B)

(828C)

(828E)

(828H)

(828I)

(828F)

(825D)

(825E)

(828G)

(828J)

(828D)

(828L)

(828K)

831 BURFEIND, HENRY
   512 N. 1st   1883
   428 N. 1st   1884
   514 Plymouth Ave   1885-1898
   522 Plymouth Ave   1899-1908
831A . Style A1J; Clear
831B . Style F5C; Clear; Half Pint, Pint

HENRY BURFEIND
FINE WINES
&
LIQUORS
514
PLYMOUTH AVE
MINNEAPOLIS
MINN

(831A)

HENRY BURFEIND
514 PLYMOUTH AVE.
MINNEAPOLIS.

(831B)

(834A)

(834B)

(834C)

(835A)

834 BURK, CHAS
    253 6th Ave S.   1896-1908
834A . Coffin; Clear; Half Pint
834B . Coffin; Clear, Half Pint

835 BURSCH BROS
    Unknown   date unknown
835A . Shot Glass

837 CALIFORNIA WINE HOUSE
    505 Wash. Ave N.   1887
    253 2nd Ave S.   1894-1897
    209-211 Nicollet Ave   1904-1908
    100 Wash. Ave S.   1910

In our great grandfather's day, as today, certain things lent an air of respectability to a company-- a distinguished name, and many years of successful business. It was also true, as now, that certain companies would misrepresent themselves, or at least stretch the truth. The proprietors of the California Wine House are a case in point.

As the bottle embossing illustrates, Julius Rees and Julius Fineman, proprietors of the Califonia Wine House, claimed to have been established in 1863. The truth of the matter is that they bought the concern after the death of the former proprietor, Max Adler, in 1900. Adler, in partnership with another man named Kohn, had operated the business at 253 2nd Ave. South since 1893. They were cigar manufacturers prior to that date. What about 1863? Well, on the cover of an issue of Antique Bottle World some years back there was a sketch of a strapsided whiskey from Kohn and Adler of Rock Island, Ill. Adler's obituary does confirm the fact that he spent time in Rock Island, but it also states that he was born in 1855, which would make him about "half pint" size in 1863. Possibly Kohn was the senior partner, perhaps the company was first founded by somebody else, or perhaps the 1863 claim was a total fabrication.

The name California Wine House, first used by Adler in 1893, would appear to be a near copy of A.M. Smith's successful California Wine Depot, which was

established in 1888. (Smith's bottles proclaim "Established 1872" which was partially true, for that was the year he first set up shop in Salt Lake City, Utah).

In any event, Rees and Fineman seem to have done well in their trade as "Importers and Wholesale Liquor Dealers", selling "Pan-American Rye", "High grade whiskey, brandies, rums, gins, etc." They moved to 209-211 Nicollet Ave. in 1903, and a few years later are also listed as proprietors of the Advance Distilling Company.

Fineman appears to have played less and less of a role in the company, being listed as secretary of the Napa Valley Wine Company in 1910, then establishing his own wholesale liquor concern at 213 1st Avenue South. This business ended in bankruptcy and Fineman drowned himself in the Mississippi River in June, 1913. Julius Rees moved the Wine House to 100-102 Washington Avenue South in 1910. Four years later he died, but his company (renamed the J. Rees Co. after his death) continued on until Prohibition.

837A . Style D4D (ABM); Clear; Half Pint
837B . Style D4D; Clear; Half Pint
837C . Style D4D; Clear; Half Pint
837D . Style D4A; Clear; Half Pint, Pint; I G CO.
837E . PACKER Jug with handle; Amber; Gallon
837H . Jug
837I . Various Corkscrews
837J . Pocket Mirror
837K . Pocket Mirror
837L . Pocket Mirror
837M . Advertising Tray
837N . Advertising Tray
837P . Coffin; Clear
837Q . Shot Glass
837R . Jug
837S . Shot Glass
837T . Shot Glass

THE CALIFORNIA WINE HOUSE
100-102
WASHINGTON AVE. SO.
MINNEAPOLIS
ESTABLISHED 1863
HALF PINT
FULL MEASURE

(837A)

(837B)

(837C)

(837D)

(837E)

(837Q)

(837S)

(837T)

CALIFORNIA WINE HOUSE
253
SECOND AVE.
SOUTH
MINNEAPOLIS

(837P)

(837H)

(837R)

(837L)

(837J)

(837M)

(BACK OF 837M & 837N)

(837N)

(837K)

840 CASINO, THE
    34-36-38 S. 6th St   date unknown
840A . Coffin; Clear; Pint
840B . Coffin; Clear; Half Pint
840C . Coffin; Clear; Half Pint
840D . Coffin; Clear; Half Pint

[CENTRAL WINE CO. - See I. Goldman]

[COMMERCIAL, THE - See Elschlager]

[CREAMERY BUFFET - See Brewery Section]

FROM THE CASNIO 34-36&38 SOUTH 6TH ST MINNEAPOLIS MINN.
(840A)

FROM THE :CASINO: 34·36&38 SOUTH 6TH ST. MINNEAPOLIS MINN.
(840B)

O. DAMM DEALER IN WINES & LIQUORS 327 CEDAR AVE MINNEAPOLIS
(849A)

FROM THE "CASINO" 38 SO.6TH ST MINNEAPOLIS MINN.
(840C)

FROM THE "CASINO" 38 SO.6TH ST. MINNEAPOLIS MINN.
(840D)

849 DAMM, OLAF
    1822 Riverside Ave
849A . Coffin; Clear; Half Pint
849B . Metal Tray

852 DAVIS, J. M.
    107 Wash. Ave N   1889-1900
    114 N. 2nd   1892-1911
Little solid information exists on Joseph M. Davis. It seems he did more to emboss his name into history through his business ventures than through his private life. He left behind a wide variety of liquor-related memorabilia, all carrying either his name or the name of his most famous product - Silver Pitcher Whiskies.

No information is to be found at this time on where Davis was born or on how he came to establish himself in Minneapolis. Davis is first listed in the 1884 business directory as a partner in the Moss and Davis wholesale and retail liquor establishment. It was not until 1890 that the partnership dissolved and Davis opened his own store (Albert Moss and his brothers Charles and Jesse opened the Moss Brothers liquor store). It is interesting to note that some Davis bottles state, "Established 1883".

During the next ten years Davis maintained both a wholesale and a retail dealership and a saloon, but the locations of these establishments were frequently changed to various North Minneapolis addresses.

In 1902, according to the Minneapolis Tribune, F.C. Pratt, bookkeeper to the J.M. Davis Wholesale Liquor Co., was arrested and charged with the embezzlement of about $12,000. The news story goes on to say that Davis had hired a private detective to establish Pratt's guilt. By 1915 the business was listed as:
J.M. Davis Mercantile Co, J.M. Davis, Proprietor. Mail Order House., Merchandise, Wholesale Wines and Liquors 106-108 North 2nd.

The word "merchandise" is most significant here. In the face of impending Prohibition (enacted in 1920), Davis seems to have seen the inevitable. It appears he was attempting to establish a new business in which he might continue after Prohibition was enacted. It appears, however, that his attempt to establish a new business was not successful. His directory listing for 1920 gives only a residential address - no business is listed.

852A . Coffin, Clear; Half Pint
852B . Coffin; Clear; Half Pint
852C . Style D3B; Clear: Half Pint
852D . Miniature Squat Brandy; Clear
852E . Squat Brandy; Clear; Quart
852F . Silver Water Pitcher, engraved "Silver Pitcher Whiskey"
852G . Back Bar Decanter "Silver Pitcher Rye"
852H . Back Bar Decanter
852J . Shot Glass
852K . Back Bar Decanter "Silver Pitcher"
852L . Mechanical Pencil

J.M. DAVIS SILVER PITCHER MINNEAPOLIS (852D)

38 SILVER PITCHER TRADE 1883 MARK RYE
(852G)

SILVER PITCHER
(852H)

SILVER PITCHER
(852K)

ESTABLISHED 1883 J.M. DAVIS WHOLESALE WINES & LIQUORS 107 WASHINTON AVE N MINNEAPOLIS MINN.
(852A)

ESTABLISHED 1883 HEADQUARTERS SILVER PITCHER WHISKIES 107 WASH AVE.N. MINNEAPOLIS MINN.
(852B)

ESTABLISHED 1883 J.M. DAVIS WHOLESALE WINES & LIQUORS 107 WASHINGTON AVE.N. MINNEAPOLIS MINN. FULL ½ PINT
(852C)

SILVER PITCHER RYE J.M. DAVIS SOLE PROPRIETOR MINNEAPOLIS, MINN. FULL QUART
(852E)

(852J)

(852F)

(852F)

(858E)

(857A)

(855A)

dRYERs
FamilyLiquor
319 Hennepin
AVE.
MINNEAPOLIS

(858A)

855 DENNELL, E. L.
  220 Central   1898-1899
  203 Central   1900-1901
  1516 S. 7th   1902-1905
  117 S. E. Main   1906-1910
855A . Coffin; Clear

857 DONAHUE, J.C.
  116 1st Ave. S.   1895-1898
  226 Henn. Ave.   1899-1910
  250 1st Ave. S.   1900
  30 Wash. Ave. N.   1902
857A1. Coffin; Clear

858 DRYER
  319 Henn. Ave   after 1910
858A . Style D4D (ABM); Clear; Pint
858B . Watch Fob
858C . Shot Glass
858D . Shot Glass
858E . Mug, Yellow Glaze

(858B-BACK)

(858B-FRONT)

(MINEATURES-852D

(852E)

(858D)

(858C)

21

861 DUFAUD WINE & LIQUOR CO.
   316 Henn. Ave
861A . Shot Glass "Tierney's Golden Rye"   1905-1906
861B . Shot Glass

862 DUPONT, JOS. W.
   311 Henn. Ave.   1900-1901
   25 S. 4th   1902-1908
862A . Coffin; Clear; Half Pint

864 EISLER, ADOLPH
   311 N. E. Main   1886-1887
   307 N. E. Main   1888-1890
   210 Henn. Ave   1891-1908
   109 Wash. Ave S.   1910
864A . Shot Glass
864B . Shot Glass
864C . Jug
864D . Corkscrew
864E . Purse Mirror
864F . Jug
864G . Shot Glass
864H . Jug
864J . Shot Glass

(861B)

(861A)

(862A)

(864H)

(864F)

(864E)

(864C)

(864A)

(864B)

(864J)

(864G)

867 ELLIOTT, C. H. & BRENNAN, F. E.
  415 Henn. Ave   1896
867A . Coffin; Clear; Pint

870 ELSCHLAGER & HASER - The Commercial
  250 1st Ave S.   1894
870A¹. Style A1J; Clear; Pint

873 FEILZER, JOHN A. (German Beer Hall)
  800 N. E. Marshall   1885-1886
  507 Wash. Ave N.   1887-1888
  27 Nic. Ave   1890-1894
  401 Plymouth Ave   1895-1896
  505 Wash. Ave N.   1897
  326 20th Ave N.   1899
873A . Coffin; Clear; Half Pint

876 FINEMAN, JULIUS J. (See Calif. Wine House)
  111 Wash. Ave.   date unknown
876A . Shot Glass

879 FJELLMAN, CHAS
  1223 Wash. Ave S.   1887-1889
  1225 Wash. Ave S.   1890-1893
879A1. Coffin; Clear; Half Pint

882 FJELLMAN, JOHN
  425 Wash. Ave S.   1887
  247 Cedar Ave S.   1892-1908
882A1. Coffin; Clear;

885 FORD, JAMES
  302 1st Ave S.   1886-1908
  49 Wash. Ave S.   1899-1910
  113 Wash. Ave S.   1899-1900
  229 Wash. Ave S.   1896-1898
885A . Coffin; Clear; Half Pint
885B . Coffin; Clear; Half Pint
885C . Coffin; Clear; Pint
885D . Style J9J; Clear; Half Pint, Pint; MCC
885E . Coffin; Clear; Half Pint
885F . Coffin; Clear; Half Pint

F.C.H.ELLIOTT
F.E.BRENNAN
E & B
415 HENNEPIN Ave.
MINNEAPOLIS
(867A)

THE COMMERCIAL
ELSCHLAGER
&
HASER
250 FIRST AVE. SO.
MINNEAPOLIS
(870A)

J. A. FEILZER
GERMAN
BEER HALL
401
PLYMOUTH AVE. N.
MINNEAPOLIS
(873A)

CHAS FJELLMAN
1225
WASHINGTON
AVE. SO.
MINNEAPOLIS
(879A)

JOHN FJELLMAN
247
CEDAR AV.
MINNEAPOLIS
MINN.
(882A)

FULL MEASURE
ESTABLISHED
1886
JAMES FORD
302 1ST AVE SO
49 WASH AVE SQ
MINNEAPOLIS
(885D)

ESTABLISHED
1886
JAMES FORD
302 1ST AVE. S.
49
WASHINGTON AVE. S.
MINNEAPOLIS, MINN.
(885B)

ESTABLISHED
1888
JAMES FORD
302 1ST AVE. S.
49
WASHINGTON AVE. S.
MINNEAPOLIS, MINN.
(885C)

ESTABLISHED
1886
JAMES FORD
302 1ST AVE. SO.
118 WASH AVE SO.
MINNEAPOLIS
(885F)

(876A)

(885A)

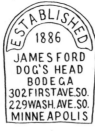
(885E)

(888A)

A.FREDERICKSON
1818
WASHINGTON
AVE. NO.
MINNEAPOLIS
(891A)

(894A)

GLADER & ERICKSON
324-2ND
AVE-S.
MINNEAPOLIS, MINN.
(897A)

CHAS GLUCK
401
WASHINGTON
AVE. SO.
MINNEAPOLIS
(903A)

GOLDMAN
ST. LOUIS
WINE CO.
229
WASH. AVE. NO.
MINNEAPOLIS
MINN.
(909A)

THE CENTRAL WINE Co.
M. R. GOLDMAN, PROP.
129
NICOLLET AVE.
MINNEAPOLIS
(912A)

GRAVES BROS.
259 6TH AVE. SO.
MINNEAPOLIS, MINN.
(914A)

888 FRECH, HERMAN
  14 N. 6th   1903-1908
  18 N. 5th   1910
888A . Style M7I; Clear

891 FREDERICKSON, ALFRED
  1814 Wash. Ave S.   1888-1890
  1818 Wash. Ave N.   1891-1895
891A . Coffin; Clear; Half Pint

894 GLADER, P. M.
  1107 Wash. Ave S.   1902-1905
  324 2nd Ave S.   1905-1910
894A . Style H7N; "Clear"

897 GLADER, & ERICSON
  324 2nd Ave S.   1905
897A . Style H7N; Clear; Pint

900 GLOBE WINE CO.
  248 Henn. Ave   1906
900A . Corkscrew "Lock Horn Bitters"

903 GLUCK, CHARLES
  401 Wash. Ave S.   1893-1895
903A . Coffin; Clear; Pint

906 GLUCK, F. P. & CO.
  401 Wash. Ave S.   1885-1888
  407 Wash. Ave. S.   1890
  255 1st Ave S. & 429 Wash. Ave S. 1891-1892
  106 2nd Ave N   1891-1898
906A . Shot Glass "Minnetonka Rye"
906B . Shot Glass "Old Wilson Rye"

909 GOLDMAN, ISAAC (St. Louis Wine Co)
  229 Wash. Ave N.   1890-1893
909A . Coffin; Clear; Half Pint

912 GOLDMAN, M. R.
  330 2nd Ave S.   1894-1895
  129 Nic. Ave   1896-1897
912A . Coffin; Clear; Half Pint

(906B)   (906A)

(915A)

914 GRAVES BROS
  259 6th Ave S.   ?
914A . Coffin; Clear; Half Pint

915 GREEN, C. G.
  2626 E. 26th   1903-1906
915A . Coffin; Clear; Half Pint

918 HALL, ANDREW & CO.
  501 Cedar Ave   1906-1910
  909 19th Ave S.   1906
918A . Style D4A; Clear; Pint; J.B. DO.

919 HANZLICK & LUDWIG
  965 Central Ave   1902-1910
919A . Coffin; Clear
919B . Shard only

921 HARTMAN, PHILLIP
  1329 S. 6th   1875-1899
  1331 S. 6th   1900-1910
  1910 Directories list Hartman's Business as
"Hartman's Cafe & Summer Garden"
921A . Coffin; Clear; Pint
921B . Coffin; Clear

924 HELLER, B
  418 3rd Ave N.   1909
924A . Liquor Decanter
924B . Shot Glass "Lesterbrook Rye"

930 HOFF & HARRIS - The Sliding Mirror
  306 1st Ave S.   1895-1900
930A . Coffin; Clear; Pint; Half Pint

934 HOFFMAN, C.A. - THE VALLHALA
  105 Wash. Ave S.   1896-1903
934A . Coffin: Clear: Pint

935 HOOKWITH & WEED
  310 Henn. Ave.   1903-1906
935A . Blue & White Mug

[INTERNATIONAL BEER HALL - See Louis Mauer]

936 JAAX, HUBERT
  2032 N.E. Marshall   1891-1893
  1830 N.E. Marshall   1894-1898
  2501 N.E. Marshall   1898-1910
936A . Coffin; Clear; Half Pint
936B . Coffin: Clear: Half Pint

HALL & CO.
501 CEDAR AVE.
MINNEAPOLIS, MINN.
(918A)

(919A)

HANZLICK & LUDWIG
965 CENTRAL AVE.
MINNEAPOLIS, MINN.

PHILIP HARTMAN
COR.
14TH AVE &
6TH ST. SOUTH
MINNEAPOLIS
MINN.
(921A)

PHIL. HARTMANN
14TH AVE.
&
6TH ST. S.
MINNEAPOLIS, MINN.
(921B)

C.A. HOFFMAN
105
WASH. AVE. SO.
VALHALLA
IMP. WINE &
LIQUORS
MINNEAPOLIS
(934A)

THE SLIDING MIRROR
HOFF
&
HARRIS
306 FIRST AVE. S.
MINNEAPOLIS
(930A)

HUBERT JAAX
WINES
&
LIQUORS
MARSHALL ST.
N.E.
MINNEAPOLIS
(936B)

HUBERT JAAX
WINES
&
LIQUORS
1830
MARSHALL ST.
N.E.
MINNEAPOLIS
(936A)

(935A)

(917A)

(924B)

(924A)

25

ST. LOUIS SAMPLE ROOM PAUL JANIKULA 215 WASH. AVE N. MINNEAPOLIS

(937A)

EAST SIDE LIQUOR HOUSE WINES, LIQUOR & CIGARS CHAS. JOHNSON PROP'R 965 CENTRAL AVE. MINNEAPOLIS

(939B)

CHAS. JOHNSON 105 VALHALLA WASH AVE So MINNEAPOLIS, MINN.

(939A)

M. KJELGREN WINES & LIQUORS 309 CEDAR AVE. MINNEAPOLIS FULL PINT

(945A)

KLASSY & SEIBEL WINES & LIQUORS 1231 WASHINGTON AVE. N. MINNEAPOLIS

(948A)

(939C)

(951B)

UMPIRE BOURBON

(942G)

KLEIN & PAUNTZ WINES & LIQUORS 36-38 SO. 6TH ST. MINNEAPOLIS, MINN.

(951A)

937 JANIKULA, PAUL
   315 Wash. Ave N.   1895-1897
937A . Coffin; Clear; Pint

939 JOHNSON, CHAS - The Vallhala
   957 Central Ave   1895-1901
   111 Wash. Ave S.   1902
   105 Wash. Ave S.   1903-1906
   28 S. 6th   1908-1910
939A . Coffin; Clear; Pint
939B . Coffin; Clear; Pint
939C . Shot Glass

941 KELLY, JAMES L.
   The Winsor Hotel   1892-1895
   244 Henn. Ave.   1896-1901
941A1. Style E1OJ; Clear

942 KELLY & STEINMETZ
   17 Wash. Ave. N.   1906-1912

942B . Back Bar Decanter, engraved "Monogram" and "KSL Co" Monogram
942C . Back Bar Decanter, engraved "Umpire" & "KSL Co"
942D . Pinch Bottle Decanter, engraved "Umpire Bourbon" & "KSL Co."
942E . Handled Glass Jug, etched "Umpire - Bourbon Whiskey...etc.", Ground Pontil
942F . Back Bar Decanter

945 KJELGREN, MAURITZ
   314 Cedar Ave   1887
   327 Cedar Ave   1888-1892
   307 Cedar Ave   1893-1900
945A . Coffin; Clear; Pint

948 KLASSY & SEIBEL
   1231 Wash Ave N.   1887-1895
948A . Coffin; Clear; Pint

951 KLEIN, ISRAEL & PAUNTZ, IGNATZ
   36 S. 6th   1904-1908
   38 S. 6th   1910
951A . Coffin; Clear; Half Pint, Pint;
951B . Jug

(942B)

(942C)

(942D)

(942E)

(942F)

FULL MEASURE ONE HALF PINT
On. Lenihan
309 HENNEPIN AVE MINNEAPOLIS, MINN

(954A)

FRANK LINSTROM
117 WASH. AVE SO.
MINNEAPOLIS, MINN.

(957A)

(91C)

954 LENIHAN, MALACHY
    309 Henn. Ave   1908-1910
954A1. Style F5A; Clear; Half Pint

957 LINDSTROM, FRANK
    117 Wash. Ave S.   1906
957A . Coffin; Clear; Pint; Half Pint

[LINKER, J. L. - See Brewery Section]

OLE LODGORD
WINES LIQUORS
&
CIGARS
222
20TH AVE - N.
MINNEAPOLIS

(963A)

963 LODGORD, OLE
    213 N. 1st   1891-1894
    222 20th Ave N.   1895-1898
963A . Style A1J; Clear; Half Pint

966 LUNDBERG, ANDREW
    315 Wash. Ave S.
966A . Coffin; Clear; Half Pint   1899-1902

A. LUNDBERG
WINES
LIQUORS & CIGARS
315
WASH. AVE. SO.
MINNEAPOLIS, MINN.

(966A)

CARL J MAEDER
WINES
&
LIQUORS
229 MAIN ST N.E.
MINNEAPOLIS

(969A)

969 MAEDER, CARL
    229 Main St. N.E.   1892, 1896-1902
969A . Coffin; Clear; Pint

    MAGNUSON, H.
    Address unknown   date unknown
    . Shot Glass "Old King Cole"
    . Shot Glass "Old King Cole"

(91E)

972 MAURER, LOUIS - International Beer Hall
    507 Wash. Ave N.   1895-1908
972A . Style A1J; Clear; Pint; Half Pint

973 MELGORD, JOHN
    220 Henn. Ave   1906-1910

[MELGORD & ORBECK - See Brewery Section]

978 MENGELKOCH, H. & CO.
    327 Plymouth Ave   1897-1902
Hubert Mengelkoch's parents were pioneers of
Hennepin County; coming from Germany in the early
1850's, they settled in Plymouth Township. Hubert
was one of eleven children. In 1888 at the age of
27, he came to Minneapolis with his brother Jacob
and established a grocery store at 329 Plymouth
Ave. In 1892 they were joined by another brother,
Henry, and together they opened a saloon next door
at 327. The three shared and alternated the work
load until the next year when Jacob left to open
his own saloon at 311 20th Ave. No. (Broadway).
Brother Jacob later moved up the street to 320 20th
Ave. -- what became known as the Crown Sample
Rooms. Henry Mengelkoch also left after a time to
begin a business in hides and tallow, so Hubert
enlisted the help of a fourth brother, Clemens.
Hubert continued to live in North Minneapolis and
operated his businesses with an assortment of
partners until his death in April of 1909.
978A1. Coffin; Clear; Half Pint

J. L. LINKER
28 SOUTH SIXTH ST.
MINNEAPOLIS
MINN

(91F)

THE
INTERNATIONAL
BEER
HALL
LOUIS MAURER
MANAGER
WINES & LIQUORS
507 WASH AVE N
MINNEAPOLIS

(972A)

H. MENGELKOCH & CO.
WINES LIQUORS
&
CIGARS
327
PLYMOUTH AVE
MINNEAPOLIS

(978A)

(984A)

MOSS BROS.
WHOLESALE
&
RETAIL
LIQUOR DEALERS
114 HENNEPIN AVE
MINNEAPOLIS
MINN.

(987A)

THE CROWN
WINES LIQUORS
& CIGARS
SAMPLE ROOMS
J. MENGELKOCH
311
20TH AVE. N.
MINNEAPOLIS

(981A)

JACOB MENGELKOCH
311
20TH AVE. N.
MINNEAPOLIS
MINN.

(981B)

(987B)

(987C)

FROM
F.P. MURPHY'S
FAMILY
LIQUOR STORE
925 CEDAR AVE.
MINNEAPOLIS

(993A)

FROM
F.P. MURPHY'S
FAMILY
LIQUOR STORE
925 CEDAR AVE.
MINNEAPOLIS

(993B)

(996B-
LEFT
SIDE)

(996B-
RIGHT
SIDE)

981 MENGELKOCH, JACOB - Crown Sample Room

311 20th Ave N.	1898-1903
325 20th Ave N.	1904-1910

981A . Style A1J; Clear; Half Pint, Pint
981B . Style A1J; Clear; Half Pint

984 MILLER BROS

103 1st Ave N.	1907-1918

984A . Shot Glass

987 MOSS BROS

114 Henn. Ave	1890-1899
116 Henn. Ave	1900-1904
101 Wash. Ave N.	1905-1910

987A . Coffin; Clear; Half Pint
987B . Style F5A; Clear; Pint
987C . Corkscrew

990 MOSS & DAVIS

227 Wash. Ave N.	1885-1886

993 MURPHY, F. P.

925 Cedar Ave	1892-1900
923 Cedar Ave	1901-1905

993A . Coffin; Clear; Half Pint
993B . Coffin; Clear; Half Pint

996 NAPA VALLEY WINE CO.

308 Henn. Ave	1888-1910

It is interesting to note that many of the early liquor dealers billed themselves as Wine Houses, Wine Depots, or Wine Companies because those of us who dig find many more whiskey flasks than wine bottles. Perhaps when the Temperance movement was strong it was more socially acceptable to advertise their less potent products, especially wine, which had the sanction of Biblical usage as well. This most likely is the case with the Napa Valley Wine Company, which was formed in 1888 by Joseph Paulle, Louis Gross, and Nels Nelson. The business occupied the basement and 1st floor of a 4 story brick building at 308 Hennepin Avenue, which ironically, was on the same block as the Minnesota Anti-Saloon League headquarters. The officers of the Napa Valley Co. shuffled around a bit in its early years, with only Ludwig Gross staying with the firm; by 1897 he was both president and treasurer. Like most turn-of-the-century liquor dealers, they sold wholesale and retail. Some details on the business can be found in an article which appeared in the Minneapolis Journal in 1903: "The business of the above wine company was established some 20 years ago by L. Gross, its present president. He can justly claim credit for having first introduced to the city and state the finest grades of California wines and brandies. The wines of this company enjoy a high reputation for their purity and bouquet and many of the best known physicians prescribe the leading brands of this well known and reliable house". Ads from this period list a number of products including 8-year old Port, Angelicas and Muscatel at $1.00 per gallon or 25¢ per quart bottle, and "Oris" Pure Rye or "Ursus" whiskey at 95¢ per full quart.

On April 10, 1908, the building at 308 Hennepin caught fire, causing $20,000 damage. Gross was forced to sell out his entire smoke-damaged inventory at 1/2 wholesale prices. The business never seems to have fully recovered, and in 1913 its creditors forced it into bankruptcy. Gross carried on a sort of mail order liquor business for a few years; then, in 1917, we find his last listing in the Minneapolis city directory as president and treasurer of the Colonial Tire and Rubber Company. After 1917 he moved to Duluth where he died in 1929.

In addition to the embossed whiskey bottle, (which is by no means common) there are a number of interesting artifacts from the Napa Valley Company, including a ceramic whiskey nip in the shape of a little dog, a whiskey jug, and the elusive bitters embossed CURRAN'S HERB BITTERS/PEPSINIZED on one side and THE NAPA VALLEY WINE CO./MINNEAPOLIS on the other.

996A . Style D3A; Clear
996B . Dog with leg raised, Figural pottery bottle
996C . Watson #374: bright light green, H8-1/4 x L4-3/8 x W2-1/2 - See Pat. Medicine Section for drawing
996D . Jug

997 NELSON, A.C.
    1117 Wash. Ave S.   1902-1905
997A1. Coffin: Clear

998 NELSON, ERICK
    28 Main St S.E.   1881
    13 Main St S.E.   1882-1883
    2 Main St N.E.   1885-1893
998A . Coffin; Clear

(997A)

(998A)

(999A)

(999B)

(1004A)

CURRAN'S HERB BITTERS (996C)
PEPSINIZED

THE NAPA VALLEY WINE CO.
MINNEAPOLIS, MINN.

(996D)

NAPA VALLEY WINE Co. 308 HENNEPIN AVE. MINNEAPOLIS MINN.

(996A)

NORDEEN & LUND WINES & LIQUORS LABOR TEMPLE 730 4TH ST. SO. MINNEAPOLIS

(1005B)

NELSON & BOHLIG UNION TEMPLE 26 & 28 WASHINGTON AVE SO. MINNEAPOLIS

(1002A)

NORDEEN & LUND No. 800 FOURTH ST MINNEAPOLIS MINN.

(1005A)

NORDEEN & LUND WINES & LIQUORS 730 SO. FOURTH ST. MINNEAPOLIS

(1005C)

999 NELSON, NELS
    718 3rd Ave N.E.   1895
    120 S. 2nd   1896-1898
    229 Nic. Ave   1899-1902
    229 Wash. Ave S.   1902-1910
999A . Coffin; Clear; Half Pint
999B . Style D4A; Clear; Pint
999C . Tray, Colored

1002 NELSON & BOHLIG
    26 Wash. Ave S.   1896-1899
1002A . Style Unknown; Clear

1004 NIERENHAUSEN, J.N.   1898-1909
    124 Henn. Ave.
1004A . Coffin; Clear; Pint

1005 NORDEEN & LUND
    800 S. 4th   1892-1894
    730 S. 4th   1895-1900
    329 Cedar Ave   1899-1900
1005A . Coffin; Clear; Quart
1005B . Coffin; Clear; Half Pint
1005C . Coffin; Clear; Pint

(1008A)

(1025A)

(1023A)

(1026A)

1008 NORTH STAR WINE CO.
312-314 20th Ave N.   1895
205 Cedar Ave   1896
1008A . Coffin; Clear; Half Pint

[NORTHWESTERN BOTTLING CO. - See Brewery Section]

1014 O'DONNELL & CO   ?
Address unknown
1014A . Shot Glass

1017 O'HERN, WM. F.
927 Cedar Ave   1903-1910
Billy O'Hern, along with partner John P. Collins,
started a saloon at 917 Cedar Ave. So. in 1902.
Collins left the business a year later, but O'Hern
continued in business at the same address for
years, even to the point of selling soft drinks in
his establishment once Prohibition was enacted.
1017A . Style D4J; Half Pint
1017B . Style D4G; Half Pint
1017C . Mug
1017D . Pocket Mirror
1017E . Opener

(1017D)

(1017H)   (1017J)

(1017A)

(1017K)

(1017B)

(1017I)

(1017C)

(1017L)

1017F . Opener
1017G . Opener
1017H . Style D4G; Clear; Abm & Bimal; Half Pint
1017I . Trade Card

[OLIMB, I. E. - See Brewery Section]

1023 OLSON & FJELLMAN
103 Wash. Ave S.   1900-1901
1023A . Coffin; Clear; Half Pint

1025 OLSON, F. L.   ?
413 Central Ave
1025A . Coffin; Clear; Half Pint

1026 OLSON & RYBERG
413 Central Ave   1902-1906
1026A . Style D4G; Clear; Pint; Half Pint

1029 ORBECK, EDWARD
427 Cedar Ave   1896-1906
24 N. 5th   1910

1032 OSWALD, J. C.
Pence Opera House   1867-1873
17 Wash. Ave N.   1874-1905

There have been some distinguished men in the history of the Minnesota liquor industry. Some became known even outside of the state, such as A.M. Smith and George Benz. Others were influential in the growth of Minneapolis, such as Isaac Weil and Jonas F. Brown. However, there is one man who is virtually unknown to the Minneapolis bottle collector because he seems to have left no embossed or paper labelled bottles or "go-withs" to mark his passing. Yet this man was in the liquor business for over fifty years. He was a pioneer of Minneapolis. He was a State Senator. He raised race horses of world renown. And his native wines were known far beyond Minnesota borders. This man was John Conrad Oswald.

J.C. Oswald was born in the villge of Oberaach, Canton Thurgau, Switzerland on May 20, 1824. At age 16, he apprenticed to a cotton manufacturer, Godfrey Scheitlin. In two years his industry and aptness were rewarded by his appointment as overseer, which he diligently pursued for the next five years.

In 1847 he joined the tide of emmigration which flowed toward the shores of America. While in New York he was appointed the agent of a large tract of land in West Virginia. He met Ursula Scheitlin, an old girlfriend and also the sister of his former employer. They soon married and she accompanied him to the scene of his labor for the next ten years. It was a wild region and the locality offered none of the comforts and conveniences of life.

He opened a country store, cleared and cultivated a farm and met with fair success. Five children were born while the Oswalds were in the South. Only one survived.

In 1857, he sold out and came to Minneapolis, where Godfrey Scheitlin, his former employer and now brother-in-law, had preceded him. He opened a general store with his brother Henry Oswald and after a year bought out his brother's interest. He moved his stock goods to the old land office buildings in lower town. In the spring of 1859 he took a new partner, Mathias Nothakel. The firm continued in business until 1862, when both members sold out.

He then bought a 160 acre farm named "Oak Grove," which was on the site of the present Bryn Mawr area of Minneapolis. He raised tobacco and made a success of it for two years, but the crop was destroyed by frost in August 1863 and the attempt was never repeated.

He had a fondness for horses, which he bred and raised. His mare brought him nine colts, every one a trotter and some breaking world records.

His knowledge of wine making in the valleys of his native land directed his attention to the adaptation of the fruits of this country for wine. In 1858, he and Godfrey Scheitlin experimented in the manufacture of native fruit wine. The experiments proved a great success. In 1862 Oswald constructed a wine cellar on his farm, and engaged in the manufacture of wine on an extensive scale. "J.C. Oswald's Native Wines" became celebrated and brought orders from distant places.

About 1866 he added to the wine business that of distilled liquors and established the first wholesale wine and liquor business in Minneapolis. The first location was an old stand at the corner of First Street and Hennepin Avenue. In 1867 he moved to No. 3 Pence Opera House and apparently bought out a Mr. Thornton, a grocer who ran an ad in the 1867 Minneapolis Tribunes for "fine wines and liquors" (one would guess that the wines came from Oswald himself).

In 1874 he erected a four-story brick store at No. 17 Washington Avenue North, where he stayed until his death. In 1881 he associated with Mr. Theophil Basting, who had long been manager of the business and also his son-in-law. The firm's name was J.C. Oswald and Co. In that same year he had a huge, elegant home built at 1322 Hennepin Avenue.

Oswald always took an active interest in public affairs. He was on the Board of Commissioners who directed the building of the present County Courthouse in Minneapolis. He was instrumental in the building of the first electric street car system. For many years he was a member of the Park Board. During these years the foundation of the magnificent park system of the city was laid, and its plans largely perfected.

Oswald was a distinguished-looking man. He had piercing eyes, white hair surrounding a bald top and a white General Custer style mustache and goatee. In 1887 he was elected to the State Senate and he held the office four years. At this time he sold his farm, 119 acres of it going for nearly one-half million dollars.

At the time of his death, on June 13, 1905, J.C. Oswald was Vice-President and Director of the Germania Bank and Director of the F&M Bank. Shortly after Oswald's death, Basting closed the J.C. Oswald and Co. doors for the last time.
1032A . Pottery Handled Decanter

1035 PERSON, OSCAR
229 20th Ave N.   1909-1910
1035A . Style D4D; Clear; Pint
1035B . Corkscrew

1038 PETERSON, F.E.
323 20th Ave N.   1894-1896
1038A . Embossing from Clear Shard

(1035A)

(1038A)

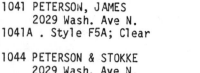

JAS. PETERSON
2029 WASH. AVE NO.
MINNEAPOLIS, MINN.

(1041A)

PETERSON & STOKKE
2029 WASH AVE NORTH
MINNEAPOLIS

(1044B)

PETERSON & STOKKE
2029
WASH AVE NO.
MINNEAPOLIS

(1044A)

S.J. RICHARDSON
516 HENNEPIN
&
221 CENTRAL
NEAPO
MINN

(1050A)

C.H.A. RICHTER
311 HENNEPIN AVE.
MINNEAPOLIS

(1053A)

1041 PETERSON, JAMES
    2029 Wash. Ave N.   1899-1906
1041A . Style F5A; Clear

1044 PETERSON & STOKKE
    2029 Wash. Ave N.   1892-1898
                                   1907-1909

1044A . Coffin; Clear; Pint
1044B . Style F5A; Clear

[PLYMOUTH BEER HALL - See Adolph Wolff]

1050 RICHARDSON, S. J.
    105 Wash. Ave N.   1886
    516 Henn. Ave   1888
    245 1st Ave S.   1890
    30 S. 6th   1890-1892
    221 Central Ave   1890-1891
1050A . Clear fragment - probably Quart size

1053 RICHTER, C. H. A.
    317 N. Wash. Ave   1878-1883
    311 Henn. Ave   1883-1897
1053A . Picnic - (Single K8P); Clear; Half Pint, Pint

1056 ROBITSHEK, S.
    1429 Wash. Ave S.   1890-1910
1056A . Paper label found on back of California Wine
       House reads "Family Liquor Store - S.
       Robitshek"

[ROGER, J. G. - See TOOZE'S]

1059 ROMAN & PERSON
    229 20th Ave N.   1890-1910
1059A . Coffin; Clear; Half Pint, Pint, Quart

1061 RUD, ANTHONY
    1842 S. 9th
1061A. Metal Adv Tray   1902-1910

1062 S & L WINE CO.
    1509 Wash Ave S.   1904-1905
1062A . Coffin; Clear; Half Pint
1062B . Coffin; Clear; Half Pint

1065 SAMPSON & LUNDBERG
    1329 Wash. Ave S.   1890-1898
1065A . Coffin; Clear

1066 SAXRUD, C. E.
    810 Central Ave   ?
1066A . Coffin; Clear; Half Pint

1068 SCHIEK, FRED
    122 Henn Ave   1887
    49 Wash Ave S.   1888-1893
    45-47 S. 3rd   1894-1910
1068A . Drinking Mug
1068B . Drinking Mug
1068C . Drinking Mug

1071 SCHERVEN, PAUL
    829 Cedar Ave   1892-1894
    901 Cedar Ave   1895-1898
    805 Cedar Ave   1901-1902
    629 Cedar Ave   1903
1071A . Style A1J; Clear; Half Pint
1071B . Coffin; Clear; Half Pint
1071C . Coffin; Clear; Half Pint

S&L
WINE CO.
1509
WASH. AVE.
SOUTH
MINNEAPOLIS, MINN.

(1062A)

S. & L.
1509
WASHINGTON Av.
SOUTH
WINE COMPANY

(1062B)

ROMAN & PERSON
229
20TH AVE NO.
MINNEAPOLIS

(1059A)

SAMPSON & LUNDBERG.
WINES
LIQUORS & CIGARS
1829
WASH. A
MIN

(1065A)

LIGHT HOUSE
LIQUOR STORE
C. E. SAXRUD
810
CENTRAL AVE
MINNEAPOLIS

(1066A)

(1068A)

(1071A)

(1071B)

PAUL SCHERVENS
LIQUOR
STORE
901 CEDAR AV.
MINNEAPOLIS

(1071C)

WM. J. SHEEHAN
WHOLESALE LIQUORS
253 HENNEPIN AVENUE
PHONE T.C. 1211   MINNEAPOLIS
(1077A)

(1077B)

(1080A)

involved surveying, farming and being a common "dead broke tramp." Finally, in 1872, he was in Salt Lake City, Utah when he found his calling; he opened his first California Wine Depot. Smith started his first store with $10 capital and a shaky credit rating, but good advertising, good wares and good investments soon made him a financial success. So much so, in fact, that in 1876, he closed up shop and moved to Philadelphia where preparations for the great Centennial were in progress. Here he set up his second depot. Sadly, he was too liberal granting credit and his business failed. Smith picked up the pieces, borrowed more money and started over. With much hard work he again built up his trade and in 1886 set up a small branch in Minneapolis (said to be no more than boards laid across two barrels). When this venture seemed assured of success, Smith sold his Philadelphia store and his California Wine Depot became a permanent fixture on Hennepin Avenue.

[SCHULENBERG, MATHIAS - See Brewery Section]

1077 SHEEHAN, W. J. & CO.
    117 Wash. Ave N.   1882-1884
    24 Henn. Ave.   1885-1889
    123 Wash. Ave N.   1890-1895
    253 Henn. Ave.   1901-1906
1077A . Style J10A; Clear:
1077B . Style D3A; Clear; Pint

1080 SHORBA. GEORGE
1080A . Calendar

[SIXTH STREET BODEGA - See Brewery Section]

1083 SMITH, A. M.
    249 Henn. Ave   1888-1910
    Most early liquor dealers pass on and off of the stage of history leaving few details of their life for later researchers to unearth. This is because society at that time regarded saloon keepers as low and unworthy characters of whom the less said the better. So we are indeed fortunate that Andrew Mason Smith decided to set down his life story in a book called Up and Down in the World or, Paddle Your Own Canoe.

A.M. Smith was born Hans Lykkejaeger on February 4, 1841 in Juteland, Denmark. His family was poor so the lad was apprenticed to work in a foundry; work which soon drove him to run away to sea. His career as ship's cook, London street vagabond and seaman make for interesting reading; at one point he jumped ship in Brazil, was captured by natives and feared he was to be eaten! In the late 1850's he was serving on American ships, so, when the Civil War broke out he signed on with the Union Navy (he also did a stint in the Army fighting Indians in California). His career in America also

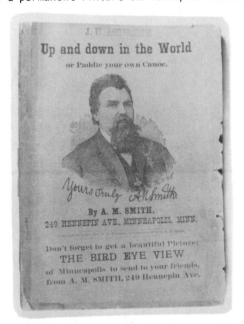

(1083AM-SMITH'S PORTRAIT PROUDLY GRACED THE COVER OF HIS AUTOBIOGRAPHY)

Smith's business soon became one of the largest of its kind in the city and was famous for its numerous advertising give-aways including calendars, trays, dominoes, almanacs, shot glasses, corkscrews, brushes, etc. For a number of years Smith also ran The California Restaurant next to his Depot. This later became a delicatessen and grocery store.

33

(1083A)

A.M.SMITH
1892
249 HEN Av.
MINNEAPOLIS
MINN.
CALIFORNIA
WINE DEPOT
ESTABLISHED
1872
FULL ½ PINT

(1083B)

A.M.SMITH
1896
249 HEN. Av.
MINNEAPOLIS
MINN.
CALIFORNIA
WINE DEPOT
ESTABLISHED
1872
FULL 1 PINT

(1083C)

A.M.SMITH
1900
249 HEN. AV.
MINNEAPOLIS
MINN.
CALIFORNIA
WINE DEPOT
ESTABLISHED
1872
FULL 1½ PINT

(1083D)

A.M.SMITH
1903
249 HEN. Av.
MINNEAPOLIS
MINN.
CALIFORNIA
WINE DEPOT
ESTABLISHED
1872
FULL ½ PINT

(1083E)

A.M.SMITH
1907
249 HEN. Av.
MINNEAPOLIS
MINN.
CALIFORNIA
WINE DEPOT
ESTABLISHED
1872
FULL 1 QUART

(1083F)

A.M.SMITH
1909
247 & 249 HEN. Av.
MINNEAPOLIS
MINN.
CALIFORNIA
WINE DEPOT
ESTABLISHED
1872
FULL PINT

(1083G)

A.M.SMITH
1914
247-249 HENN AVE
MINNEAPOLIS
ESTABL. 1872
FULL QUART

(1083H)

A.M.SMITH
BODAGA
248 HEN. Av.
MINNEAPOLIS
MINN
CALIFORNIA
WINE DEPOT
ESTABLISHED
1872

(1083I)

A.M.SMITH
BODAGA
249 HEN. Av.
MINNEAPOLIS
MINN.
CALIFORNIA
WINE DEPOT
ESTABLISHED
1872

(1083J)

A.M.SMITH
BODEGA
249 HEN. Av.
MINNEAPOLIS
MINN.
CALIFORNIA
WINE DEPOT
ESTABLISHED
1872

(1083K)

A.M.SMITH
247-249 HENNEPIN AVE
MINNEAPOLIS

(1083L)

Smith's trademarks were his various "Crescent Brand" beverages. In addition to this local trade he did a large mail order business (largely to dry counties one would suppose).

Andrew M. Smith died of his Civil War wounds in July 1915, with his son Author Mason Smith taking over the business. Prohibition, of course, closed his doors in 1919 but the Smith interests diversified to include the Universal Car Agency and a sand and gravel business.

Of all the individuals whose bottles we collect today, perhaps A.M. Smith would have best understood our hobby. He was obviously fascinated with go-withs and trinkets, and was quite the collector in his own right, being a world-recognized authority on rare coins and the author of an encyclopedia of rare coins.

1083A . Cumming's (Style K8A); Clear; Half Pint
1083A2. Cumming's (Style K8U); Clear; Half Pint
1083B . Style D3A; Clear; Half Pint, Quart
1083B2. Style D3A; Amber; Quart
1083B3. Style J3Y; Clear; Half Pint
1083B4. Style D3W; Clear; Half Pint
1083C . Style J3Y; Clear; Half Pint, Pint
1083D . Style D3A; Clear; Half Pint, Pint

A.M.SMITH
CRESCENT
PALE BEER
MINNEAPOLIS

(1083AZ)

A.M.SMITH
CRESCENT
BEER
MINNEAPOLIS, MINN.

(1083BA)

A.M.SMITH
1892
249 HEN Av.
MINNEAPOLIS
MINN.
CALIFORNIA
WINE DEPOT
ESTABLISHED
1872
FULL 1 QUART

(1083B2)

34

(PAGES FROM THE SMITH AUTOBIOGRAPHY)

1083E . Style D3A; Clear; Half Pint, Pint
1083F . Style D3A; Clear; Half Pint, Pint
1083G . Style D3A; Clear; Pint
1083H . Style D3A (ABM); Clear; Half Pint, Pint, Quart
1083I . Coffin; Clear; Pint
1083J . Coffin; Clear; Half Pint, Pint
1083K . Coffin; Clear; Half Pint
1083L . Machine made packer Jug (without handle eyes), Clear; Gallon; C.B.CO.
1083M . Shot Glass
1083N . Shot Glass
1083P . Shot Glass
1083Q . Shot Glass
1083R . Shot Glass

1083S . Shot Glass
1083T . Shot Glass
1083U . Safety Razor
1083V . Dominoes
1083W . Can Opener
1083X . Jack Knife
1083Z . Juice Strainer
1083AA . Funnel
1083AB . Egg Boiler?
1083AC . Match Safe
1083AD .
1083AE . Teapot
1083AF . Mug (markings on base)
1083AG . Knives, Forks, Spoons

(1083M)

(1083N)

(1083R)

(1083AQ)

(1083P)

(1083Q)

(1083S)

(1083T)

(1083AJ)

(1083AH)

(1083AR)

(1083AK-FRONT)

(1083AK-BACK)

(1083AL)

1083AH . Adv Tray (colored litho)
1083AJ . Adv Tray (colored litho)
1083AK . Adv Tray (wording on back)
1083AL . Style B6G; Amber; Strap side
1083AM . Paperback Book - Biography of A. M. Smith
1083AN . Letter Opener w/Jackknife (no photo)
1083AP . Deck of Playing Cards
1083AQ . Shot Glass
1083AR . Vienna Art Plate, Adv "Wines, Brandies,
          Pure Olive Oil, etc., on back
1083AS . (not pictured) Shot Glass "1913-1914"
1083AT . Etched Beer Glass
1083AU . Jackknife
1083AV . Birds eye view map of Minneapolis, dated 1892
1083AW . (not pictured) Beehive Jug, all white glaze
1083AX . (not pictured) Magazine called the "AMSCO
          Monthly"

(1083BD)

(1083AT)

(1083AP-BOX)

(1083AP-FRONT AND BACK OF CARDS)

(1083AE)

(1083Z)

Freut euch des Lebens
ni noch das Lämpchen glüht
Pflücket die Rose
th sie verblüht.

(1083AF)

(1083AA)

(BASE OF 1083AF)

(1083X)

(1083AU)

(1083W)

(1083BH)

(1083U)

(1083BF)

1083AZ . LS; Aqua; H9-1/2 x D2; Root
1083BA . HFC; Amber; H9-3/4 x D2-7/8; NBBG CO. 881
1083AZ2 HFC; Amber; H11-3/4 x D3-7/8
1083BC . Cork Adornment
1083BD . Jug
1083BE . Various Corkscrews
1083BF . Advertising Calendar
1083BG . Shoe Polish Brush (not pictured)

(1089A)

(1083AC)

(1086A)

(1092A)

(1083V)

(1085A)

(1083AB)

1085 SODINI, J. C.
    14 N. 1st   1892
    229 S. 2nd & 1227 N.E. Main   1893
    229 S. 2nd & 220 Wash. Ave S.   1894
    208 Wash. Ave S.   1898
1085A . Coffin; Clear; Half Pint

1086 SPORRONG & HOFFMAN
    505 Wash. Ave N.   1890-1894
1086A . Coffin; Clear; Half Pint

1089 STEARN BROS
    324 1st Ave S   1894-1906
    19 S. 5th   1901-1904
1089A . Corkscrew

1092 STERLING BRANCH
    Unknown   ?
1092A . Coffin; Clear

(1083BE)

(1098C)

(1098F)

(1098G)

(1098B)

(1098A)

[ST LOUIS WINE CO - See Issac Goldman]

1098 STOCKHOLM WINE CO.
    1207 Wash. Ave S.   1898
    103 Wash. Ave S.   1899-1910
1098A . Coffin; Clear
1098B . Coffin; Clear; Half Pint, Pint
1098C . Style D3H; Clear; Half Pint
1098D . Coffin; Clear; Half Pint
1098E . Corkscrew
1098F . Coffin; Clear; Half Pint
1098G . Style D4G; Clear

(1098D)

1101 SVENSON, M.D. - CROWN SAMPLE ROOM
    311 20th Ave N.   1894-1896
1101A . Style A1J; Clear; Half Pint, Pint

1103 THOMPSON & JOHNSON
    409 Central Ave   1887-1895
    411 Central Ave   1896-1906
1103A . Coffin; Clear; Pint
1103B . Coffin; Clear; Half Pint
1103C . Coffin; Clear; Pint

1104 THOMPSON & OLSON
    617 Central Ave   1908-1910
1104A . Coffin; Clear; Half Pint, Pint
1104B . Coffin; Clear; Half Pint

1107 THOMPSON, J. B.
    629 Central Ave   1902-1903
    617 Central Ave   1904-1907
1107A . Coffin; Clear; Pint

(1101A)

(1103A)

(1103C)

(1107A)

(1104A)

(1103B)

(1113A)

[THORESEN, ANCHOR - See Brewery Section]

1113 TOBIASON, TOBY
   1001 Wash. Ave S.   1906-1907
1113A . Style H7N; Clear; Half Pint, Pint

1116 TOOZE'S - J. E. Rogers
   301 S. 3rd   1897-1900
   516-518 Henn.   1897-1910
   32 S. 5th   1897-1907
   29 S. 4th   1902-1910
   46 S. 4th   1902-1907
   324 4th Ave S.   1904-1910
   Old Colony Bldg   1903

Little did Mr. Rogers, a retired minister, know that when he nicknamed his son Tooze the name would not only stick to him for life but would become even more familiar and better known that his proper name.

Tooze's business career was one without parallel in the commercial life of Minneapolis. Born a poor farm boy in Illinois, he came to the Twin Cities at the age of 18 and worked at such jobs as waiter at the Nicollet Hotel and bell boy at the St. Louis Hotel until he started his first saloon, The Mint, on Washington Ave. No. with a capitol of just $225. In 1896, at age of 27, he opened the TOOZE WINE CO. at 301 So. 3rd. At his death he owned the Rogers Hotel and Cafe 25-29 So. 4th, The Unique Theater 520 Hennepin Ave., The Empress Theater on Wabasha in St. Paul, a delicatessen and restaurant 516-518 Hennepin, The Chamber of Commerce Cafe at 4th & 4th Minneapolis, extensive property in northern Minnesota, Mexico mining property, and a chicken ranch at Mound. In the planning stages was a truly magnificent hotel - one bigger and better than Minneapolis had ever seen, one to serve as a monument to the city. In between, he had owned 7 other saloons and restaurants. His estate was valued at $165,000.

His Midas touch was admired and respected by all, and his saloons, restaurants and hotel were considered models of perfection in every way. He once said, "Work is my play, my relaxation is auto rides where we usually talk business. That's far more interesting than anything else. I have 11 different enterprises on my hands and manage them

all just as I did my 7 saloons, simply by being systematic. When I start a business I spend every minute at it working constantly. I learn every possible thing there is to know about it. In a restaurant this would include how many servings per pound of every given meat and vegetable, how much it costs to operate the range per hour, so by the time the food reaches the customer I know to a penny what the profit on each item is. I have a prominent former Minneapolis bank president in my accounting office who does this type of summary for me and I am paying him well you may be sure. This is the only way to make a business pay a profit yet meanwhile improve on the service and quality."

"I then turn it over to my manager who sends in daily reports. If receipts go down I investigate. If I hear complaints I investigate and enter it into my records. Once a week I meet with my employees, talk with them briefly and ask for suggestions, then use all the good ones. I want them to think of their enterprise as an automobile, they are the chauffeurs. I cannot tolerate lack of ambition in my employees. I know what can be done. I hope that I train them well enough and hire them with enough ambition so that some day they run me competition. I also believe in sharing profits with my employees for they have earned them."

Not only did Tooze have the Midas touch with money, but with people. He drew friends like a magnet, and people valued his friendship for its sincerity and candidness. He practiced love-never preached it, always had time to chat, for Tooze never forgot his early poverty nor the helping hands he got along the way. To charitable things he gave generously of both his time and money. The thoroughness and vigor with which he entered business carried over into his charities. If an

1908 VIEW OF TOOZES LIQUOR STORE-MHS PHOTO COLLECTION

(1116E)

appeal met his sympathy he informed himself of all details and gave not only money but his time, business acumen and physical self. Many times he heard of someone who was destitute and helped get them back on their feet, all anonymously. If that person needed hospitalization Tooze would personally take him there, visit him, pay his bills both at the hospital and home, then help find the man employment when he was able to work again. He truly believed and followed his business motto - "He best serves himself who best serves others."

He was a timid man about some things and notably quick to blush and back away when complimented, especially on his charitable acts.

Every Thankgiving while he owned the Rogers Hotel and Cafe he invited all the newsboys of the city there for dinner. There they dined in the elegantly decorated rooms and were the most important guests of the day. He would walk among them complimenting them, giving words of encouragement, calling many of them by name for he had a fabulous memory for names and faces. In 1911 there were 400 of these boys there and they had planned a small surprise testimonial to him. Somehow he got wind of it and retired to his room, 140 on the second floor, and stayed until they had all departed. The newsboys not to be thwarted went out into Nicollet Avenue below his window and held up all traffic while they stood giving cheers to Mr. Rogers.

He loved children, though he had none of his own, and spent about $5,000 a year on them. At the Unique Theater he annually gave free performances. The lobby would be heaped with thousands of bags of candy to be given away. He also was very active in Boys Club and sponsored a baseball team for 10 years.

(1116G)

Tooze had very definite ideas on liquor, the liquor business and saloons, some quite unorthodox for men of his profession. To quote him, "When I started my first saloon I knew there were many dangers about it, but I believed it could be run right. I have neither allowed myself to be influenced adversely by it nor conducted it in a way to bring discredit. I simply put before the people that which they want, and served them honestly. Any employee serving liquor to an intoxicated man meets with instant dismissal, even if both men involved are close friends of mine. A ban is put on serving any man who is using money to drink that is needed by his family. A man should not use liquor if he cannot do so without abusing it."

"I stopped drinking 26 years ago. My advice to any man would be not to drink. If all drinking were to be eliminated I would be as pleased as anyone. I would rather serve them tea than liquor or beer, but so long as people want to drink with their meals and in between their meals and prefer to patronize hotels and restaurants that afford such opportunities, I will sell them drinks."

"My bar in the Rogers Cafe is also a soda fountain - my own invention. It draws not only wines, liquors and beer but soda and mineral waters. As a result people are quite as apt to take a soft drink as something intoxicating. I hope to equip all my buffets with this type of fountain bar."

(1016I)

"I think if all people had to sit down to drink and all saloons served food there would be less intoxication. The worst, most ridiculous thing, was when the temperance extremists got the city council of Minneapolis to prohibit the free lunches. The saloon keepers had wanted them abolished because they were expensive and kept people from drinking. They couldn't get the ordinance passed but the temperance cranks did it for them, thus promoting intemperance!"

John E. Rogers died of shock following a five hour operation for intestinal adhesions. He was awake throughout the majority of the operation and in his own inimitable fashion was instructing the many doctors. He had been ill for just a few days. Although he knew his time had come he was calm and relaxed until the end. His affairs had been put in order many years before for he had endured 8 serious operations in as many years. He had formed a corporation that was to be instated by his executors upon his death. They were told to continue in his various enterprises for a term of ten years unless they deemed it advisable to

(1116F-FRONT) (1116F-BACK)

liquidate before that. The estate was then to be divided into equal parts - one to go to his wife, the other to be divided by his sister and four brothers. A liberal allowance was to be given his wife meanwhile.

By request of the thousands of his friends his body was laid in state so that they all might say their last goodbyes. Funeral services were private with fellow Elks acting as pallbearers.

From the time he owned the Unique Theater he had had church services held there each Sunday morning for people who would not or could not ordinarily get to church. The Sunday following his funeral a memorial service was held there for him. Not another person could be crowded into the theater and there were about 500 left outside so a second service was held.

1116A . Style D3L; Clear; Half Pint, Pint
1116B . Style D3W; Clear
1116C . Miniature Decanter, Clear
1116D . Style D3W; Clear; Pint
1116E . Mug
1116F . Metal Trays, front & back view

(1122A)

(1119A)

Walla Valley Wine Co
246 HENNEPIN AVE.
MINNEAPOLIS
FULL ONE PINT
(1125A)

(1125B)
WALLA VALLEY WINE HOUSE
246 HENNEPIN AVE.
MINNEAPOLIS
FULL HALF PINT

1116G . Ash Tray/Match Holder
1116H . Corkscrew
1116I . Dinner Plate

[TUGMAN, B. - See WET GOODS STORE in BREWERY SECTION]

1119 WAIDT, PAUL
     1801 Wash. Ave N.   1891-1894
1119A . Coffin; Clear; Half Pint

1122 WALIN, CHAS. - Five of Hearts Saloon
     718 S. 4th   1895
     601 Wash Ave S.   1900
     309 Wash Ave S.   1896-1900
     319 Wash Ave S.   1901-1903
1122A . Coffin; Clear; Half Pint

1125 WALLA VALLEY WINE HOUSE
     246 Henn. Ave   1892-1895
1125A . Style J12A; Clear; Pint
1125B . Style F5J; Clear

Tooze's

(1116C)

(1116H)

Tooze's
TRADE MARK
ZZ
MINNEAPOLIS
(1116A)

Tooze's
518-518
HENNEPIN AVE
301 3RD STR SO
34 5TH STR SO
MINNEAPOLIS
(1116B)

Toozes
TRADE MARK
ZZ
MINNEAPOLIS
(1116D)

(1128A)

(1131A)

GUST. WARMELIN
WINES
&
IORS

(1131B)

1128 WANG, OLAUS
    601 Cedar Ave   1894-1901
    913 Cedar Ave   1902
1128A . Coffin; Clear; Half Pint

1131 WARMELIN, GUSTAV
    2615 E. 25th   1891
    2619 E. 25th   1892-1895
1131A . Coffin; Clear; Half Pint
1131B . Coffin fragment; Clear

1134 WEIL, ISAAC
    210 Henn Ave   1880-1889
    110 Henn Ave   1890
    40 & 42 S. 6th   1891-1901
    42 & 44 S. 6th   1902-1904

In 1866, when Isaac Weil was just 18, he decided to leave his native land of Bohemia for America. He worked in New York for a time, then moved to Chicago where he was a witness to the great fire of 1871. While in Chicago, he met and married Hannah Bachrach and in 1874 their first son, Jonas, who was later to become a lawyer, was born.

Minnesota was being widely proclaimed as the most beautiful, healthful, opportunity laden state to be found. In 1879 the Isaac Weil family decided to give it a try. According to his grandson, he was a large but very gentle, well liked and admired man. His somewhat bushy hair was snow white by the time he was 26 and he wore a large white walrus type mustache.

(1134V-WEIL'S PORTRAIT APPEARED ON THIS COMMERA-TIVE COIN STRUCK FOR HIS 75TH BIRTHDAY)

He is not listed in the directories until 1881 when he opened a saloon at 210 Hennepin Avenue. The following year he added his wholesale and retail outlet. The next significant dates seem to be: 1887 when he became known as Isaac Weil & Co.; 1891 when he moved to 42 South 6th; and the following year when he expanded to 40 - 42 South 6th Street.

Downtown at that time had many fancy bars that catered to the business man. Weil's was a place where any man was made to feel welcome. The back bar was 50 feet of ornate mirrors and beautifully carved wood. On it were not the vast variety of bottles we have today, but a few barrels and 20 to 25 decanters. More barrels were in racks at the ends of the bar. Whiskey sold for 10¢ a shot or 25¢ a half pint. The front bar was also a thing of beauty and had the usual brass rail and spitoons, but no stools. The rest of the saloon was filled with small tables and chairs.

1905 saw a large spurt of growth for the Weils whose slogan was EVERYTHING DRINKABLE. Isaac took three of his 5 sons into the business, moved to 42 - 44 South 6th Street and added another outlet at 39 - 41 South 3rd Street. Isaac became president of Isaac Weil & Sons, Charles was vice president and treasurer, Benjamin was the secretary and Hermann acted as clerk until 1911 when he became branch manager. All were still living at home with their folks.

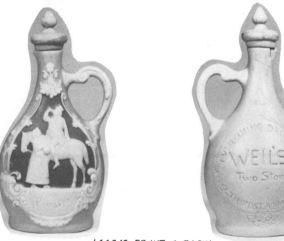

(1134I-FRONT & BACK)

The company became incorporated in 1906 and remained an apparently steady, stable company until 1918, when with Prohibition the talk of the industry, they all split to go into different fields. Charles became vice president - treasurer of the Emporium, 715 Nicollet, a store that specialized in woman's millinery and clothing. Benjamin became a broker and Hermann was a district agent for a life insurance company.

For some years preceding this closing date, Isaac Weil went to Europe once a year, taking one child along each time. While there, he personally chose all the wines, liquors and liqueurs he would import. He also took time to visit the factories so that he might personally order all the whiskey nips that he gave away, mostly in December with his famous nickel lunches. There are about 50 varieties according to a grandson.

(1134S)

(1134L)

(1134K)

(1137M)

(1134M)

(1134H)

(1134J-BEAUTIFULLY DETAILED WHISKEY NIP)

(1134F)

44

Isaac Weil died December 24, 1925, at the age of 78, Charles in 1929 at age 50, Jonas in 1933 at age 58. All had been extremely active in civic and Jewish affairs of the area. Isaac served for many years as president of the Temple of Israel. So active and well known was Jonas that officials of various departments of the city participated in his funeral.

In 1934 the firm of Isaac Weil & Sons was started up once again, this time at 28 South 6th Street. Hermann acted as President & treasurer and William the youngest of the brothers was manager. There was a tunnel from this store to the Hotel Radisson a block away. Bell hops frequently made the trip over there for the guests.

In 1938, their last year, they moved to 100 South 4th Street. 1938 shows William as a salesman for Schenley Distillers Corp., and so ended another of Minneapolis' great liquor establishments.

1134A . Style D3U; Clear
1134B . Coffin; Clear; Half Pint and Pint
1134C . Coffin; Clear; Half Pint
1134D . Packer Jug; Clear; Half Gallon
1134E . Style D3B; Clear; Quart
1134F . Pottery Barrel; blue & white
1134G . Pottery Teapot; green; glazed
1134H . Handled Pottery Pitcher; yellow & white
1134I . Pottery; German Greenware
1134J . Pottery; German; blue glaze
1134K . Shot Glass
1134L . Shot Glass
1134M . Shot Glass
1134N . Jug
1134P . Jug
1134Q . JUG
1134R . Metal Tip Tray
1134S . Shot Glass
1134T . Style D3B; Clear; Half Pint
1134U . Cork Adornment
1134V . Commemorative Coin, one coin minted for each of Weil's children
1134W . Monogrammed calling card holder dated 1909
1134X . Head of walking stick

1137 WEIL, ISAAC & SONS
    42 & 44 S. 6th   1905-1907
    39 & 41 S. 3rd   1905-1907
1137A . Style D3B; Clear; Quart
1137B . Style D3X; Clear
1137B2. Style D3W; Clear
1137C . Style D3A; Clear
1137D . Style D4A; Clear; Half Pint and Pint
1137E . Style D3X; Clear
1137F . Style D4D; Clear; Half Pint
1137H . Pottery; dark brown glaze
1137I . Pottery Jug
1137J . Taper Cordial
1137K . Pottery Jug; Cobalt Blue Glaze
1137L . Pottery Jug

1140 WEIL, ISAAC & SONS, INC.
    42 & 44 S. 6th   1908-1909
    39 & 41 S. 3rd   1908-1910
1140A . Style D3A; Clear; Private Mold; ABM
1140B . Style D4G; Clear; Half Pint AND Quart

1143 WEIL & GARDNER   ?
    242 Henn. Ave
1143A . Coffin; Clear

(1134P)

(1134N)

(1137K)

(1137I)

(1137L)

(1134Q)

(1137H)

(1134X)

(1137J)

(1134R)

(1134A)

(1134C)

(1134B)

(1134D)

(1134E)

(1134T)

(1137C)

(1137A)

(1137B)

(1137D)

(1137E)

(1137F)

46

(1134G)

(1134Z)

(1140A)
(1140B)

(1152A)

(1143A)

1146 WESTERN CONSOLIDATED DISTILLING CO.
    Address unknown   1906-1914
1146A . Jug

[WET GOODS STORE - See Brewery Section]

1152 WOLFF, ADOLPH - Plymouth Beer Hall
    226 Plymouth Ave   1894-1898
 Soon after selling his saloon, Wolff went to work
as a foreman for the Massolt Bottling Company.
1152A . Coffin; Clear; Pint

(1146A)

LATE ARRIVALS

(920A-CHRISTIAN HANSTAD IN
BUSINESS 1908-1910+)

(999C. NELS NELSON)

THE CRYSTAL
JOHN T. HART PROP'R
21 N. WASHINGTON AVE.
MINNEAPOLIS, MINN.

(922A. COFFIN)

J. C. OSWALD & CO.

Wholesale Dealers and Importers

Wines and Liquors

17 Washington Avenue North,

MINNEAPOLIS, - - MINNESOTA.

AST CH
LUDWIG
65 CENTRAL

(?)

DEUTSCHER RATHSKELLER
T.C. PHONE 656
J.N. NIERENHAUSEN
124 HENP. AVE.
MINNEAPOLIS, MINN.

(1004A)

J. M. DAVIS,

SILVER PITCHER RYE & BOURBON.

TRADE MARK
ESTABLISHED 1883.

Wholesale Dealer in

Fine Whiskies,

Brandies and

Wines.

In Bond or Tax Paid.

114 North Second St.,

Minneapolis, Minn.

R. SILBERSTEIN
108
CENTRAL AVE.
MINNEAPOLIS
MINN.

(1082A. COFFIN)

SHOURBA & MARTONN
WINES & LIQUORS
1500
SECOND ST. SO.
MINNEAPOLIS

(1079A)

1207
WASH. AVE. S
TELEPHONE
1207
MINNEAPOLIS

(?)

HENRY THOMPSON
WINES
LIQUORS
&
CIGARS
718 3RD AVE. N.E.
MINNEAPOLIS
MINN.

(1106A)

CALIFORNIA WINE HOUSE
253 SECOND AVE. SOUTH
MINNEAPOLIS
FULL   ½ PINT

(837W)

JAMES L. KELLY
WINES & LIQUORS
244 HENNEPIN AVE. MINNEAPOLIS

(941A)

(1061A RUD WAS IN BUSINESS 1902-1910+)

(CORKSCREWS)

(1068B)

(1081A-LOUIS SIEVERS IN BUSINESS 1892 ONLY)

(1068C-VIEW OF LID)

(SIDEVIEW OF 1068C & 91D)

(91D-VIEW OF LID)

49

(970B)

(970A)

(849B)

(810C)

(852L)

(1032A)

(1003A)

(1134AB)

50

2
ST PAUL
WHISKEYS

(1201D)

1201 ABERLE, DANIEL & CO.
    409-411 Sibley   1885-1904
    129 E. 3rd St   1905-1918
1201A . Back Bar Decanter "Melbrook"
1201B . Back Bar Decanter "Golden Link"
1201C . Jug "Golden Wedding Rye"
1201D . Metal Tray

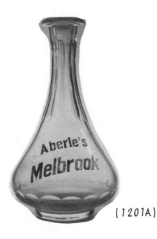

(1201A)

(1201B)

(1201E)

(1201C)

(1204A)

(1204C)

ST. AUGUSTINE BITTERS

ABERLE, WESTHEIMER CO.

SOLE PROPRIETORS

ST. PAUL, MINN.

(1204B)

1204 ABERLE - WESTHEIMER
174-178 W. 7th St   1897-1904
In 1892 Ferdinand Westheimer and his sons Eugene,
Morris and Lee came from St. Joseph, Mo. and opened
a wholesale liquor store at 282 Jackson.

The following year David Aberle started a liquor
store at 127 E. 3rd. From 1894 to 1896 the company
was listed and Aberle and Rose at 174-178 W. 7th
(Seven Corners) St. Paul.

In 1897 the two businesses merged and formed the
Aberle-Westheimer Liquor business.

Sometime during 1900 Westheimer left the business
and went to work for Sternberg, Weil & Co. a
clothing manufacturer. Thus ended the partnership
of the two (1897-1900).

David Aberle kept the name Westheimer on the record
books and advertised as Aberle-Westheimer & Co.
until 1904 when he moved his liquor business
to 129 E. 3rd. He remained in business there until
he died in 1916. He called the business D. Aberle
and Sons. Jacob Westheimer formed his own liquor
business.

The first St. Augustine Bitters to be found was dug
in a dump in Scanlon, Minnesota in 1973. Six whole
bottles and about twenty broken bottles were dug
the following year in the Irene, South Dakota dump.
1204A . Coffin; Clear; Half Pint
1204B . See Bitters Chapter of the Book; Amber;
         H9-1/4 x L4-1/4 x W2-1/4
1204C . Style D3B; Clear; Quart

1207 BENZ, GEORGE
110 E. 3rd St   1881-1887

1210 BENZ, GEORGE & SONS
6th & Main St.   1887-1918
George Benz was born in Osthofen Germany in
1838. He immigrated to America in 1853, settling
first in Chicago, then three years later coming
to the frontier town of St. Paul, Minnesota
Territory. There he opened the "United States
Billiard Hall and Restaurant", which he ran until
1865 when he entered the distilling and wholesale
liquor business with a Major C.J. Becht. After
Becht's death in 1878 Benz was sole owner of the
thriving business.

Back in 1861, Benz had married Miss Rose
Voehringer, who bore him 5 sons and 3 daughters.
Several of these sons became involved in the family
business: George G., who went to Europe to get a
PhD in Chemistry before entering the firm; Herman,
who opened a Benz branch office in Duluth in the
1880's; and Paul, who played a lesser role. In
1887 the company was renamed Geo. Benz and Sons to
reflect their increased role in the business.

GEORGE BENZ
ST. PAUL.
GEO. BENZ & SONS, DISTILLERS AND WHOLESALE
MERCHANTS.

At the height of its power the Benz organization
was impressive indeed. Their headquarters at 110
E. 3rd Street occupied three stories. In addition
they used the cellars of several adjacent buildings
for storage of their wines, liquors, ginger ale,
porter and mineral water. Besides their Duluth
branch they maintained an outlet in Minneapolis and
held controlling interests in distilleries in
Eminence, Kentucky and Baltimore.
From Benz's newspaper ads it would seem the
mainstays of his trade were his "Uncle Sam Monogram
Whiskey" and his "Pickwick Rye". But the Benz
bottle most sought after by collectors is the
famous "Geo. Benz and Sons Appetine Bitters" which
was advertised as "A tonic, an appetizer, a
cocktail bitters..." This product seems to have
been introduced in the 1890's; when subjected to
analysis in 1905 it was found to contain 36.95%
alcohol. While its medicinal properties were
dubious at best there is no question that this
bitters, with its elaborate scrollwork, and various
sizes and colors, is among the very finest of
Minnesota bottles.

GEORGE BENZ STORE AT 218 HENNEPIN
AVE IN MINNEAPOLIS IN 1915-(MHS
PHOTO COLLECTIONS)

George Benz died January 11, 1908 at the age of 69, and his sons carried on the business. Around 1918 the Benz clan (perhaps seeing Prohibitionist handwriting on the wall) abandoned the liquor trade and went into real estate. At this too, they prospered, and present day St. Paul is home to quite a few of old George's descendants.

1210A . Miniature Cylinder Whiskey; Clear; H4-1/4
1210B . 3" diameter cylinder; Clear and Amber
1210C . Miniature base embossed; Clear Cylinder
1210D . Backbar decanter
1210E . Back Bar Decanter "Old Blue Ribbon Bourbon"

1210F . Mini Pottery Jug, white glaze, "Old Days Pure Rye"
1210G . Multi colored Pottery Pitcher, "Old Blue Ribbon"
1210H . Back Bar Decanter "Pickwick Rye"
1210I . Back Bar Decanter "Uncle Sam's Monogram"

1210J . Jug
1210K . Metal Adv Sign
1210L . Metal Adv Sign
1210M . Adv Tray
1210N . Private Mold; Amber; H8 x L3-1/2 x W3-1/2; H6-1/2 x L3 x W3; H4-1/2 x L2 x W2; Base "Pat. Nov. 23, 1897"
1210N2. Private Mold; Black Amethyst; H8 x L3-1/2 x W3-1/2; Base "Pat. Nov. 23, 1897"
1210Q . Private Mold; Amber; H3-1/2 x L1-1/2 x W1-1/2

A LINE-UP OF BENZ'S MANY FINE AND POPULAR PRODUCTS

(1210F)

(1210T)

(1210AE)

(1210AB)

(1210U)

(1210I)

(1210AC)

(1210H)

(1210D)

(1210G)

(1210E)

(1210AD)

(1210Y)

(1210X)

1210R . Same mold as 1210N1 but without side panel
        embossing; Amber; H8 x L3-1/2 x W3-1/2; Base
        "Pat. Nov. 23, 1897"
1210S . Tin Advertising Sign
1210T . Back Bar Decanter "Old Days Rye"
1210U . Back Bar Decanter "Appetine Bitters"
1210V . Sign, Bas-relief, Plaster, about 24" x 36"
1210W . Style D3W; Amber; Base Embossed
1210X . Half Gallon Flint Glass Jug
1210Y . Back Bar Decanter "Old Blue Ribbon"
1210Z . ABM Screw Cap; Amber; "BENZ" on shoulder
1210AB . Fancy Decanter

(1210B)

(1210S)

(1210J)

(1210Z)

(1210N)

(1210V)

(1210R)

(1210Q)

(1210K)

(1210M)

(1210L)

55

(1210A)

(1210C)

GEO. BENZ
& SONS

(1210W)

(1213G)

(1213L)

(1214B)

P. J. BOWLIN & SON
ST. PAUL
MINN

(1214B)

1213 BOWLIN, P. J.
        314 Sibley   1885-1908
        145 E. 5th   1909

Patrick J. Bowlin came to St. Paul with his parents
when a lad of ten years, remaining a resident of
St. Paul until he died. He was engaged in the
wholesale liquor business for about a half a
century. He was born in County Tipperary, Ireland,
August 17, 1847. His parents were Jeremiah and Ann
(Chasen) Bolin. They came to America in 1849, and
located in Boston. In 1857 they moved to St. Paul
where Jeremiah Bowlin engaged in business as a
railroad contractor.

Patrick J. Bowlin attended the Cathedral School and
also night school sessions. It was in the 60's
that he secured a position as bookkeeper in the
employ of Griggs Brothers, wholesale grocers,
brewers, and distillers. He remained with that
concern until it retired from business on the 1st
of September, 1869. He then embarked in the
wholesale liquor business on his own as senior
member of the firm of Bowlin & Flannagan, which was
changed to Bowlin & McGeehan on the 1st of July
1883. Fourteen years later (1897) the business was

incorporated under the name of P.J. Bowlin & Son,
which maintained a continuous and successful
existence until 1919, when Prohibition went into
effect. Mr. Bowlin was also the head of the Bowlin
Realty Company, extensive owners of business
properties in St. Paul, which was established about
1912. He usually was successful in whatever he was
associated with, and he long ranked among the
substantial and enterprising businessmen of the
city.

On the 9th of April 1872 Mr. Bowlin married Miss
Josephine Bevan (who passed away on March 7, 1884)
and had 8 children. P.J. Bowlin died on February
4th, 1923 at age 76.

Bowlin's leading brands of Whiskey were Humbolt
Rye, Camp Nelson Bourbon, Hazel Grove Bourbon, and
White Rose Rye Whiskey.

(1213E)

(1213K)

DIGESTINE
BITTERS
P.J. BOWLIN LIQUOR CO.
SOLE PROPRIETORS
ST. PAUL MINN.

(1213F)

DIGESTINE
BITTERS
P.J. BOWLIN & SON
SOLE PROPRIETORS
ST. PAUL MINN.

(1214A)

(1214A)

(1213B)

(1213C)

(1213D)

(1213H)

(1213M)

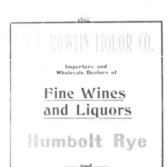

(1213J)

(1214C)   (1261B)

(1216B)

COLUMBIA
WINEHOUSE
BRENCK&KRENT
460,462 & 464
WABASHA ST
ST PAUL
FULL ½ PINT

(1216A)

1213B . Silver Gilded Back Bar bottle, engraved
        "Humbolt Whiskey"
1213C . Back Bar Decanter "Camilla Brandy"
1213D . Pottery Jug "White Rose Rye",4 Sizes Known
1213E . Metal Adv Sign
1213F . Private Mold; Amber; H8 x L3-1/2 x W3
1213G . Private Mold; Amber; H3-1/4 x L1-1/2 x W1-1/4
1213H . Back Bar Decanter "Camp Nelson Bourbon"
1213J . Tin Sign, 32" x 44"
1213K . Silver Covered Metal Hip Flask

1214 BOWLIN, P.J. & SON
1214A . Private Mold; Amber; H8 x L3-1/2 x W3
1214B . Base embossed miniature; clear

1216 BRENCK & KRENT - Columbia Wine House
      460 Wabasha   1894-1902
1216A . Style Unknown; Clear; Half Pint
1216B . Jug

1219 CALIFORNIA WINE HOUSE
      42 E. 7th   1886-1918
1219A . Shot Glass
1219B . Shot Glass
1219C . Shot Glass
1219D . Shot Glass
1219E . Shot Glass

(1219B)

(1219A)

(1219C)

(1219D)

(1219E)

(1225A)

1222 DEER PARK DISTILLERY CO.
      159 W. 3rd   1905-1908
1222A . Jug
1222B . Jug
1225 ECONOMY
      Address unknown   date unknown
1225A . Shot Glass

1228 EGGERT, FRED
      484 Robert   1901-1912
1228A . Coffin; Clear; Half Pint

1231 EPSTEIN, L. & CO. (sold "MAPLE LEAF RYE")
      373 JACKSON   1899-1910
1231A . Coffin; Clear; Half Pint

(1222A)

(1222B)

(1228A)

(1231A)

1234 ESCH, JACOB
      33 E. 7th   1901-1918
1234A . Shot Glass
1234B . Jug

1237 FINK, MORRIS
      306 E. 7th   1902-1912
1237A . Coffin; Clear; Half Pint
1237B . Shot Glass
1237C . Jug
1237D . Jug
1237E . Jug
1237F . Style D4G; Clear; Pint

(1234B)

(1234A)

(1237B)

(1237D)

(1237A)

(1237E)

(1237C)

(1237F)

1240 GRUENTER, AUGUST
    Address unknown   date unknown
1240A . Leather covered flask with ground lip & screw
        cap

[HAGGENMILLER, CHAS. - See Brewery Section]

1243 HAYNER, DISTILLING COMPANY (Branch)
    32 E. 5th   1905-1917
1243A . Cylindrical; Clear; Quart; Fluted neck & base
1243A2. Cylindrical; Amber; Quart; Fluted neck & base
1243A3. Flask; Clear; Pint; Fluted neck & base,
        "Design Pat Nov 30 1897"

1249 HILLSDALE DISTILLERY CO.
    317 Minnesota St   1905-1918
1249A . Cork Adornment

1252 HIRCHMAN & CO. (Minnesota Club Rye Whiskey)
    605 E. Minnehaha   1892-1918
1252A . Back Bar Decanter
1252B . Back Bar Decanter
1252C . Back Bar Decanter
1252D . Metal Adv Tray
1252E . Cordial; Amber; Pint
1252F . Back Bar Decanter

(1243A)

(1249A)

(1252D)

1246 HERZ, A.
    297 E. 7th   1903-1918
1246A . Miniature with Paper Labels
1246B . Shot Glass
1246C . Shot Glass
1246D . Metal Tray
1246E . Shot Glass

(1246B)

(1246C)

(1246A)

(1246D)

59

(1252A)

(1252C)

(1252B)

(1252F)

(1261A)

A.HIRSCHMAN&CO.
(1252E)

1254 HOLLISTER DISTILLING CO.   ?
1254A . Beer Bottle Label

1255 HOUSE OF ST. CROIX
    Address unknown   date unknown
1255A . Leather covered Flask with ground lip & screw
     cap
1255B . Back Bar Decanter
1255C . Back Bar Decanter

1258 HURLEY BROS
    322 Sibley   1892-1901
    318 Robert St   1902-1913
1258A . Shot Glass
1258B . Watson #374; Dark Amber; H7-3/4 x L4-1/4 x
    W2-1/2 - See Pat. Medicine section for drawing
1258C . Watson #253; Light Amber; H8 x L4-1/4 x W2-1/2
    See Pat. Medicine section for drawing
1258D . Watson #374; Amber; H7-3/4 x L4-1/4 x W2-1/2
    See Pat. Medicine section for drawing

(1255B)

(1255C)

1261 KUHL, B. & CO.
    194 E. 3rd   1885-1918
1261A . Back Bar Decanter

1264 LOW PRICE LIQUOR STORE
    Address unknown   date unknown
1264A . Shot Glass
1264B . Shot Glass

(1261B)

(1258A)

(1264A)

(1268A)

GEO. H. MOHR
WINES
&
LIQUORS
446
WABASHA
ST. PAUL

(1273A)

1268 METZGER, LEWIS
    140 E. 3rd   1905-1918
1268A . Shot Glass "Maryland Old Rye"
1268B . Glass Jug
1268C . Jug

1269 METZGER, ZIEN & CO
    140 E. 3rd   1903
1269A .
1269B . Jug "Dr. Bopps Hamburger Bitters"

MICHAUD BROS.
INC.
WINES & LIQUORS
ST. PAUL

(1270C)

MICHAUD BROS.
WINES
&
LIQUORS
ST. PAUL

(1270A)

MICHAUD BROS.
WINES
&
LIQUORS
ST. PAUL

(1270B)

(1270E)

1270 MICHAUD BROS
    425-427 Wabasha   1895-1918
1270A . Coffin; Clear; Half Pint, Pint
1270B . Coffin; Clear; Half Pint
1270C . Coffin; Clear; Half Pint
1270D . Jug
1270E . Butter Crock
1270F . Jug ; 1270G1. Jug; 1270H1. Jug

[MINNESOTA CLUB - This Rye Whiskey was a Private
Label Product of A. Hirschman of St. Paul]

1273 MOHR, GEO. H.
    446 Wabasha   1886-1900
1273A . Style A1J; Clear; Pint

1276 MONFORT & CO.
    5 E. 3rd   1867-1889
1276A . Cylindrical; Amber; Quart
1276A2. Cylindrical; Clear; Quart

(1270J)

(1270D)

(1270H)

(1270F)

(1270G)

(1276A2)

1279 PERKINS, W. L.
309-319 Robert St.   1872-1891
339 E. 7th   1892-1918

Peabody, Lyons and Company was established in 1859 in a small two-story stone building on Third Street, St. Paul. George P. Peabody and Maurice Lyons continued business until 1872, when Mr. George Peabody sold out his entire interest to Charles Peabody.

W.L. Perkins was born in New York in 1849. Eventually he was attracted by the discovery of gold in California and went to the West Coast. There he married and in 1868 his son W.L. Perkins Jr. was born. He remained in California until 1872, then came to St. Paul to settle up the estate of Geo. Peabody (his brother-in-law), and remained in St. Paul because of the health of his wife.

In 1879 Perkins and Mr. Lyons bought out Charles Peabodys interest, and needing more room for their fast increasing business, moved their business to a larger building at 319 Robert Street. The new company name was Perkins, Lyons and Company. In 1891 W.L. Perkins, Jr. was admitted to the partnership and the business became known as W.L. Perkins and Co. Their leading brands were Nonpariel Rye and Gibson Whiskey. They kept a full stock of California wines and brandies in addition to a very large stock of imported wines, brandies and rum. They also sold a full line of all the favorite brands of bourbon and rye whiskies of Kentucky, such as Hermitage, O.L.C. Nelson, Anderson, McBrayer, Carlisle, etc. They continued in business until Prohibition.

1279A . Sweet Wine (seal on shoulder); Clear; Quart
1279B . Flask (seal on side at base); Green; Half Pint
1279C . Back Bar Decanter "Old Red Still"
1279D . Handled Glass Jug "Old Red Still"
1279E . Back Bar Decanter "Non Pareil Rye"
1279F . Miniature with Paper Labels

(1282B)

(1282D)

(1282A)

1282 ROCHE, JNO. G.
Robert near w. Cor 5th St   1892-1907
1282A . Style F5A; Clear; Half Pint
1282B . Style F5A; Clear; Half Pint
1282D . Milk Glass Shot Glass

(1279B)
(1279A)

(1279A2)

(1279D)

(1279E)

(1279C)

(1279F)

(1282G)

(1285A)

(1285B)

(1282J)

(1282H)

(1285F)

(1285D)

1282E . Jug
1282F . Jug
1282G . Jug
1282H . Jug
1282J . Lettered Brandy; Clear; H 12-1/4 x D. 3-1/2

1285 SANDELL BROS.
    275-277 E. 7th   1901-1918
1285A . Shot Glass
1285B . Shot Glass "Private Stock"
1285C . Jug
1285D . Jug
1285E . Jug
1285G . Sign
1285H . Sign
1285J . Calendar

(1282E)

(1282F)

(1285C)

63

(1285J)

(1285E)

(1285G)

(1285H)

1895-1917

1288 SAN FRANCISCO WINE CO.
     498 St. Peter
1288A . Style F5A; Clear
1288B . Jug
1288C . Shot Glass
1288D . Jug
1288E . Shotglass

(1288A)

(1288E)

(1288B)

(1288C)

(1288D)

1289 SCHEIN, SAMUEL B.
    362 Jackson   1910-1911
    372 Minnesota   1912-1916
1289A . Squat Bitters; Amber; H7-7/8 x L3-1/4 x W2-7/8

1290 SCHMITT & RICHTER
1290A . Aqua; Strap Side Flask; "H.FRANK PAT
        AUG 6TH 1879" on base

1291 SHERMAN HOUSE WHISKEY
1291A . Leather covered Flask

1294 SIMON, B.
    299 E. 7th   1888-1902
 B. Simon also manufactured a bitters later produced
by Samuel B. Schein. See BITTERS section also.
1294A . Style F5A; Clear; Half Pint, Pint
1294B . Coffin; Clear

1297 SNELLING LIQUOR STORE
    Address unknown   date unknown
1297A . Shot Glass

[STERLING WINE HOUSE - See Welz-Mangler & Co]

1303 THEOBALD, WM.
    198 W. 3rd   1901
1303A   Shot Glass "Old Yucca Rye"

SIMON'S
AROMATIC STOMACH
BITTERS

(1289A)

SAMUEL B. SCHEIN
PROP. & MNFR.
ST. PAUL, MINN.

B. SIMON
COR 7TH AND
BROADWAY
ST PAUL   (1294B)

B. SIMON'S
WINE & LIQUOR HOUSE
COR, 7TH & BROADWAY, ST. PAUL

(1294A)

(1290A)

(1294C)

(1291A)

(1297A)

(1303A)

(1305A)

(1305B)

(1305C)

1305 WEILER, NIC & SON
    622 W. University
1305A . Metal Adv Tray
1305B . Metal Adv Tray
1305C . Metal Adv Tray

1897-1904

(1306D)

(1306E)

(1306F)

(1306G)

1306 WELZ-MANGLER & CO. - Sterling Wine House
    41 E. 7th (cor Seventh & Cedar)   1894-1917
    466 Wabasha (Wabasha & Ninth)   1914-1918
1306A . Style D3B; Half Pint
1306B . Style D3B; Clear; Pint
1306C . Back Bar Decanter "Fine Whiskies"
1306D . Jug
1306E . Jug
1306F . Jug
1306G . Jug
1306H . Hidden Bottle Novel, Title on cover reads
       "ABER NIT A NOVEL BY G. WIZ HOWGOOD"

1308 WESTHEIMER, FERDINAND & SONS
    282 Jackson

1892-1896

(1306A)

(1306B)

(1306C)

(1306H)

(1306H)

LATE ARRIVALS

RESIDENCE OF GEORGE BENZ

(1246F)

(1246E)

(1505B)

(1206A)

(1268D)

(1268B)

(1210AG)

(1210AF)

(1260A)

(1252G)

(1282K)

(1210AH)

3

MINNESOTA
WHISKEYS
(EXCLUDING MINNEAPOLIS & ST PAUL)

Brainerd

W40 COATES, JOHN LIQUOR CO.   date unknown
W40A. Jug

Cannon Falls

W50 SWANSON, OSCAR   date unknown
W50A. Jug

Duluth

W85 SMITH, MARTIN   date unknown
W85A. Backbar decanter
W85B. Leather covered flask

W90 ZIEN, J.D.   date unknown
W90A. Shotglass

W91 ZIEN, J.D. & CO.   date unknown
W91A. Backbar decanter

East Grand Forks

W95 SKAREN & OLSON   date unknown
W95A. Jug

(W40A)

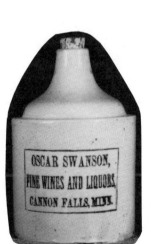

(W50A)

(W85A)

(W85B)

(W90A)

(W91A)

(W95A)

Ely

W100 SKALA, JOS   date unknown
W100A. Jug

Fergus Falls

W140 BENDER, C. J.   date unknown
W140A. Jug

Kittson County

W200 SUNBERG, G.   date unknown
W200A. Amber; Strap Sided Flask; Double Roll Lip. A
       spectular pioneer bottle that could be the
       prize in many collections.

Lester Prairie

W220 ENGELS, EUGENE   date unknown
W220A. Pocket Whetstone

Little Falls

W225 CARLSON, C.E.   date unknown
W225A. Jug

Mankato

W240 HOLSTEIN & MILLER   date unknown
W240A. Jug

Moorhead

W300 DIEMERT, W.H.   date unknown
W300A. Mini Jug

W301 DIEMERT & MURPHY   date unknown
W301A. Jug

(W100A)

(W140A)

(W200A)

(W225A)

(W220A)

(W240A)

(W301A)

THOMAS ERDEL
FINE LIQUORS
RIDGE AVE NEAR
NORTH BRIDGE
MOORHEAD, MINN.

(W305A)

(W300A)

(W310A)

(W315A)

(W320B)

(W320A)

(W320C)

(W325A)

W305 ERDEL, THOMAS	date unknown	W320 PEDERSON, MERCHANTILE CO	date unknown
W305A. Coffin flask		W320A. Jug	
		W320B. Jug	
W310 HANSON & PETERSON	date unknown	W320C. Jug	
W310A. Jug			
		W325 RUSTAD, A. J.	date unknown
W315 HIGGINS, ASKE, CO.	date unknown	W325A. Jug	
W315A. Jug			

New Brighton

W340 DAVIS, J. T.   date unknown
W340A. Coffin Flask

(W340A)

(W400A)

(W410A)

(W420A)

(W430A)

(W440A)

Red Wing

W400 CARLSON, FRANK A.   date unknown
W400A. Jug, 5-1/2 Tall

W410 KEMPE, J. & CO.   date unknown
W410A. Amber; Strap Sided Flask; Double Roll Lip

W420 LADNER BROS   date unknown
W420A. Jug

W430 RED WING LIQUOR CO.   date unknown
W430A. Jug

W440 SEUFERT, L. J.   date unknown
W440A. Jug

Rochester

W450 ABERWALD, J.J.   date unknown
W450A. Style G5Q, Clear

W455 DEVILLIERS, A.W.   date unknown
W455A. Metal Advertising Tray

W456 DEVILLIERS, C.H.   date unknown
W456A. Metal Advertising Tray

(W455A)

(W456A)

KENTUCKY CLUB
J.J.ABERWALD
(W450A)   ROCHESTER, MINN.

(W500A)

(W510A)

(W520A)

(W601A)

St Cloud

W500 CALIFORNIA WINE HOUSE   date unknown
W500A. Jug

W510 MUTSCHLER, MARTIN   date unknown
W510A. Jug

Stillwater

W520 OLD SHIELDS   date unknown
W520A . Backbar Decanter; Clear Flint Glass; engraved
     letters filled with red; ribbed neck; polished
     pontil

Wabasha

W600 CALLAHAN, STEPHAN   date unknown
W600A. Jug

W601 SCHMIDT, E. M.   date unknown
H601A. Jug

Winona

W620 DIETZE, JOHN   date unknown
W620A. Jug
W620B. Jug

W630 GRIESEL BROS.   date unknown
W630A. JUG-BROWN TOP
W630A2. JUG-WHITE TOP, SAME MARKINGS AS 630A

(W620A)

(W600A)

(W630A)

(W630C)

(W620B)

73

W635 HAUSMANN, EDWARD   date unknown
W635A. Self-framed tin sign

W640 HOFFARTH, JOS.   date unknown
W640A. Jug
W640B. Jug
W640C. Shotglass
W640D. Shotglass

W650 HOLLINGWORTH, F. S.   date unknown
W650A. Amber; Strap Sided Flask; Pint; Double Roll
       Lip

W660 SCHMIDT & BEUTNER   date unknown
W660A. Amber; Strap Sided Flask; Pint; Double Roll
       Lip

(W640C)

(W635A)

(W640B)

(W650A)

(W660A)

(W640A)

(W640D)

4

MINNEAPOLIS

DRUGGISTS

Enter if you will, via your imagination, a typical drugstore circa 1900. Its storefront has the traditional mortar and pestle sign hanging above the door, with several large display windows, each with a colorful display of patent medicines, sewing notions or fancy soaps on sale within. Pass through the open doors and you are in a long, well-lit room lined on either side by elegant hardwood cases with glass fronts, and by long rows of shelves. One large section is devoted to patent medicines, row upon row of them, dozens of varieties each packed in colorful cardboard boxes. Leaning over another case, filled with fancy soaps and perfumes, is a young clerk flirting with a lady customer while casting an occasional glance to the back of the store to be certain that his employer is not scowling at him. Other cases and shelves contain stationery, photography supplies, flower seeds, flypaper, hot water bottles and many other items. At one end of the store is a glittering marble and brass soda fountain serving up floats, fizzes, sarsaparilla and the like, while in the very back of the store stands the prescription counter with its scales, ledgers and the ornate porcelain jars from which drugs are ladled. Present your prescription and the druggist will measure, grind and mix the ingredients, pour them into a bottle and hand it to you. Look down at it and you will see a

small clear bottle with the name and address of the store embossed on one side and a paper label describing the contents affixed to the other.

Such then is the story behind the druggist bottles so commonly found and all too often scorned by bottle collectors. Their history goes back to the earliest days of Minnesota; the first drugstore in this area was said to have been Dewey and Collier's opening in St. Paul in 1848. Other stores sprang up throughout the 1850's, mostly in river towns such as St. Paul, St. Anthony and Winona. Many of these early establishments sold not only patent and prescription medicines but also locally gathered herbal mixtures, such bulk products as Kerosene and paints, and liquor "for medicinal purposes." The bottles used were generally clear, round, unembossed and probably pontilled.

The first druggist bottles embossed with the name and address of the store began appearing in this area in the mid 1870's, with widespread usage starting about ten years later. This type of bottle became popular after perfection of the "slug plate" mold which allowed glassmakers to use a single bottle mold with a snap-in plate of embossing to make personalized bottles for many

TYPICAL DRUGGIST BOTTLE STYLES

INTERIOR VIEW OF KNIGHTS PHARMACY, CIRCA 1915

different pharmacists at a reasonable cost. These bottles were usually rectangular or "semi-oval," ranging in size from one ounce to one quart. The vast majority were clear, although some were made in amber to protect light-sensitive medicines, while a very few came in blues, greens, or milk glass for fancy cosmetic products. Pharmacy bottles were generally embossed with the name and address of the druggist, perhaps with some decorative feature such as a monogram, mortar and pestle or animal figure. Of course many drug stores, especially smaller ones, could only afford unembossed bottles.

The pharmacy trade in the late 19th and early 20th century was a very competitive field, with partnerships constantly forming and dissolving, established firms changing addresses or adding additional stores, and medicines being dispensed at grocery stores, department stores and patent medicine shows. Some old businesses came out of this turmoil, such as drug store/post office combinations, drug store/jewelry stores, Scandinavian Apothecaries, even a drugstore and bakery and a drug store/public library. Embossed druggist bottles, which span the time period of circa 1875 to 1915, are among the few reminders of this colorful past.

PHARMACY IN PIONEER DAYS IN THE CITY OF MPLS.
(by Henry Rauch, reprinted from the proceedings of the Minnesota Pharmaceutical Association 1935)

Way back in the year 1879 in the City of Minneapolis, I first saw the light of day in a drug store owned by my uncle, George Huhn, and located at 123 Nicollet Avenue. Those were happy days for the independent pharmacist for the reason that competition was clean and we did not know anything about the cutter nor the chain store or department stores.

The pharmacist did not have a mere existence, he was blessed with more than a living in those happy and prosperous days. The drug store of any size carried a large paint department which helped to remunerate the owner with a fair profit.

The pharmaceutical manufacturing companies were not in existence then; the pharmacist was compelled to make his tinctures, fluid extracts, solid extracts, elixirs, ointments and what not. He was classed as an up-to-date druggist and did not lose sight of the scientific end of his profession. Soda fountains were few, only about one-half dozen in the city. A large number of the drug stores in the early days did not sell cigars or cigarettes or tobacco. I know we didn't handle them at the drug store I apprenticed in. The largest and best equipped drug stores were located in the down-town districts. Most of the business in all lines was at that time done in what we called Bridge Square, which comprised the area from the old-time Nicollet Hotel to the Great Northern Depot. First Street was one of the busiest streets in the City. Most of the farmers that came to the City from 20 or more miles away came by the way of First Street due to the fact that the wood market, hay market and the market house were all located on Bridge Square. The pioneer pharmacists of the City of Minneapolis that were doing business in those early days were as follows: George Huhn and Company, located at 123 Nicollet Avenue; T.K. Gray, located at 108 Hennepin Avenue. This latter store is still doing business at the old stand. Messrs. Webster and Churchill in the old Nicollet Hotel did a very large and lucrative business. Mr. Webster, by the way, was a member and secretary of the State Board (of Pharmacy) for many years. S.W. Melendy, located on Nicollet Avenue near Washington, ran an up-to-date pharmacy; his store was one of the few stores in our City that had a tile floor. Voegeli Brothers, who had their first and most popular drug store in our City, was located in what we called the Central Block on the corner of Washington Avenue and Hennepin. This store had no equal in the City of Minneapolis. It was a household word over the City, "Where will I meet you?" "Meet me at Voegeli's Corner." Spink and Company, located at the corner of First Avenue South and Washington, did a little wholesaling in connection with their retail department. J.H. Hofflin and Company, located at First Avenue South and Washington, had one of the best corners in the City. W.C. Colbroth was located on Washington Avenue South between Nicollet Avenue and First Avenue South. Alfred Backdahl, across from the Milwaukee Depot, did a very nice business. This store was the headquarters

ONE DRUGGISTS
METHOD OF
DELIVERING HIS WARES

for the Scandinavian trade. A.D. Thompson on First Avenue South and Third Street did a large prescription business, a number of doctors being located in the same building. Gamble and Ludwig, located at the corner of Hennepin Avenue and Third Street, did a large paint business in connection with their drug store. Danek and Shumpik had a store at the corner of 20th Avenue North and Washington.

O.B. Skinner was located at 29th and Washington Avenue North. Gormley and Moran were located on Central and 24th. Roses's Drug Store, run by the father of George Rose, was located on Central Avenue between 2nd and 3rd Streets. C.A. Pardoe had a drug store on Lake and Bloomington for many years. Mr. Williams is now the oldest actively engaged pharmacist in the drug business in the United States. Truman Griffin at 26th and Hennepin Avenue, and J.O. Peterson at 15th Avenue and Washington Avenue South, too had a large Scandinavian following. J.O. was one of the most successful druggists in our City. On Lake and Hennepin there was Frank J. Gould and the Washburn drug stores. We must not forget the old Doctor Sanderson Drug Store on Central and 5th Street. Doctor Sanderson was at the time considered one of the best posted botanists in the United States and the Doctor got the proper and earned recognition by our government at Washington.

I am afraid the pharmacists of today will never equal the pharmacists of the past unless the government makes the necessary and very essential laws to regulate the drug stores so that druggists will get not only an existence out of his business but a good living, to which he certainly is entitled as a recognized professional man.

(1603A)

```
┌──────────────────────┐
│   ALLEN BROS.        │
│   PHARMACISTS        │
│   1020 HENNEPIN AVE. │
│   MINNEAPOLIS        │
└──────────────────────┘
```

```
╭──────────────────────╮
│  ALLEN BROS.         │
│  TOILET CREAM        │
│  1020 HENNEPIN AVE.  │
│  MINNEAPOLIS, MINN.  │
╰──────────────────────╯
```
(1603B)

1600 ADAMS, SAMUEL E.	
1924 Western Avenue	1884-1886
1603 ALLEN BROS	
1020 Hennepin Avenue	1884-1894
1538 Nicollet Avenue	1898-1910

1603A . **; 1603B . Style Unknown; 1603C . Style ? ; Aqua; H5-7/8 x W2 x D7/8

1606 ALLEN & DORSEY	
Jackson & 7th	1876-1877
1609 ALTHER, C.A.	
301 Hennepin Avenue	1892
1612 AMES, A.A.	
250-52 Nicollet Avenue	1895-96
302 Nicollet Avenue & 21 S. 3rd	1897
20 S. 3rd	1898
54 S. 3rd	1899
1615 AMES, F.W.	
405 Washington Avenue South	1883-1884
500 Hennepin Avenue (West Hotel)	1885-1887
1615A **	
1616 AMES, F.W. & CO.	
243 - 4th Avenue South	1882

Minneapolis in the 1880's was quite a boomtown. The lumber and milling industries were flourishing, and the population was growing rapidly. New railroads provided the means for moving freight and people. Business opportunities in this era abounded, (except for women and minorities) and many individuals of ambition and foresight found success. Like so many men of this time, Frederick Ames changed his occupation many times, hoping to find his pot of success at the end of the rainbow.

Ames was born on July 5th, 1858, the youngest son of Dr. Alfred Elisha Ames, who was one of the pioneers of early St. Anthony. He graduated from the Minneapolis High School in 1876 and from a seminary school in Massachusetts three years later. He then returned to Minneapolis, working in real estate and civil engineering for a few years. In 1882, Fred Ames opened his first drugstore at 243 4th Avenue South. Only in the drug business for five years, he moved twice; to 405 Washington Avenue in 1883, and to 500 Hennepin Avenue in 1885. His Hennepin Avenue store was below the West Hotel, largest in the city, and it was known as the "West Hotel Drug Store." It was operated by the Weinhold brothers after Ames' departure in 1887.

For two years ('83-'85) Fred Ames' drug store was located under Ames Hospital. The hospital, it turns out, was not named for Fred Ames; rather for his older brother, Albert Alonzo Ames. A. A. Ames, a doctor and several years older than Fred, ran the hospital. It only lasted a few years, beginning in 1882. It was most likely a small operation, with perhaps 10-20 beds. Several of these small hospitals sprang up in the early days of Minneapolis; a few of them survived to become more modern-day hospitals. Dr. A.A. Ames was elected mayor of Minneapolis in November of 1882, and he most likely went on to more profitable ventures. Possibly A.A. Ames never intended to operate the hospital indefinitely; rather he used it more or less as a political steppingstone to the mayor's office.

After spending some time as a cashier at the Bank of Minneapolis, Fred Ames was called upon to serve as an officer in the U.S. Army. The Phillipine Insurrection was heating up, and Ames, who had been active in the Army Reserves for many years, was promoted to Colonel, commander-in-chief of the 13th Minnesota company just before the group left for San Francisco. This was early in 1899, and the 13th was sent to the front after reaching Manila.

Trouble soon developed, however, when Ames' company began seeing heavy combat. Fred Ames claimed that he was stricken with malaria, and left the front for treatment in Manila. Ames, it seems, was seen about the streets of Manila, enjoying himself and seemingly in good health. Rumors began to circulate, and his company, still engaged at the front, began to speak openly of Ames' cowardice. The doctors who examined him could find nothing wrong-no sign of malaria. Soon afterward, the 13th Minnesota was called out of combat and sent back to San Francisco. This was not popular with the men; being sent home with victory so close at hand. An attempt was made by some in the company to strip Ames of his command. This was a slow process; at first Gov. Link of Minnesota interceeded in favor of Ames, but later withdrew his support. Meanwhile, back in San Francisco, Ames had rejoined his company, and, professing innocence to charges of cowardice and

J.O.
PETERSON

E.P.
SWEET

HENRY
VOEGELI

C.A.
ROBINSON

T.K.
GRAY

78

 (1633A)

FRED. W. AMES
PHARMACIST
MINNEAPOLIS, MINN.
(1615A)

FRED W. AMES & CO.
PRESCRIPTION DRUGGISTS
4TH AVE S. NEAR WASHINGTON
UNDER AMES HOSPITAL
(1616A)

bribery, won the troops over. He was apparently a man of some charisma, and due to the company's change of attitude, he retained his command and received an honorable discharge.

Ames returned to Minneapolis after the conflict and managed his brother's re-election campaign. A.A. Ames was re-elected mayor of Minneapolis and appointed his brother Fred Police Chief in December of 1900. Albert A. Ames was quite a character himself. A four-time mayor of Minneapolis (the final time, in 1900, he won without party endorsement, causing some political hard feelings against him), he was a tall man with a booming voice. He was popular during his time in office, but he had enemies, as well. As a mayor he was controversial at times. Besides installing his brother in an important job, he also offered Northfield bank robber Cole Younger (who could not legally leave Minnesota) a police appointment and occasionally attended meetings while intoxicated. As a boy, he was the first person to walk across the first suspension bridge between Minneapolis and St. Anthony. This was in 1855.

The political scene in the days of A.A. Ames was a dirty business. Ames had, over the years, some secret organizations dedicated solely to his re-election. Two of these were the "Ames Guards" and the "Knights of Fidelity". Most likely there were other organizations just as intent opposing him. Graft and corruption were commonplace in almost all levels of government, and charges flew frequently between political rivals. Men of power and wealth did as they pleased; the result was crooked politics. Both Fred and Albert Ames faced charges of bribery, extortion, and conspiracy in 1902. These charges were probably brought to the public's attention by rival politicians who had been burned by the elder Ames two years before. Public pressure forced both of the Ames brothers to resign their respective government posts within a week of each other, in August of 1902. Fred Ames was tried and found guilty of taking a $15 bribe from a "lady of the town." He was sentenced to six and one-half years in Stillwater State Prison. He was pardoned in December of 1904 and moved with his family to Oakland, California in 1910. Albert Ames left Minneapolis for reasons of "health" and moved several times to avoid having to return and go on trial. There was speculation as to where he was headed; first it was Mexico, then Canada. He was seen on a train in New Hampshire, apprehended, and brought back to Minneapolis. After a long trial he was cleared of all charges, largely because a jury of citizens could not be found that would convict him. He remained popular, in spite of the proceedings against him. He died in 1911.
1616A **

1618 ANDERSON, C.L.
Corner Helen & 2nd   1859

1621 ANDERSON'S DRUG CO.
104 Washington Avenue South   1904-06

1624 ANDERSON'S DRUG STORE
104 Washington Avenue South   1902-03

1627 ANDERSON, E.J.
728 - 11th Avenue South   1896-97

1630 ANDERSON, O.F.
1229 S. 5th   1885
615 Cedar Avenue   1886-97

1633 ANDRUS BUILDING PHARMACY (See F.W. Peterson)
833 Andrus Bldg   1901-10
1633A **

1636 ANGIER, A.E.
106 Fort-Seven Corners   1876

1639 ARNEBERG & NELSON
402 Cedar Avenue   1895

1642 ARNOLD, JACOB
300 S.E. 9th   1890
2 E. Lake   1894

1645 ARNOLD & CO.
2 E. Lake   1895-96

1648 ARNOLD & LASHER
2 E. Lake   1888

1651 ARVIDSON, E.N.
2603 Stevens Avenue   1906-07
1827 E. Lake   1908-10

1654 ARVIDSON & STULTZ
2603 Stevens Avenue   1904-05

1657 AUDITORIUM LIBRARY PHARMACY
1031 Hennepin Avenue   1907-09

1660 AUNE, MARTIN
1500 Hennepin Avenue   1902-09

1663 AVERY, H. N.
2550 Nicollet Avenue   1884-85

1666 BABENDRIER, G.A.
84 S. 7th   1908

[BABENDRIER & VAN NEST - See Mpls Pharmacy Co]

1672 BACHARACH, HARVEY (Quality? Drug Store)
2447 4th Avenue South   1909-10

1675 BACHDAHL, ALFRED
313 Washington Avenue   1873-88
1675A **; 1675B **; 1675C **

(1675A)
ALFRED BACKDAHL
313 WASHINGTON AVE.
MINNEAPOLIS, MINN.

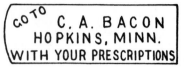

ALFRED BACKDAHL
313 WASHINGTON AVE.S.
MINNEAPOLIS

(1675B)

ALFRED BACKDAHL
MANUFACTURING CHEMIST
313 WASHINGTON AVE.
MINNEAPOLIS, MINN.

(1675C)

A. BACKDAHL & CO.
313 WASHINGTON AVE
MINNEAPOLIS, MINN.

(1678A)

GO TO C.A. BACON
HOPKINS, MINN.
WITH YOUR PRESCRIPTIONS

(1681A)

Geo. T Beull & Co.
MINNEAPOLIS

(1709A)

BEBB & HOFFMAN
PHARMACISTS
MINNEAPOLIS

(1711A)

B-M BEST MATERIALS
Bell-McCord Drug Company
MINNEAPOLIS

(1717A)

MANUFACTURING BENNESON & RAICHE AND DISPENSING
CHEMISTS
MINNEAPOLIS
MINN.

(1729A)

BERNARD & GIBBS
400-2ND AVE S.
MINNEAPOLIS, MINN.

(1741A)

CATARACT DRUG STORE
WEBSTER BENNER & Co
MINNEAPOLIS

(1726A)

BIGELOW'S
ELECTRIC LINE DRUG STORE
MINNEAPOLIS, MINN.

(1744A)

1678 BACHDAHL & CO, ALFRED
   313 Washington Avenue   1809-95
   313 Washington Avenue, 283 Cedar Avenue 1896-98
   313 Washington Avenue   1899-1910
1678A **

1681 BACON, C.A.
   Hopkins   1903-06
1681A **

1684 BAECKMAN, A.L.
   402 Cedar Avenue   1907-10

1687 BALDWIN, WALTER I.
   3009 Hennepin Avenue   1885

1690 BALDWIN, W.W.
   2 E Lake   1900

1693 BALL, G.A.
   2200 Hennepin Avenue   1907-08

1696 BALL'S PHARMACY
   2200 Hennepin Avenue   1909-10

1699 BANKS & PIKE
   501 2nd Avenue South   1885

1702 BARKER, F. I.
   2 E. 26th   1907-10

1705 BARCK, G.W.
   1533 Franklin Avenue South   1882
   608 Washington Avenue South   1883

1708 BATHRICK & ADAMS
   102 Central Avenue   1874

1709 BEALL, GEO & CO.   ?
1709A **

1711 BEBB & HOFFMAN
   228 20th Avenue North   1886-87
1711A **

1714 BELDEN & COPP CO.
   130 S 2nd   1908-09

1717 BELL - McCORD DRUG CO.
   528 Nicollet Avenue   1906
   395 Syndicate Arcade & 23 Syndicate Blk 1907
1717A **

1720 BELL, R.M.
   721 Nicollet Avenue   1908

1723 BECKER, R.A.
   161 E. 7th   1876-77

1726 BENNER, WEBSTER (CATARACT DRUG STORE)
   Washington & 2nd Avenue   1871-73
   603 Washington Avenue South   1874-78
1726A **

1729 BENNESON & RACINE
         ?   ?
1729A **

1732 BERG, O. J.
   501 Washington Avenue South   1894

1735 BERGQUIST, LEONARD
   316 Cedar Avenue   1907-10

1738 BERNARD, J.A. & CO.
   400 2nd Avenue South   1886

1741 BERNARD & GIBBS
   400 2nd Avenue South   1887-1892
1741A**

1744 BIGELOW'S (ELECTRIC LINE DRUG STORE)
         ?   ?
1744A **

1747 BIGELOW, MRS. C.A.
   2601 Stevens Avenue South   1882
   199 S. 26th   1883
   2 E. 26th   1884-1906

1750 BIGELOW'S (MOTOR LINE DRUG STORE)
     ?   ?

1750A **

1753 BIGELOW, E.B.
    Washington & Helen   1871-73

1756 BIGELOW, E.B. & CO.
    Washington & Helen   1867-69

1759 BIGGS, E. H.
    30 E. 3rd   1876-77

1762 BINGENHEIMER, G.A. (Oak Park Drug Store)
    529 Plymouth Avenue   1889-94
    2001-2003 4th Avenue South   1895
    642 6th Avenue North   1898
    642 & 1320 6th Avenue North   1899-1905
1762A **; 1762B **; 1762C **

1768 BOERICKE & TAFEL
    604 Nicollet   1890-91

1771 BOOCK, H. F.
    29 Washington Avenue North   1874

1774 BOOTH, C.E.
    500 E. 24th   1890-91

1777 BOSTON BRANCH PHARMACY - D.W. HAM
    1201 3rd Avenue South   1878
1777A **

1780 BOYD, WATSON H.
    621 - 17th Avenue South   1887

1783 BREDE & ERKEL
    1228 N.E. Main   1904

1786 BREIDENBACH BROS (Owl Drug Store)
    600 Hennepin Avenue   1908

1789 BRIDGE SQUARE DRUG CO.
    109 Nicollet Avenue   1907

1792 BRIGHT & SCHMIDT
    129 Nicollet Avenue   1893

1795 BRINSMAID, CHARLES H
    735 S 10th   1884

1798 BROSIUS, E.F.
    1402 N.E. Marshall   1890-93

1801 BROWN & CO.
    1331 Nicollet Avenue   1887-88

1804 BROWN, G.G.
    Division & 3rd Avenue S.E.   1883

1807 BROWN, MRS. L.A. - CRESCENT DRUG STORE
    1331 Nicollet Avenue   1885-86

1810 BROWN, H.O.
    1323 Nicollet.Avenue   1887

1813 BROWN, L.F.
    600 Washington Avenue S.E.   1905-10

1816 BROWN, R.F.
    1331 Nicollet Avenue   1889

1819 BROWNLEE DRUG CO.
    101 Washington Avenue South   1906-10
1819A **; 1819B **

1822 BRYANT, C.
    Woodmans Block   1859

1825 BUEHLER, HENRY
    1538 Nicollet Avenue   1896-97
    747 N.E. Adams   1897-99
    758 N.E. Adams   1900-10
1825A **

1828 BUFFUM, HARRY (Pioneer Drug Store)
    2423 Central Avenue   1906-1910

1831 BUNDY BROS.
    1st & 13th Avenue North   1874-75

1834 BUNDY & WOOSTER
    128 Washington Avenue South   1878

1837 BUNGE, DR. H & CO.
    Bridge Square   1874

BIGELOW'S
MOTOR LINE DRUG STORE
MINNEAPOLIS, MINN.

(1750A)

BOSTON BRANCH PHARMACY
1201-3RD AVE. SOUTH
MINNEAPOLIS, MINN.

(1777A)

G.A. BINGENHEIMER
DRUGGIST
PLYMOUTH AVE & 6TH ST
MINNEAPOLIS

(1762B)

G.A. BINGENHEIMER
DRUGGIST
PLYMOUTH & 6TH ST.

(1762A)

C.A. BINGENHEIMER
PHARMACIST
MINNEAPOLIS, MINN.

(1762C)

(1819A)
BROWNLEE DRUG
OPEN ALL NIGHT
101 WASHINGTON AVE S. MINNEAPOLIS MINN.

BROWNLEE DRUG CO.
OPEN ALL NIGHT
101 WASHINGTON AVE.S. MINNEAPOLIS, MINN.

(1819B)

(1825A)
HENRY BUEHLER
DRUGGIST
MINNEAPOLIS, MINN.

THE PUBLIC DRUG CO. STORE

VOEGELI'S PHARMACY AT 7TH & NICOLLET

VOEGELI'S WEST HOTEL STORE

CHAS CIRKLER'S STORE AT 602 NICOLLET

```
┌─────────────────────────┐      ┌──────────────────────────┐      ┌──────────────────────┐
│    CABLE & JUDD         │      │   GEO. S. CHURCHILL      │      │  GEO. S. CHURCHILL   │
│    DRUGGISTS            │      │     DRUGGIST             │      │    PHARMACIST        │
│                         │      │ NICOLLET HOUSE DRUG STORE│      │    MINNEAPOLIS       │
│   MINNEAPOLIS, MINN.    │      │  MINNEAPOLIS, MINN.      │      │                      │
└─────────────────────────┘      └──────────────────────────┘      └──────────────────────┘
       (1858A)                         (1895A)                          (1895B)
```

```
┌──────────────────────────┐     ┌──────────────────────────┐     ┌──────────────────────┐
│  ▧  M. CHILSTROM         │     │ HILL & SCHELDRUP         │     │  Cirkler's           │
│     DRUGGIST             │     │ PHARMACISTS              │     │                      │
│                          │     │ NICOLLET HOUSE           │     │  MINNEAPOLIS, MINN.  │
│   MINNEAPOLIS, MINN.     │     │ MINNEAPOLIS              │     │                      │
└──────────────────────────┘     └──────────────────────────┘     └──────────────────────┘
      (1892A)                         (1898A)                          (1901A)
```

1840 BURCH, G.S.
    717 3rd Avenue South   1900-01

1843 BURKE Bros.
    2405 W. 42nd   1904-08, 1910
    4201 Queen Avenue South, &   1909
    4316 Upton Avenue South

1846 BUSETH, NILS
    415 Washington Ave. So. & 1500 E. Franklin   1888
    1500 E. Franklin   1889

1849 BUSH, G.W.
    1229 Nicollet Avenue   1902-06
    428 2nd Avenue South   1908-10

1852 BYRNES, WILLIAM J.
    1229 Western Avenue   1887-89

1855 CABLE, F.M. (Nicollet House Drug Store)
    15 Nicollet House Block   1881

1858 CABLE & JUDD (Nicollet House Drug Store)
    3 Nicollet House Block   1879-80
1858A **

1861 CARON, ARRESTIDE
    738 Adams   1891

1864 CASE, J. W.
    208 Western Avenue   1906-10

1867 CAVANAUGH, C.A.
    2525 Emerson Avenue North   1904

1870 CENTRAL DRUG CO.
    501 Central Avenue   1906-10

1873 CHADBOURNE & JOFFOSS
    2423 Central Avenue   1904

1876 CHERRY, D.S.
    23 Central Avenue   1887

1879 CHILDS, E.
    Washington Avenue & 2nd Avenue North   1884
    228 20th Avenue North   1885

1882 CHILSTROM, C.E.
    2 W. Lake   1903-09

1885 CHILSTROM DRUG CO.
    1 E. Lake   1910

```
        (1901C)
     ╱──────────╲
    │ CHAS H. CIRKLER │
    │ DRUGGIST&CHEMIST │
     ╲ MINNEAPOLIS ╱
      ╲──────────╱
```

```
        ╱────────────────╲
       │  CHAS H CIRKLER   │
      │  DRUGGIST&CHEMIST   │
       │ MINNEAPOLIS MINN  │
        ╲────────────────╱
            (1901B)
```

1888 CHILSTROM & CO.
    301 E. Lake   1890-91
    2 W. Lake   1892-94

1892 CHILSTROM, MATILDA
    2 W. Lake   1895-1902
1892A **

1895 CHURCHILL, G.S. (Nicollet House Drug Store)
    15 Washington Avenue South   1902-1910
1895A **; 1895B **

1898 CHURCHILL & SCHELDRUP (Nicollet House Drug Store)
    15 Washington Avenue South   1900-01
1898A **

1901 CIRKLER, C.H.
    26 S Washington   1884-85
    316 Nicollet Avenue   1886-93
    602 Nicollet Avenue   1894-1901
    602 Nicollet Avenue & 49 S. 6th   1902-1903
    602 Nicollet Avenue   1904-1908
    602 Nicollet Avenue & 49 S. 6th   1909-10

Charles Cirkler apparently got his start in the drug and medicine trade in 1883, when he was a clerk for the J.R. Hofflin Co., one of Minnesota's largest dealers in drugs and patent medicines (Liebig's Sarsaparilla, Liebig's Corn Cure, Higgin's Balsamic Lotion.)

By 1884 Mr. Cirkler was in business for himself.

More important for collectors of local bottles are Cirkler's own products. Since he was doing business in a period which favored exotic names for patent medicines, it is not surprising that his most popular product seems to have been "CIRKLER'S ORIENTAL BALM."

(1916A)

(1924A)

(1927A)

(1966A)

(1921A)

THE PRESCRIPTION STORE OF W.A.COFFIN 928 PLYMOUTH AVE. MINNEAPOLIS COR. DUPONT, MINN.

W. A. Coffin DRUGGIST CAMDEN PLACE MINNEAPOLIS, MINN.

(1921B)

W. C. COLBRATH DRUGGIST MINNEAPOLIS, MINN.

(1927B)

WASHINGTON LOTION CROCKER & THOMPSON MFR'S MINNEAPOLIS, MINN.

(1966B)

WASHINGTON SCHOOL DRUG STORE 601-8TH AVE. S. MINNEAPOLIS

(1966C)

His other products included "CIRKLER'S BORATED CREAM" and "CIRKLER'S BENZOATED CREAM", in similar bottles. The Balm is scarce, and the two creams are perhaps rarer. He also produced a couple of druggist bottle, variants. Charles was still in business as late as World War One.

1901A **; 1901B **; 1901C **;
1901D   Toilet Cream; Clear
1901E   Toilet Cream; Clear
1901F   Toilet Cream; Clear

[CITY DRUG STORE - SEE MELENDY & LYMAN]

1910 CITY HALL PAHRMACY
      129 Nicollet Avenue   1894

1913 CLARKE, A.H.
      123 Washington Avenue   1897-1901

1916 CLARK & HARRIS
      Washington & Hennepin   1886
1916A **

1919 COBB, WM S. (Deceased 9/09)
      3122 Emerson Avenue North   1909

1921 COFFIN, W.A.
      43rd Avenue North & Washington   1891-93
      4169 Washington Avenue North   1894-97
      928 Plymouth Avenue   1902-05
      1500 Crystal Lake Avenue   1908
1921A **; 1921B **

1923 COLBRATH & RUSSELL, R.P. (Novelty Drug Store)
      301 Hennepin   1883-1888

1924 COLBRATH & THOMPSON
      26 Washington Avenue   1867
      43 Washington Avenue South   1874-75
1924A **
1924B **

1927 COLBRATH, W.C.
      43 Washington Avenue South   1878-81
1927A **;
1927B **

1930 COLBRATH, W.N. (Novelty Drug Store)
      301 Hennepin   1888

1933 COLE, A.L.
      24 Washington Avenue South   1896

1936 COLLINS, F.H.
      1401 S 7th   1888

1939 COLTON & CO'S DEPARTMENT STORE
      6th & Nicollet   1882

1942 COMO DRUG CO.
      1516 Como Avenue   1909-10

1945 COMSTOCK, A.W.
      500 E. 24th   1889

1948 CONDIT & LAMBIE
      2 W. 3rd   1876

1951 COOK, MRS. CLARA A.
      202 13th Avenue North   1886

1954 COREY, C.A.
      1229 Nicollet Avenue   1907-10

1957 CORNELL, M.C.
      2558 Aldrich Avenue South   1891

1960 COWIN, G.A.
      1500 20th Avenue North   1909

1963 CROCKER, GEORGE
      2558 Lyndale Avenue South   1889
      901 Nicollet Avenue   1890

1966 CROCKER & THOMPSON
      601 8th Avenue South   1889-1910
1966A **; 1966B **; 1966C **; 1966D **

84

1969 CROSBY DRUG CO.
    426 Central Avenue   1898-1902

1972 CROSMAN, C.F.
    27 Windom-Loring Blk   1890-93

1975 CROSMAN & PLUMMER
    2nd & Nicollet Avenue   1874-78
    129 Nicollet Avenue   1879-88
1975A **

1978 CROW, C.E.
    102 Central Avenue   1894-95

1981 CROW, JAMES
    708 Hennepin Avenue   1882

1984 CROWELL, A.B.
    1012 Hennepin Avenue   1903-10

1987 CROWELL, F.W.
    3600 Lyndale Avenue South   1910

1990 DAMM, L.F.
    1403 Washington Avenue South   1878-79
    1401 Washington Avenue South   1880
    1428 Washington Avenue South   1881
1990A **

1993 DANEK, J.F.
    1228 Washington Avenue North   1891-1909
John F. Danek was born in Caledonia, Wisc., in
October of the Civil War's first year. His parents
were of Bohemian ancestry. He came to Minneapolis
at age 25 in 1885 and teamed in the drug business
with Edward Shumpik before opening his own pharmacy
four years later. This was located at 1228
Washington Ave. No., as his bottle says--"On the
corner of Wash. and Plymouth Aves." He resided at
1417 Fremont Ave. No. during most of his time in
the city. As the years passed he became secretary
of the North Side Commercial Club, and later,
president of both city and state pharmaceutical
associations. He was very active in civic
affairs. He operated his drugstore for 45 years,
from 1889 until his death in 1934. Danek turned
out an abundant quantity of embossed bottles for
many years, almost all of them are of the same
style.
1993A **; 1993B Style A5H; Aqua; H5-1/2; 1993C **;
1993D **

1996 DANEK'S PHARMACY
    1228 Washington Avenue North   1910

1999 DANEK & SHUMPIK
    1921 Washington Avenue North   1886-88
    1323 & 1921 Washington Avenue North   1889
    1228 & 1921 Washington Avenue North   1890
1999A **

2002 DANIELSON'S DRUG CO.
    2339 Central Avenue   1910

2005 DANIELSON, F.J.
    2339 Central Avenue   1909

2008 DAVIS, S.S.
    1501 Hennepin Avenue   1888-90

2010 DAVIS & BIGELOW
    424 Nicollet Avenue   1891

2013 DAY, JOHN H.
    253 Nicollet Avenue   1883

2016 DAY & CO.
    3007 Hennepin Avenue   1884

2019 DEAN, A.P.
    717 3rd Avenue South   1891-99
2019A **; 2019B **

2022 DE RAICHE, EMIL D.
    2122 4th Avenue South   1892-1900

2025 DE RAICHE DRUG CO.
    630 Hennepin Avenue   1902-05
2025A . **

(1993C)

DANEK'S
PERFECTION HAND LOTION

(1993D)

J.F. DANEK
PHARMACIST
MINNEAPOLIS

WASHINGTON SCHOOL
DRUG STORE
MINNEAPOLIS

(1966D)

L.E. DAMM
DRUGGIST
MINNEAPOLIS, MINN.

(1990A)

JOHN F. DANEK
PHARMACIST
PLYMOUTH & WASHⁿ AVES

(1993A)

CROSMAN & PLUMMER
CITY HALL DRUG STORE
MINNEAPOLIS, MINN.

(1975A)

DANEK'S
WILD CHERRY
COUGH BALSAM

(1993B)

DANEK & SHUMPIK
PHARMACISTS
MINNEAPOLIS

(1999A)

A.P. DEAN
717 3ᴿᴰ AVE.S.
MINNEAPOLIS

(2019A)

(2019B)

A.P. DEAN
717 3ᴿᴰ AVE S
MINNEAPOLIS

85

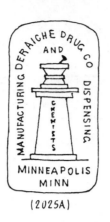

(2025A)

C. M. DEVOE
400 CEDAR AVE
MINNEAPOLIS
(2037A)

J. F. DVORACEK
DRUGGIST
1921 WASHINGTON AVE NO.
MINNEAPOLIS, MINN.
(2100A)

10TH AVE DRUG STORE
DOW & SKINNER
MINNEAPOLIS
(2076A)

OPEN ALL NIGHT
S. DRULLARD'S
MODEL DRUG STORE
MINNEAPOLIS
(2082B)

DRULLARD'S
MODEL DRUG STORE
MINNEAPOLIS, MINN
(2082A)

E. PATRICK DUBE
PHARMACIST
230-20TH AVE.NO.
MINNEAPOLIS, MINN.
(2091A)

(2028A)

MONS DE RAICHE
CHEMIST
MINNEAPOLIS
MINN.
(2028B)

2028 DE RAICHE, MONS
?   ?
2028A **;
2028B **
2028C **

2031 DE VOE & BUTLER
400 Cedar Avenue   1882

2034 DE VOE BROS
400 Cedar Avenue   1886

2037 DE VOE, CHARLES M.
400 Cedar Avenue   1883-85, 87-88
5 E. 26th   1889-91
111 E. 26th   1892-99
2613 E. 25th   1900-05
2601 E. 25th   1906-10
2037A **

2040 DILLIN DRUG CO.
101 Washington Avenue South   1902-04
101 Washington Avenue South, &   1905
828 Nicollet Avenue

2043 DINSMORE, W.E.
7th & Western Avenue   1892
2 Western Avenue   1893

2046 DONALDSON'S CO., L.S.
6th & Nicollet Avenue   1910

2049 DONALDSON'S PHARMACY
201 Donaldson's Bldg.   1908-10

2052 DONALDSON & CO., WM.
6th & Nicollet Avenue   1898-99

2055 DOUGLASS, ANNA
3451 Chicago Avenue   1893-94
3457 Chicago Avenue   1895-97, 1899-1905

2058 DOUGLASS, A.C.
1514 20th Avenue North   1889

2061 DOUGLASS, L.W. (Died 2/7/09)
1404 20th Avenue North   1886
1512-14 20th Avenue North   1887-88, 90
3457 Chicago Avenue   1898, 1906-08

2064 DOUGLASS, M.E.
1920 Lyndale Avenue North   1886

2067 DOUGLASS, M.R.
621 17th Avenue North   1891
3515 Chicago Avenue, & 203 8th Avenue N.E.   1892

2070 DOUGLASS & SON
604 20th Avenue North   1885

2073 DOW, J. NEIL (Neal) (Tenth Ave Drug Store)
1001 Washington Avenue South   1884-88

2076 DOW & SKINNER (Tenth Ave Drug Store)
1001 Washington Avenue South   1878-81
1001 & 1428 Washington Avenue South   1882
2076A **

2079 DREIS & MITSCH
114 St. Peter   1876-77

2082 DRULLARD, SOLOMON (Model Drug Store)
628 Nicollet Avenue   1884-99
2082A **; 2082B **

2085 DRULLARD, MRS. M.B.
628 Nicollet Avenue   1888

2091 DUBE, E.P.
230 20th Avenue South   1904-1907
801 N.E. 2nd   1908
2091A **

2094 DUPONT, J.W.
1903 Central Avenue   1897
2029 Central Avenue   1898

2097 DUPONT, J.G.
2029 Central Avenue   1899

2100 DVORACEK, J.F.
1921 Washington Avenue North   1914-?
2100A **

2103 DYE, A.M.
1931 4th Avenue south   1882

2106 DWYER, R.H.
    318 4th Avenue South   ?
2106A **

2109 EAGLE DRUG CO.
    1700 N.E. 4th   1910
2109A **

2112 EBERHARD & WASSER (Nicollet Drug Store)
    828 Nicollet Avenue   1909

2115 ECKSTEIN, E.J.
    400 Plymouth Avenue   1895

2118 EHRENHOLM, C.A.
    2029 S. 9th   1889

2121 EHRENHOLM & TURNER
    2029 S. 9th   1888

2124 ELLIS, D.W.
    616 Nicollet Avenue   1886

2127 EMERSON AVE DRUG STORE
    3122 Emerson Avenue North   1910

2130 ENGLUND, D.C.
    360 Monroe   1902-05
    403 Central Avenue   1906

2133 ERKEL, A.G.
    1228 N.E. Main   1908-10

2136 ESTERLEY, T.W.
    429 4th Avenue N.E.   1889-91
    701 Adams   1892-93
    700 Adams   1894-95
    700 N.E. Adams   1896-1900
    700 Adams   1901-10

2139 EUREKA DRUG STORE (See J. W. Harrah)
    1718 4th Avenue South   1891-1910
2139A **; 2139B **; 2139C **; 2139D **

2142 EXCELSIOR DRUG CO.
    301 Hennepin Avenue   1898
    301 1/2 Hennepin Avenue   1899-1900

2145 FAMILY DRUG STORE
    8 S. 7th   1884

2148 FERTE, C.E.
    8 Mississippi   1876-77

2151 FISCHER, C.F.
    1031 Hennepin Avenue   1910

2154 FISHER, W. N.
    1101 26th Avenue North   1909

2157 FLIESBURG & GOLDNER
    22nd Avenue N.E. & Central Avenue   1904
    2029 Central Avenue   1905

2160 FOELL, JACOB
    Main & 4th Avenue N.E.   1886
    Marshal & 4th Avenue N.E.   1887
    609 N.E. Marshal   1890-91
    102 Central Avenue
2160A **; 2160B **

2163 FOELL, J.J.
    402 N.E. Main   1889
    609 N.E. Main   1892
    609 N.E. Marshal & 120 Central Avenue   1893
    609 N.E. Marshal   1894

2166 FOREST HEIGHTS DRUG STORE
    (see also Wilson Bros.)
    1500 20th Avenue North   1910

2169 FORNWALT, M.L.
    828 Nicollet   1886-87

2172 FORNWALT & CO.
    2644 Lyndale Avenue South   1889

2175 FOURTH AVENUE PHARMACY
    1400 4th Avenue South   1909

J. FOELL
DRUGGIST
PURE DRUGS
MINNEAPOLIS, MINN
(2160B)

EAGLE DRUG CO.
MINNEAPOLIS, MINN.
(2109A)

EUREKA DRUG STORE
1718-4TH AVE. SOUTH
MINNEAPOLIS,   MINN.
(2139A)

J. FOELL
DRUGGIST
MINNEAPOLIS, MINN.
(2160A)

EUREKA DRUG STORE
1718-4TH AVE. So.
MINNEAPOLIS
(2139D)

Eureka DRUG STORE
(2139C)

"THE BEST IS GOOD ENOUGH"
R.H. DWYER
318 2ND. AVE. So.
MINNEAPOLIS
GUARANTEED 6 OZ.   (2106A)

EUREKA DRUG STORE
1718 4TH AVE.   SOUTH
MINNEAPOLIS,   MINN.
(2139B)

(2205B)

GARDINER'S
HOMEOPATHIC PHARMACY
MINNEAPOLIS

(2205A)

DRUGGIST
S. Gjesdahl
MINNEAPOLIS

(2219A)

(2187A)

J. P. GILMORE
DRUGGIST
MINNEAPOLIS, MINN.

(2213A)

J. P. GILMORE
PHARMACIST
MINNEAPOLIS, MINN.

(2213B)

(2246A)

2178 FRANK, D.F.
3001 Hennepin Avenue   1889

2181 FREIDLAND, MATHIAS
1533 Franklin Avenue East   1887

2184 FREIDLANDER, SAMUEL
633 1st Avenue South   1895-96

2187 FROST & CO, B.C
129 Nicollet Avenue   1889-91
2187A **

2190 FULLER & MERRILL
105 Washington Avenue North   1888

2193 GALE, C. F.
301 Central Avenue   1886

2196 GALUSHE & SCHULZE
1031 Hennepin Avenue   1906

2199 GAMBLE, J.S.
2 E. Lake   1909-10

2202 GAMBLE & LUDWIG
301 Hennepin Avenue   1893-1908
300 & 901 Hennepin Avenue   1909-10

2205 GARDINER, THOMAS (HOMEOPATHIC PHARMACY)
38 Nicollet Avenue   1869-71
244 Nicollet Avenue   1874
306 Nicollet Avenue   1888-90
410 Nicollet Avenue   1893
610 Nicollet Avenue   1895-99
22 S. 6th   1900-03
11 S. 7th   1904
723 Hennepin Avenue   1905-10
2205A . Private mold, Amber
2205B . Private mold, Clear

2208 GARFIELD PHARMACY
2123 Chicago Avenue   1910

2213 GILMORE, J.P.
105 Central Avenue   1883
105 Central Av. & 1215 S.E. 4th   1884
127 Central Avenue   1885
129 Central Av. & 401 14th Av S.E.   1886-87
401 14th Avenue S.E.   1888-90
401 14th Avenue S.E. & 800 Wash Av S.E. 1891-92
401 14th Avenue S.E. & 1229 Nicollet Av 1893-94
401 14th Avenue S.E.   1895-1902
2213A **; 2213B **

2216 GILMORE, J.R.
1215 14th Avenue S.E.   1885

2219 GJESDAHL, SVEN
2000 Riverside Avenue   1895
402 Cedar Avenue   1896-1905
1500 Crystal Lake Avenue   1906-07
1333 Franklin Avenue East   1908-10
2219A **

2222 GOES, JOHN
515 Hennepin Avenue   1880

2225 GOLDNER, J.E.
2029 Central Avenue   1906-07
1854 Central Avenue   1908-10

2228 GOODRICH & JENNINGS
2 E. Lake   1898-1908

2231 GOODSELL, W.R.
828 S. 6th   1887-88

2234 GOPHER DRUG STORE
1929 Washington Avenue South   1905-06

2237 GORMLEY & CO.
2401 Harrison   1890-91

2240 GORMLEY, JOHN
2401 Central   1892-1903

2243 GORMLEY & MORAN
2401 Central   1904-06
2339 Central   1907-08

2246 GOULD, J. FRANK
Lake & Lyndale Avenue   1885-86
Lake & Lyndale Avenue, 3001 Hennepin   1887
3001 Hennepin & 3025 Lyndale Ave So   1888
3000 S. Lyndale   1889-96
395 Syndicate Arcade   1897-1900
2246A **; 2246B **

2249 GOULD & SON, J. FRANK
2924 Lyndale Avenue South   1908-10

2252 GOWDEY & OBERT
128 Washington Avenue South   1886

2253 GRABEN & CO, OTTO H.
    642 6th Avenue North   1906-10
2255A **

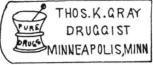

O.H. GRABEN & CO.
PHARMACIST'S
6TH AVE. NO. & LYNDALE
MINNEAPOLIS, MINN.
(2255A)

2258 GRAVES, G.H.
    930 Hennepin   1889

2261 GRAY BROS. (J.D. & T.K.)
    1st & Hennepin   1865
    42 Bridge Square   1867-73

THOS. K. GRAY
DRUGGIST
PURE DRUGS
MINNEAPOLIS, MINN
(2267A)

2264 GRAY & CO., T.K.
    108 Hennepin Avenue   1874-75

T.K. GRAY & CO.
DRUGGISTS
108 BRIDGE SQUARE
MINNEAPOLIS
(2267C)

2267 GRAY, THOMAS K.
    108 Hennepin Avenue   1878-1909

T.K. GRAY
DRUGGIST
BRIDGE SQUARE
MINNEAPOLIS, MINN. (2267B)

Thomas K. Gray was born in 1833, at Jefferson Maine. He was of Scottish descent. His father was a physician who died when Gray was four. Gray developed a taste for the knowledge and handling of medicines and drugs by a study of the medical books left in his father's library. In October 1855, he moved with his two brothers to Minneapolis, Minnesota. Oliver Gray moved south after one year in Minneapolis, John D. Gray entered the drug business with Dr. M.R. Greeley, while Thomas found work as a clerk with D.W. Ingersoll of St. Paul.

In 1857 he returned to Minneapolis and purchased Dr. Greeley's interest in the drug business and the firm of Gray Bros. was formed. They dealt in drugs, medicines, paints and oils. The store was located at 108 Bridge Square, now known as 108 Hennepin Avenue.

In 1871 John D. retired, making Thomas K. Gray the sole owner. He enlarged the scope of the business, doing a wholesale trade for many years, until the advent of the exclusive wholesale drug houses rendered it no longer profitable.

Gray married Julia Allen in 1865 and had five children.

Thomas K. Gray died in December 1909. Newspaper headlines read, "City's Oldest Tradesman Passes Into the Beyond" and went on to say, "Mpls. oldest merchant and oldest druggist in the state of Minnesota, his signs on the fences made his name widely known".

Mr. Gray was a pioneer in fence post advertising and the little tin signs tacked to posts and fence rails reading, "Go to T.K. Gray for your Drugs" would be remembered by persons who travelled over the country roads in Hennepin County.

Until two months before his death, he had continued to take part in the conduct of the store.

T.K. Gray's bottles are rare.

An interesting T.K. Gray artifact is a cook book that he had published in the summer of 1900. All the even numbered pages are advertisements for products sold by Gray, and all the odd numbered pages are recipes. The following is a list of some of the advertisements:

American Standard Stock Food, Poultry Food Worm
    Powder, and Juniper Tar.
Healing Balm--American Standard Stock Food Co.
    Mpls.

(T.K.GRAY'S DRUG STORE, 1887)

Eureka Catarrh Cure--Volk Remedy Co. Mpls.
Killimall Bug & Roach Powder--Regan & Gillford
    Mfg. Co. Mpls.
Fullers Climas Wallpaper--H.B. Fuller, St. Paul.
Prussian Spavin Cure, Stock Food, Poultry food
    and Heave Powder-Prussian Remedy Co. St. Paul.
Hazle's Headache Capsules--Hazle Mfg. Co. St.
    Paul.
Kresota--Potter Chemical Co. Mpls.
Salt Rheum & Eczema Cure--Clarkin Bros. St. Paul.
Adams Liquid Glue--Adams Mfg. Co. Mpls.
Bartholomews Hair Restorer--S. Bartholomew Mpls.
Combine Catarrh Cure--Diamond Chemical Co. St.
    Paul.
Hindoo Oil--R.E. Fisher Mpls.

2267A **; 2267B Aqua Bottle Shard
2267C ; Style A1A; H6

2270 GRAY (estate of), THOMAS K.
    108 Hennepin Avenue   1910

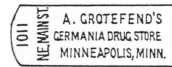

```
┌─────────────────────────┐
│   THE GENUINE           │
│  LIEBIG'S CORN CURE     │
│  GRAY & HOFFLIN         │
└─────────────────────────┘
        (2273B)
```

```
┌──┬──────────────────────┐
│1011│ A. GROTEFEND'S      │
│NE.MAIN ST.│ GERMANIA DRUG STORE │
│  │ MINNEAPOLIS, MINN.   │
└──┴──────────────────────┘
        (2292A)
```

```
┌─────────────────────────┐
│  METROPOLITAN           │
│  PHARMACY               │
│  F. H. Hainert Prop'r   │
│  MINNEAPOLIS, MINN.     │
└─────────────────────────┘
        (2304A)
```

```
      ┌──────────┐
      │ HANSEN'S │
      │  (chess  │
      │  piece)  │
      │    A     │
      │    P     │
      │    O     │
      │    T     │
      │    H     │
      │    E     │
      │    K     │
      │MINNEAPOLIS│
      │  MINN.   │
      └──────────┘
        (2237B)
```

```
┌─────────────────────────┐
│  G. A. Hallman          │
│      DRUGGIST           │
│  MINNEAPOLIS, MINN.     │
└─────────────────────────┘
        (2313A)
```

```
┌─────────────────────────┐
│  GRAY & HOFFLIN         │
│     DRUGGISTS           │
│  101 WASHINGTON AVE. S. │
│  MINNEAPOLIS, MINN.     │
└─────────────────────────┘
        (2273A)
```

2273 GRAY & HOFFLIN
101 Washington Avenue South   1878-81
2273A **; 2273B   Style A6A; Aqua, H3-3/4

2276 GREELEY & GRAY
108 Hennepin   1859

2280 GRIFFIN & DAY
2123 W. 21st   1904

2283 GRIFFIN, TRUMAN
2123 W. 21st   1905-06
2123 W. 21st & 2547 Henn Av   1907
2547 Hennepin Avenue   1908-10

2286 GRINNELL, ANDREW J.
2644 Lyndale Av. & 930 Hennepin Avenue   1887

2289 GROOCOCK, SAMUEL & SONS
Nicollet Av & 6th (Glass Block)   1883

2292 GROTEFEND, AUGUST H.F. (GERMANIA DRUG STORE)
105 Franklin Avenue North   1883
618 N.E. Marshal   1884-88
1011 N.E. Main   1889-1909
2292A **

2295 GUIWITS, F.M.
401 E. Lake   1907-10

2298 GUIWITS & JONES
2451 Bloomington Avenue   1900-04

2301 HADDEN & MOWAT
260 1st Avenue South   1897-98

2304 HAINERT, F.H. (Metropolitan Pharmacy)
528 Nicollet Avenue   1890-93
2304A **

2307 HAINERT DRUG CO.
528 Nicollet Avenue   1894

2310 HAISH, C.F.
Hopkins   1893

2313 HALLMAN, G.A.
1632 N.E. Washington   1905
1700 N.E. 4th   1908-09
2313A **

2316 HALLO, HYMAN
2 Western Avenue   1890-91

2319 HAM, C. U.
750 E. Franklin   1889

2322 HAM, D.W.
1201 3rd Avenue South   1879-80, 89-90
1205 3rd Avenue South   1882
1538 Nicollet Avenue   1895

2325 HAM, M. J.
526 Hennepin Avenue   1895

2328 HAND, R. T.
122 W. 3rd   1876

2331 HANES, L. A.
4169 Washington Avenue North   1898

2334 HANKESON, C.E.
424 Nicollet Avenue   1893

2337 HANSEN, J. P.
310 Cedar Avenue   1884-91
316 Cedar Avenue   1892-97
2337A **; 2337B **

2340 HANSEN DRUG CO.
316 Cedar Avenue   1898-1906

2343 HANSON, HENRY C.
603 Washington Avenue South   1893-95

2347 HARDING, E. M.
2 East Lake   1885-87

2350 HARDING, MRS. E.
207 East Lake   1888-89

2353 HARDING, H.G.
Nicollet & Lake   1885

2356 HARRAH, J.W. (Eureka Drug Store)
1718 4th Avenue South   1991-1910

2359 HARTER & CO, H.E.
419 Nicollet Avenue   1886-88

2362 HART'S PHARMACY
1229 Nicollet Avenue   1895-1901

2365 HARRISON, W.A.
1031 Hennepin   1908

2368 HATSCHEK, L. C.
    West Hotel   1887

2371 HAUGAN, C. E.
    390 Syndicate Arcade   1894-96
    3000 Lyndale Avenue South   1897
    701 W. Lake   1898-1910

2374 HAYNES, S.C.
    1st & Harrison   1869

2375 HAWTHORNE, E. P.
    528 Nicollet Avenue   circa 1889

2377 HEDDERLY, A. H. & Co
    245 Hennepin Avenue   1878

(INTERIOR VIEW OF E.P.HAWTHORNE'S "METROPOLITAN PHARMACY IN 1889)

2380 HEDDERLY, Edwin
    245 Hennepin Avenue   1879-80

2382 HEDDERLY, G. W.
    211 Washington Avenue North   1881

2386 HEEDELS, AVTON
    1920 Franklin Avenue East   1901

2389 HEIBERG, E.B.
    1920 Franklin Avenue East   1891

2392 HEIMANN & CO., L.C.
    717 3rd Avenue South   1902

2395 HENNEPIN AVENUE PHARMACY
    1500 Hennepin Avenue   1900-01
2395A **

2398 HENNEPIN PHARMACY
    630 Hennepin Avenue   1906-09

2401 HERRICK, FRANK H.
    124 Lake Street   1884

2404 HERRMANN, A.B.
    400 2nd Avenue South   1894-1905
2404A **

2407 HERRMANN & HAUGAN
    400 2nd Avenue South   1893
2407A **

2410 HESSELBERG, EYVIND
    402 Central Avenue   1893

2413 HICKMAN, F. M.
    2659 Dupont Avenue South   1909-10

2416 HICKS & CO, WM. K.
    1529 E. Franklin Avenue   1884-88

2419 HICKS, WM. K.
    1533 E. Franklin Avenue   1889-1910
2419A **; 2419B **

2422 HIGGINS, GEORGE E
    10 Washington Avenue South   1875
    251 Nicollet Avenue   1878
    253 Nicollet Avenue   1879
    823 Nicollet Avenue   1883
2422A **; 2422B **; 2422B2** Amber

[HIGHLAND PARK DRUG STORE - See W. G. THOMPSON]

HENNEPIN AVE PHARMACY
1500 HENNEPIN AVE.
MINNEAPOLIS, MINN.
(2395A)

A.B. HERRMANN
DRUGGIST
400
SECOND AVE.S.   MINNEAPOLIS
(2404A)

HIGGINS'
PHARMACY
MINNEAPOLIS MINN
(2422B)

TRADE WITH HICKS.
(2419A)

(2419B)

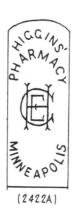

(2422A)

HERRMANN & HAUGAN
DRUGGISTS
No. 400 } MINNEAPOLIS
SECOND AVE. S.   MINN.
(2407A)

HIGH SCHOOL DRUG STORE
COR. 3ᴿᴰ AVE. SOUTH & 12ᵀᴴ ST.
MINNEAPOLIS
(2431A)

Hofflin-Thompson Drug Co
101 WASHINGTON AVE. SOUTH
MINNEAPOLIS, MINN.
(2449A)

HOFFLIN'S
MINNEAPOLIS, MINN.
(2437E)

J.R. HOFFLIN & CO.
THE DRUGGISTS
101 WASHINGTON AVE. S.
MINNEAPOLIS, MINN.
(2443A)

THE GENUINE
LIEBIG'S CORN CURE
HOFFLIN-THOMPSON DRUG Co.
(2449B)

HOFFLIN'S
DRUG STORE
MINNEAPOLIS
(2437C)

J.R. HOFFLIN Co.
THE DRUGGISTS
MINNEAPOLIS, MINN.
(2443B)

THE GENUINE
LIEBIG'S CORN CURE
J. R. HOFFLIN
(2437D)

HOFFLIN'S THE OLD DRUG CORNER
MINNEAPOLIS, MINN.
(2437B)

J.R. HOFFLIN & CO.
PRESCRIPTION
101 WASHINGTON AVE. SO.
DRUGGISTS
MINNEAPOLIS
(2443C)

HOFFLIN & CO.
(2443D)

COMPLIMENTS OF
J.R. HOFFLIN & CO.
DRUGGISTS
MINNEAPOLIS, MINN.
(2443E)

HOFFLIN & GRAY
10ᵀᴴ AVE DRUG STORE
MINNEAPOLIS, MINN.
(2446A)

HOFFLIN'S DRUG STORE
101 WASHINGTON AVE. S.
MINNEAPOLIS, MINN.
(2437A)

THE DRUGGISTS
Jos. R Hofflin Co
MINNEAPOLIS, MINN.
(2443F)

2426 HILL, A & GRUWELL, C.
Washington Avenue & 2nd Avenue South   1877

2428 HINKLEY, J. W.
319 Nicollet Avenue   1883

2431 HIGH SCHOOL DRUG STORE
3rd Avenue South & 12th Street   ?
2431A**

2434 HOFFLINS DRUG STORE
101 Washington Avenue South   1901

2437 HOFFLIN, JOSEPH R
101 Washington Av So   1882-1886
258 1st Av So (Security Drug Store)   1883-1894
2437A **; 2437B **; 2437C **;
2437D Style A6A; Aqua; 2437E1**

2443 HOFFLIN, JOSEPH R & CO.
101 Washington Avenue South   1887-93
258 1st Avenue South   1894-96
2443A **; 2433B **; 2433C Citrate of Magnesia,
Aqua; 2443D **; 2443E Dose glass, Clear;
2443F **

2446 HOFFLIN & GRAY (Tenth Ave Drug Store)
1001 S Washington   1877
2446A . Amber

2449 HOFFLIN - THOMPSON DRUG CO.
101 Washington Avenue South   1895-1900
"The Genuine Liebig's Corn Cure" is one of the
smallest bottles in a Minnesota patent medicine
collection, but nonetheless has an interesting
story. It actually comes in three different
embossings, one each from Gray and Hofflin
(1877-81), J.R. Hofflin (1882-94) and from Hofflin-
Thompson Drug Co. (1894-1901). Now, Joseph R.
Hofflin may be familiar to many Minneapolis
collectors for his numerous druggist bottles, but
he was also prominent in the local patent medicine
trade, manufacturing at various times Liebig's Corn
Cure, Liebig's Sarsaparilla (The Great Blood
Remedy), Higgin's Balsamic Lotion, and Uncle Josh's
Rheumatic Cure.

The use of the name Liebig on the corn cure is
significant, as is the word "genuine." The name
refers to a Justus Freiherr vo Liebig (1803-1873),

a highly respected German chemist and physiologist. Liebig was one of the great minds of his age, and it seems unlikely that he would lend his name to any patent medicine. Soon after his death, however, there started to appear such products as "Liebig's German Blood Tonic (an embossed bottle from out west somewhere), "Liebig's Extract of Beef" (ads say "None genuine without my signature"), and "Liebig's Corn Cure".

The use of the word "Genuine" in the name was necessary because Hofflin had a local competitor in the firm of Crosman and Plummer who put up a product called "Liebig's Corn Remover". An 1887 ad reads:
"Rated in the First Class of Standard Remedies
Liebig's Corn Remover
Manufactured only by Crosman and Plummer
druggists, Cor. Nicollet and 2nd
Warranted to cure Hard corns, Soft corns, Bunions, Warts, Callouses, Moles etc. Beware of Counterfeits."
Crosman and Plummer were in business from 1874 to 1890; little else is known about them except that Charles Crosman continued to be listed as a manufacturing chemist until 1908, putting up Liebig's Corn Remover and a Spanish Sarsaparilla, presumably paper labeled. It is impossible to say which firm put out their corn remedy first.
2449A **; 2449B Style A6A; Aqua

2452 HOLMGREN DRUG CO.
    1309 Washington Avenue South   1894

2455 HOLMES BROS
    1126 S 7th   1895

2458 HOLZSCHUH, JOHN J.
    500 Washington Avenue North   1881
    428 Washington Avenue North   1882-96
    402 20th Avenue North   1897
    2122 4th Avenue South (Owl Drug Store)   1901-04

2461 HOOPER & MATTSON
    2029 South 9th   1887

2464 HORN & KISTLER
    642 6th Avenue North   1888-92
    642 & 1320 6th Avenue North   1893

2467 HORN, S. J.
    2835 Chicago Avenue   1894-1906
    3000 Chicago Avenue   1907
    745 E. Lake   1908-10

2470 HOSKINS, A (Plymouth Pharmacy)
    312 Plymouth Avenue   1909

2473 HOWARD, GEORGE M
    AT J.O. Slemmons   1871

2476 HUGHES & SWEET
    719 3rd Avenue N.E.   1883-84

2479 HUGHES, WALTER J.
    719 3rd Avenue N.E.   1885-93
    226 Central Avenue   1894-97
    300 Central Avenue   1898-1904
    22 Washington Avenue South   1905
2479A **; 2479B **; 2479C **; 2479D Style unknown;
2479E Style A5A; Aqua; H5-1/4 x W1-3/4 x D1
2479F Style Unknown; 2479G1. Aqua; Square; H2-1/4 x W3/4 x D3/4

2482 HUGHES CUT RATE DRUG STORE
    32 Washington Avenue South   1906-10

2485 HUHN, C.H. (GEM DRUG STORE)
    208 Western Avenue   1890-98
    98 Western Avenue   1899-1910

2488 HUHN & CO, GEORGE E.
    38 Bridge Square   1869-73
    121 Nicollet Avenue   1874
    123 Nicollet Avenue   1378-84, 87
2488A **

2491 HUHN, GEORGE E.
    123 Nicollet Avenue   1885-86, 88-90

2492 HULBERG, A.O.
    941 Central Avenue   04-

2494 HUNT, P.C.
    243 Nicollet Avenue   1898

2497 HURD, G.E.
    1930 4th Avenue South   1887

2500 IVES & CO, G.A.
    519 Nicollet Avenue   1889-91
2500A **

2503 JACOBSEN, JACOB (Masonic Temple)
    226 Hennepin Avenue   1903
    526 Hennepin Avenue   1904-10
2503A **; 2503B **

W.J.HUGHES
PHARMACIST
MINNEAPOLIS, MINN.
(2479B)

HUGHES ANODYNE 710
W.J.HUGHES
MANUFACTURER
MINNEAPOLIS, MINN.
(2479E)

J.Jacobsen
MASONIC TEMPLE
MINNEAPOLIS
(2503B)

W.J.HUGHES
DRUGGIST
MINNEAPOLIS, MINN.
(2479A)

LIQUID CAMPHOLINE
W.J HUGHES MAN.F.R.
MINNEAPOLIS, MINN.
(2479F)

GEO. HUHN & CO.
MINNEAPOLIS
MIN.
(2488A)

(2500A)

GEO. A. IVES & CO.
SYNDICATE BLOCK
MINNEAPOLIS

MASONIC TEMPLE
PHARMACY
MINNEAPOLIS, MINNESOTA
J. JACOBSEN, Prop.   (2503A)

(2479C)

W.J.HUGHES
PHARMACIST
MINNEAPOLIS, MINN.

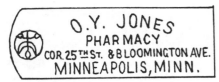

(2524A)

(2521A)

(2521B)

(2524B)

KADLEC & DANEK
DRUGGISTS
625 PLYMOUTH AVE.

(2530A)

KINPORTS
DRUG STORE
MINNEAPOLIS MINN.

(2536B)

J.H. KINPORTS
DRUGGIST
MINNEAPOLIS MINN.

(2536A)

(2536C)

2506 JENKS, J. R.
13 W 3rd — 1876

2509 JENNINGS & DAMM
711 Washington Avenue South — 1875

2512 JOHNSON & ERICKSON
1023 Washington Avenue South — 1991

2515 JOHNSON & HARRAH
1718 4th Avenue South — 1889-92

2518 JOHNSON & CO, P.
2000 Riverside Avenue — 1896

2521 JONES, HENRY
2841 Chicago Avenue — 1888
2835 Chicago Avenue — 1889-93
2521A **; 2521B **

2524 JONES PHARMACY, O.V.
2451 Bloomington Avenue — 1905-10
2524A **; 2524B **

2527 JOSEPH, J.P.
312 Plymouth Avenue — 1910

2530 KADLEC & DENEK
625 Plymouth Avenue — 1892-1898
2530A **

2533 KAMPFF & CO, GEORGE
115 Central Avenue — 1909-10

2536 KAY, E. M.
4301 East 50th Street — 1910

2539 KELLY & THOMPSON
1337 Nicollet Avenue — 1895

2542 KENWOOD PHARMACY
2123 W. 21st — 1910

2545 KERKER, F.X.
1307 Washington Avenue North — 1882
1309 Washington Avenue North — 1883-93
529 Plymouth Avenue — 1895-1907
1101 26th Avenue North — 1909

2548 KERKER & SON, F.X.
2557 Lyndale Avenue South — 1910

2551 KERSTEN, H.T.
1223 S. 7th — 1908

2554 KILGORE, WILLIAM
Nicollet between 2nd & Washington — 1867

2557 KING & PATTERSON
1131 3rd Avenue South — 1888-92

2560 KING & CO, WILLIAM D.
1131 3rd Avenue South — 1893-1910

2563 KINPORTS, JOHN H.
735 S. 10th — 1885-95
2558 Lyndale Avenue South — 1896-1907
2536A **; 2563B **; 2563C **

2566 KISTLER, C. M.
642 & 1320 6th Avenue North — 1896-97

2569 KLENERT BROS.
401 S. 10th — 1906-10

2572 KLINE, A. J.
2600 Bloomington Avenue — 1891-1910
2572A **; 2572B **; 2572C **; 2572D **;
2572E1 Style A5A; Aqua; H5-1/4 x W1-3/4 x D1

2575 KLINE & BURGER
2600 Bloomington Avenue — 1888-1890
2575A **

2578 KLINGSPORN, THEORDORE
4316 Upton Avenue South — 1910

2581 KNOX BROS.
500 Hennepin Avenue — 1888

(2572A)

A.J.KLINE
MINNEAPOLIS

(2572B)

(2572C)

(2572D)

DR. HOOPERS O
PENETRATING I
A.J.KLINE & CO. L
MINNEAPOLIS , MINN.

(2572E)

(2575A)

2584 KOCH, L.W.
1229 Western Avenue 1894-95

2587 KOZLOWSKI & WIRKUS
1700 N.E. 4th 1908

2590 KRUCKEBERG, H.C.
2621 E. 25th 1891
2701 E. 25th 1892-1904
2630 E. 25th 1905-10
2590A **; 2590B **

[K.S. & A (KENNEDY, SUFFELL, & ANDREWS) - See Patent
Medicine Section]

2596 LAKE STREET DRUG CO.
2701 E. Lake 1909-10
2596A **

2599 LAKE STREET PHARMACY
620 E. Lake 1906

2602 LAKE, W.E.
1600 Western Avenue 1908-10

2605 LAMBERT, EDWARD (Red Cross Store)
637 3rd Avenue South 1910
629 3rd Avenue South 1909
717 3rd Avenue South 1905

2608 LANE, RUFUS, H. (Palace Drug Store)
501 Hennepin Avenue 1886-1907
2608A **; 2608B **

2611 LANES DRUG STORE
1331 Hennepin Avenue 1908-10

2614 LANE & SUMMERS
501 Hennepin Avenue 1885
2614A **

2617 LANTZ, HENRY
1300 Como Avenue 1887

2620 LANTZ & SON, HENRY
1300 Como Avenue 1888-96

2623 LAPAUL, G. F. (Physician & Surgeon)
203 Washington Avenue North 1888-92
24 Washington Avenue North 1893-97
2623A **

2626 LAPENOTIERE, E. M.
2001 4th Avenue South 1896-1910
Edward Murray LaPenotiere, druggist, inventor, and
bird-watcher, was born in Woodstock, Ontario,
Canada on February 19, 1844. Educated at Caradoc
Academy in Toronto, he worked as a chemist in that
city for two years before joining a firm of chemists

(2590B)

(2596A)

(2590A)

RUFUS H.. LANE
COR.5 TH ST. & HENNEPIN AVE.
OPPOSITE WEST HOTEL
MINNEAPOLIS, MINN.

(2608A)

501 HENNEPIN AVE.
Rufus H. Lane
MINNEAPOLIS, MINN.

(2608B)

LANE & SUMMERS
COR 5TH ST. & HENNEPIN AVE.
OPPOSITE WEST HOTEL
MINNEAPOLIS, MINN.

(2614A)

(2623A)

in New York City. At the end of five years he moved west for his health and engaged in the drug business for himself, first in Cedar Rapids, IA, then at Grand Junction, IA. In June of 1892 he came to Minneapolis and opened a drug store in the Masonic Temple, two years later moving to 2001 4th Avenue South where he remained until retire- ment in 1911. He died at his home on August 29th, 1912. LaPenotiere was descended from a rather distinguished English family. His grandfather, Capt. Frederick LaPenotiere, commanded the Schooner "Pickle" under Lord Nelson in the Battle of Trafalgar. LaPenotiere designed and patented an aeroplane which probably was never built.
2626A **

2629 LA PENOTIERE & CO, E. M.
    (Masonic Temple Pharmacy)
    526 Hennepin Avenue   1893
2629A **

2632 LAMBIE & CO, BETHUNE
    2 W. 3rd   1877

2635 LARRABEE, B. H. PHARMACY
    2200 W. Boulevard   1904-07

2638 LARRABEE, R. C.
    3001 Hennepin Avenue   1894

2641 LARSON, A.E.
    230 20th Avenue North   1909-10

2644 LASHER, C. W.
    259 10th Avenue South   1883, 86
    1801 Washington Avenue North   1884
    2 East Lake   1891-93

2647 LATZ, F. W.
    1401 Washington Avenue South   1890-1905

2650 LATZ, HENRY E. (Seven Corners Drug Store)
    1428 Washington Avenue South   1889-1905
    235 Cedar Avenue   1906-10
2650A **

2653 LATZ, H. & F. E.
    1401 Washington Avenue South   1381-88
2653A **; 2653B **

2656 LAWS, YNGVAR
    2000 Riverside Avenue   1890-94

2659 LAWS DRUG CO.
    408 Nicollet Avenue   1895-1900

2662 LAWS & STEIN
    424 Nicollet Avenue   1894

2665 LEIGH, C. E.
    628 Nicollet Avenue   1891-1903
2665A **

2668 LEONARD, W. H.
    Nicollet & 1st   1859-65

2671 LEONARD & CO, W. H.
    Nic. between 2nd & Wash. (Centre Block)   1867

2674 LEVY, B. L.
    3101 Nicollet Avenue   1893-94
    3047 Nicollet Avenue   1895-1910

2677 LEXINGTON DRUG STORE
    1036 Nicollet Avenue   1909-10

2680 LILJA, GUSTAV
    2216 Franklin Avenue East   1890
    2260 Franklin Avenue East   1891-93

2683 LINCOLN, L.T.
    3000 Hennepin Avenue   1907-10

2886 LINCOLN & GOULD
    3000 Hennepin Avenue   1904-06
2886A **

2689 LINDEN HILLS DRUG STORE
    4316 Upton Avenue South   1908-10

2692 LINDSAY & POMEROY
    1229 S. 5th   1886-87
    1223 S. 7th   1889-90

2695 LION DRUG STORE (See also Peter Mark)
    123 Washington Avenue South   1890-93
2695A **

2698 LION PHARMACY
    24th & Central Avenue   ?
2698A **; 2698B **; 2698C **

2701 LITTON, EDWARD E. & CO.
    3001 Hennepin Avenue   1890

2704 LITTON, EDWARD E.
    3001 Hennepin Avenue   1891-93

H. & F. W. LATZ
14TH AVENUE
SO. MINNEAPOLIS

(2653A)

Seven Corner Drug Store
Henry Latz
Minneapolis, Minn.

(2650A)

E. M. LA PENOTIERE
DRUGGIST
2001-4TH AVE. S.
MINNEAPOLIS, MINN.

(2626A)

(2665A)

CHAS. E. LEIGH
PHARMACIST
MINNEAPOLIS

(2629A)

MASONIC TEMPLE PHARMACY
E. M. LA PENOTIERE & CO.
MINNEAPOLIS, MINN.

(2695A)

LION DRUG STORE
123 WASHINGTON AVE. So.
MINNEAPOLIS, MINN.

H. & F. W. LATZ
CHEMISTS
14TH
AVENUE
DRUG STORE
MINNEAPOLIS
SO. MINN.

(2653B)

LION PHARMACY
24TH & CENTRAL AVE.
MINNEAPOLIS, MINN.

(2698A)

LION PHARMACY
24TH & CENTRAL AVES.
MINNEAPOLIS, MINN.

(2698B)

LION PHARMACY
24th & Central Ave.
MINNEAPOLIS, MINN.

(2698C)

Lonergan's Drug Store,
Scandinavisk Apotek.
230 20th Ave. N., Minneapolis, Minn.

(2710A)

H.R. LOUGHLIN & CO.
CHEMISTS
MINNEAPOLIS

(2713A)

H.R. LOUGHLIN & CO.
CHEMISTS
MINNEAPOLIS, MINN.

(2713B)

2707 LIVINGSTONE, ANDREW
    2203 Harrison   1890
    2029 Harrison   1891
    2029 Central Avenue   1892-96
    517 14th Avenue S. E.   1897-1910

2710 LONERGAN'S DRUG STORE (Scandinavisk Apotek)
    230 20th Avenue North   1914-1918
2710A **

2713 LOUGHLIN & CO, H. R.
    428 Central Avenue   1891-97
2713A **; 2713B **

2716 LOWERY HILL DRUG STORE
    1824 Lyndale Avenue South   1909-10

2719 LUDINGTON, THOMAS E.
    501 2nd Avenue South   1886

2722 LUND, J. G.
    1400 4th Avenue South   1910

2725 LYMAN BROS.
    424 Nicollet Avenue   19878-79

2728 LYMAN & TUCKER
    2 Centre Block   1869

2731 LYMAN & WILLIAMS
    2 Centre Block   1871-73

2734 LYNG & CO, K.
    1908 Riverside Avenue   1885-89
2734A **

2737 MAILER & CO.
    41 14th Avenue S. E.   1884

2740 MAJERUS BROS.
    1011 N. E. Main   1886

2743 MARCHBANK, WM.
    1020 Hennepin Avenue   1894-96
    1014 Hennepin Avenue   1897
    1012 Hennepin Avenue   1898-1902

2746 MARK, P.
    5th & 13th Avenue South   1886

2749 MARK, P. M. (Lion Drug Store)
    123 Washington Avenue South   1880-91
Most Scandinavians who, in the early seventies,
ventured into business life, located in the vicinity
of the Milwaukee station. Their principle business
block was on the corner of Helen Street (Second
Ave. So.) and Washington, which later was remodeled
and made into the St. James Hotel. Directly across
the street from this building, on Washington
Avenue, was the first Norwegian drug store in
Minneapolis, established in the late sixties by
Peter M. Mark (Mork). In accordance with the
Norwegian custom of naming a drug store for some
animal, Mark called his establishment LO
veapotheket (Lion Drug Store), and over the door
and projecting out over the sidewalk was a big
gilded lion. In 1892 Mark closed his business and
moved to Fosston, Minnesota, but the gilded lion
remained and the shoe store which moved in became
the Lion Shoe Store.
    Taken from My Minneapolis, By Carl
    G.O. Hansen. Privately published,
    Minneapolis, 1956.

2749A **

2752 MARSH, ALANSON H.
    3006 Minnehaha Avenue   1886-93
    Hopkins   1894-1902

2755 MARSHALL & CO.
    617 Monroe   1894-95
    360 N. E. Monroe   1896-1901
    1325 Nicollet Avenue   1902-1909
    1342 Nicollet Avenue   1910

2758 MARTIN, J. B.
    44 Washington Avenue South   1882
    423 Nicollet Avenue   1883

2761 MARTTY, SAMUEL
    103 13th Avenue North   1880

2764 MARTTY & SON
    103 13th Avenue North   1881

2767 MASONIC TEMPLE PHARMACY
    526 Hennepin Avenue   1894-1903

K. LYNG & CO
PHARMACISTS
MINNEAPOLIS

(2734A)

PETER M. MARK
MINNEAPOLIS

(2749A)

MATHIS & FRIEDLANDER
505 WASHINGTON AVE S. &
2016 CEDAR AVE.

(2773A)

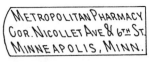

(2809A)

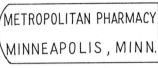

(2809B)

(2800A)

2770 MATHIS, W. D.
309 2nd Avenue South — 1892

2773 MATHIS & FRIEDLANDER
505 Wash Ave So — 1884
501 Wash Ave So & 1533 E. Franklin — 1885-86, 88
501 Wash Ave So & 203 Wash Ave No — 1887
1543 E. Franklin Ave — 1889
501 Wash Ave So & 1541 E. Franklin — 1890-91
2773A **

2776 MATTHEWS, C. M.
913 Minnehaha Avenue — 1890

2779 McCALL DRUG CO.
400 2nd Avenue South — 1906-08

2782 McCALL DRUG CO (INC)
400 2nd Ave So — 1909-10

2785 McMAHON, H. C.
517 14th Avenue S. E. — 1889

2788 McMASTERS, S. R.
122 W. 3rd — 1877

2791 McMILLAN, T. J.
Hotel Plaza — 1906

2794 MEACHEM, JOHN M.
1020 Hennepin Avenue — 1883

2797 MEIER, ERNEST
1210 Wash Ave So — 1882-88
1300 Wash Ave So — 1889-93
283 Cedar Ave — 1894-95

2800 MELENDY & LYMAN
3 Nicollet House Block — 1874-75
241 Nicollet Avenue — 1878-91
421 Nicollet Avenue — 1892-93

This story begins in 1868, which finds George Lyman in business with a Mr. Tucker in the "center block" of Minneapolis. An 1868 ad for this company billed them as "Jobbing and Retail Druggists," and listed some of their wares including: "True Farina Cologne, Prime Bay Rum, genuine ostrich feathers and lamb's wool dusters, wines and liquors for medicinal use, Congress Water by the single bottle or dozen, and Polar Soda Water." Around 1870 the firm underwent one of the management changes so typical of the early drug business, with Tucker being replaced by Mr. Williams.

Samuel Melendy was born in Lowell Mass. in 1841 and entered the drug business at age 15. He came to Minneapolis in 1871 to become a clerk with Lyman and Williams. He must have been a very industrious fellow, because in 1875 he bought out Williams and the company became Melendy and Lyman.

Melendy got top billing because Lyman devoted much of his time to a related concern, Lyman Brothers (George & Frederick) wholesale drugs. This must have been quite a cozy arrangement, with Lyman Brothers selling wholesale at 425 Nicollet and Melendy & Lyman selling retail at 241 Nicollet.

Melendy and Lyman stayed in business until 1893, when Melendy retired and was instrumental in establishing the School of Pharmacy at the University of Minnesota.

Lyman Brothers added some partners in 1884 and became the Lyman-Eliel Drug Company, or L.E.D. Co. for short. A good idea of what sort of trade they did can be found in the pages of the Northwestern Pharamacist, which was a sort of newsletter for the drug trade combined with an L.E.D. Company wholesale catalogue. Their inventory is quite impressive; they stocked about 2000 different patent and proprietory items including such exotic stuff as Begg's Little Giant Pills, Chinese Rat Destroyer, Kirk's Medical Skin Enamel, McAllister's All Healing Ointment and so on. They also sold quite a number of locally made medicines (Gregory's Scotch Bitters, North Star Lung & Throat Balsam, Monitor Liniment, Rheumatox, etc.) including a line of their own preparations under the Richards' Chemical Company trade name. These included Richards' Bitters, Richards' Blackberry Balsam, Richards' Root Beer, Richards' Sarsaparilla and about a dozen others. Unfortunately it would appear that the Richards' bottles were all paper label only. In fact the only embossed L.E.D. Co. bottles known are the many bottom embossed pharmacy bottles which they sold in great numbers to the smaller druggists who couldn't afford to buy direct from the glass houses.

The Lyman-Eliel Drug Company did a brisk trade from their headquarters at 100-104 Washington Avenue No. until 1905, when a corporate shake-up occurred with Lyman retiring (and going into the investment business). The company was known as the Eliel-Jerman Drug Company for a few years, then underwent another name change in 1907. What actually happened was a merger of the Eliel-Jerman Drug Company with Kennedy-Andrews, wholesale druggists, and Winnecke and Doerr, wholesale cigars & tobaccos. The new company was known as The Minneapolis Drug Company.

The Minneapolis Drug Company survived the Depression and was eventually purchased by a large Eastern conglomerate. They seem to have gone out of business sometime in the late 1950's or early 60's, closing out an almost century long chapter in the history of the Minneapolis pharmacy business.
2800A **

2803 MERWIN DRUG CO.
700 20th Avenue North — 1908-10

2806 METROPOLITAN DRUG STORE
130 SO. 3rd — 1908-10

2809 METROPOLITAN PHARMACY - [See also F. H. Hainert & E. P. Hawthorne]
2809A **; 2809B **

MEURER'S PHARMACY
MINNEAPOLIS, MINN.
400 CENTRAL AVE.
(2812A)

A.H. MILLER & CO.
DRUGGISTS
630 HENNEPIN AVE.
MINNEAPOLIS, MINN.
(2818A)

DRUG DEP'T
Minneapolis
Dry Goods Co
(2825A)

MINNEAPOLIS PHARMACY CO.
Babendrier & Van Nest
HOMŒOPATHIC PHARMACY
MINNEAPOLIS, MINN.
(2830A)

ANTI-CHAP
MINNEAPOLIS PHARMACY Co.
BABENDRIER & VAN NEST
MINNEAPOLIS, MINN.
(2830B)

MINNEAPOLIS PHARMACY CO.
HOMŒOPATHIC PHARMACY
MINNEAPOLIS, MINN.
(2830C)

MINNEAPOLIS Pharm. Co.
BABENDRIER & Van Nest
MINNEAPOLIS MINN.
(2830D)

J. H. MOODY
DRUGGIST
2423 CENTRAL AVE.
MINNEAPOLIS
(2842A)

FRANK J. NAGEL
→ PHARMACIST ←
MINNEAPOLIS.
(2869A)

Frank J. Nagel
Pharmacist,
MINNEAPOLIS, MINN.
(2869B)

Frank J. Nagel.
Pharmacist
MINNEAPOLIS, MINN.
(2869C)

NAGEL'S DRUG STORE,
No. 1105 26TH AVE. NORTH
MINNEAPOLIS, MINN.
(2869D)

2812 MEURER, J. J. (Meurer's Pharmacy)
    8 S. E. 4th   1907-10
    400 Central Ave   ?
2812A **; 2812B **

2815 MEWHIRTER, H. D.
    717 3rd Avenue South   1903

2818 MILLER & CO., A. H.
    628 Hennepin Avenue   1889
    630 Hennepin Avenue   ?
2818A **

2821 MILLER, W. H.
    Exchange & 4th   1876-77

2824 MILNE, H. J.
    230 20th Avenue North   1908

2825 MINNEAPOLIS DRY GOODS CO.
2825A **   ?

2827 MINNEAPOLIS PHARMACY (B. B. Fullerton, Mgr.)
    Western Av & N. 7th   1886

2830 MINNEAPOLIS PHARMACY CO.
    604 Nicollet Avenue   1892-94
    608 Nicollet Avenue   1895-1903
    35 S. 6th   1904-06
    17 S. 6th   1907
    84 S. 7th   1908-10
2830A ** Round cornered tall blake; Clear; H7-1/2
2830B **; 2830C **
2830D - Amber

2833 MINNEHAHA DRUG CO.
    1920 Franklin Avenue E.   1897

2836 MONAHAN, J. A.
    602 20th Avenue North   1888-89
    1121 Washington Avenue North   1890-94
    1500 Hennepin Avenue   1895-99

2839 MONAHAN, T. H.
    502 20th Avenue North   1886
    602 20th Avenue North   1887

2842 MOODY, J. H.
    2505 Harrison Avenue   1888
    2423 Harrison Avenue   1889-91
    2423 Central Avenue   1892-1903
2842A **

2845 MOORE & CO, JOSEPH B.
    1931 4th Avenue South   1884

2848 MOORE & MUNGER
    1331 Nicollet Avenue   1884

2851 MORAN, M. T.
    929 20th Avenue North   1910

2854 MORGAN DRUG CO.
    1101 26th Ave No & 1807 Plymouth Ave 1910

2857 MOREY, A. L.
    500 E. 24th   1895

2860 MUELLER, C.
    1210 Washington Avenue South   1886

2863 MUNNS, J. F.
    813 S. E. 4th   1896-1904

2866 MURRISON & CO, JAMES
    Merchants Block   1867-71
    44 S. Wash Ave   1874
2866A . Style C1G; Aqua

2869 NAGEL, F. J.
    230 20th Avenue North   1902-03
    1105 26th Avenue North   1904-06
    1101 26th Avenue North   1907-08
2869A **; 2869B **; 2869C **; 2869D **

2872 NELSON & CO, E.
   2404 Riverside Ave   1887
   2406 Riverside Ave   1888
   2400 Riverside Ave   1889-93

2875 NELSON, G. W.
   1005 3rd Ave N. E.   1896-99
   941 Central Ave   1900-04

2878 NELSON, NELS
   1827 E. Lake   1910

2881 NELSON, N. P.
   2400 Riverside Ave   1894

2884 NELSON, O. H.
   1918 Franklin Ave E   1897

2887 NEWELL & CO., EL. L.
   2644 Lyndale Ave So   1888

2890 NEW STORE PHARMACY, THE
   615-629 Nicollet Ave   1899-1905
2890A **

2893 NICHOLS, B. H.
   4252 Nicollet Avenue   1909-10

2896 NICOLLET DRUG STORE - See also Savory & Whitaker
   828 Nicollet Avenue   1908-09

2902 NORA PHARMACY
   1309 Washington Ave So   ?
2902A **

2905 NOBLE & FRENCH
   Lake & Minnehaha   1882

2908 NORGREN, G. P.
   401 W. Lake   1908

2911 NORGREN MEDICINE CO.
   401 W. Lake   1910

2914 NORGREN & LAMBERT
   401 W. Lake   1909

[NOVELTY DRUG STORE - See Colbrath & Russell]

2920 NYE, ALEXANDER M.
   1931 Hennepin Avenue   1883

2923 NYE, WALLACE G.
   400 13th Ave No   1882, 84-87
   400 Plymouth Ave   1883, 88-94
   "Wallace G. Nye was a druggist when he first
launched his craft for himself, and to this day, he
would have been a druggist if he had not been
possessed of a thirst for politics."
                        --Minneapolis Journal, 1906.

Wallace G. Nye-druggist, businessman, and mayor of
Minneapolis, was born in Oshkosh, Wisconsin, on the
7th of October, 1859. He operated a drug store in
Chicago for a short time before coming to Minneapolis and setting up a second drug business in
1881. He operated his shop at 400 Plymouth Ave.
North until 1894-that's when he was bitten by the
political bug. Leaving the drug trade, he dabbled
in many things; bonds, insurance and the Commercial
Club. He was elected to the School Board, the Park
Board, served as the City Comptroller, and, in 1913,
he was elected mayor of Minneapolis. He served as
mayor for 2 terms, his last year being in 1916.
2923A **

2926 OAK LAKE DRUG STORE
   100 Western Ave   1888

2929 OAK PARK DRUG STORE
   1320 6th Ave No   1894
2929A **

2932 OAK STREET DRUG STORE
   800 Wash Av S.E.   1909

2935 OAK STREET PHARMACY
   800 Wash Av S. E.   1910

2938 OBERG, CARL E.
   3757 Chicago Ave   1910

2941 OGG BROS.
   3128 Wash Ave No   1991

2944 OGG, J. J.
   236 25th Avenue North   1892-1901

2947 OLANDER, M. L.
   1223 S. 7th   1908

2950 OLIVER AVENUE DRUG STORE
   2024 Crystal Lake Av   1901-02

2953 OLIVER, J. M.
   2024 Crystal Lake Av   1903, 05-10

2956 OLIVER, J. E.
   2024 Crystal Lake Av   1904

2959 OLIVER & SHIPMAN
   529 6th Ave So   1885

2962 OLSON & CO, S. E.
   5th & 1st Ave So   1892-93
2962A **; 2962B **

2965 OPERA HOUSE DRUG CO.
   528 Nicollet Avenue   1895-96

THE NEW STORE
PHARMACY
MINNEAPOLIS, MINN.
(2890A)

NORA PHARMACY
1309 WASHINGTON AVE. S.
MINNEAPOLIS, MINN.
(2902A)

NYE'S DRUG STORE
PLYMOUTH AVE.
MINNEAPOLIS
(2923A)

OAK PARK PHARMACY
1320-6TH AVE. NO.
MINNEAPOLIS
(2929A)

S.E. OLSON & CO.
TOILET DEPARTMENT
MINNEAPOLIS
(2962A)

DRUG DEPARTMENT
S.E. OLSON CO.
THE BIG STORE
MINNEAPOLIS, MINN.
(2962B)

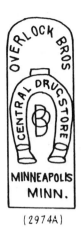

(2974A)

C. M. PARDOE & CO.
DRUGGISTS
COR. LAKE & BLOOMINGTON AVE.
MINNEAPOLIS

(2989A)

Parker Bros.
Prescription Druggists
Minneapolis

(2992A)

PABODY & WHITAKER
DISPENSING CHEMISTS
MINNEAPOLIS, MINN.

(2980A)

A M PERSALL
MINNEAPOLIS, MINN.

(3034B)

A.M. PERSALL
THE DRUGGIST
MINNEAPOLIS, MINN.

(3034A)

PIONEER
DRUG STORE
EST'D
1855
PABODY & WHITAKER
MINNEAPOLIS
MINN.

(2980B)

PATTERSON & KLINE
DRUGGISTS
2600 BLOOMINGTON AVE.
MINNEAPOLIS, MINN.

(3010A)

2968 ORIENTAL DRUG STORE
1538 Nicollet Avenue 1895

2971 OUSDAHL, EVEN (Scandia Drug Store)
402 Cedar Avenue 1891

2974 OVERLOCK BROS.
102 Central Avenue 1880-84
226 Central Avenue 1885-87
226 Central Ave & 3101 Nic Ave 1888-90
208 Central Ave 1891-92
2974A **

2977 OWL DRUG STORE
600 Hennepin Avenue 1909-10

2980 PABODY & WHITAKER, C. S. (Pioneer Drug Store)
Wash Av & Henn Av 1878-85
2980A **; 2980B **

2983 PANORAMA DRUG STORE
2644 Lyndale Ave So 1888

2986 PARDOE, C. M.
1525 E. Lake 1899-1910

2989 PARDOE & CO., C. M.
1525 E. Lake 1890
2989A **

2992 PARKER BROS
2006 Cedar Ave 1890-91
2006 Cedar Av & 1529 Franklin Ave. 1892-94
1529 Franklin Av & 1815 Franklin Ave. 1895-96
2992A **

2995 PARKER, J. W.
3101 Nic Ave 1892

2998 PARKER & PROCTOR
630 Hennepin Avenue 1890

3001 PARSON, O. M.
221 Nic Ave 1874

3004 PATTEE, IRVIN
2603 Stevens Ave 1903

3007 PATTERSON & CHILSTROM (High School Drug Store)
1201 3rd Ave So 1881-86

3010 PATTERSON & KLINE
2600 Bloomington Ave 1887
3010A **

3013 PAYNE, G. A.
2900 Wash Ave No 1908

3016 PEABODY, O. M.
2123 Chicago Ave 1906
2900 Wash Ave No 1905

3019 PEABODY & GIFFORD
2123 Chicago Ave 1907-10

3022 PECK, C. C. (13th Av Drug Store)
1229 S. 5th 1882

3025 PECK & RANDALL
529 6th Ave So 1884

3028 PELTZER, H. M
3404 University Ave S.E. 1908
3400 University Ave S.E. 1909-10

3031 PENNINGTON, HENRY
828 Nicollet Avenue 1906-07

3034 PERSALL, A. H.
1402 N.E. Marshall 1894
2000 Crystal Lake Av 1895-98
929 20th Avenue N 1899-1909
3034A **; 3034B **

3037 PETERSON & CO., J. O.
233 Cedar Ave 1888
3037A **

3040 PETERSON, J. O.
1501 Wash Ave So 1889-1910
1501 Wash Ave So & 1333 Franklin Ave 1907
Swedish born J.O. Peterson started his drug store
in a little frame building at 1501 Washington Ave.
South (Seven Corners). He was 25 years old at the
time. It was a family business and all ten
children helped--six of them graduated from the
University of Minnesota in Pharmacy.

(3040A)

(3040C)

SAPPHINE

(3043A,3970A)

(3040D)

J.O.PETERSON & CO.
DRUGGISTS
MINNEAPOLIS, MINN
(3037A)

J.O. PETERSON
MINNEAPOLIS
(3040B)

PIERSON'S PHARMACY
253 NICOLLET AVENUE
MINNEAPOLIS, MINN.
(3049A)

E. M. PIKE
PHARMACIST
COR. 2ND & 5TH ST.
(3052A)

E.M. PIKE
MINNEAPOLIS, MINN.
(3052B)

Live leeches imported from Norway, "nervousness" drops and gum asofetida (an offensive smelling sap from a large ivy type plant, found in Central Asia and used in medicine for stomach disorders) were good sellers in Peterson's Drug Store, at Seven Corners, when it opened its doors for the first time in 1888-long before the era of aspirin and miracle drugs. Peterson had a great many Swedish remedies he would make up. He made his own pills. He had a pill roller and percolated a lot of his tinctures and fluid extracts used for prescriptions.

He made cough syrup by the barrel an old time remedy brought from Sweden, and called it Peterson's Luna Balsam. When aspirin became available, the Petersons imported it in one ounce cartons and put it in 5 grain capsules. An ounce of aspirin then cost 85¢.

In 1923 J.O. Peterson died of stomach disorders (maybe his gum of asafetida didn't work?). At the time of his death there were two stores and a third was under construction. By 1963 there were four stores and about three million prescriptions filled.

In recent years flowing green plants, round tables and mugs of beer have occupied the J.O. Peterson building, replacing the druggists counters and shelves. It has been converted into a bar and restaurant.
3040A **; 3040B **; 3040C Citrate of Magnesia; 3040D Dose Glass

3043 PETERSON, F. W. (Andrus Bldg. Pharmacy)
    833 Andrus Bldg.   1903-04, 09
Comparatively few people know that J.O. Peterson had a brother, Frank, who was also a pharmacist. He was a clerk in his brother's store from 1892-1900. In 1901 he began his own venture, the Andrus Building Pharmacy. The place of business was described as being small but well kept up and well stocked. Among this stock was a line of his own preparations, under the brand name of "Sapphine". In fact, the Sapphine Chemical Company appears in the 1905 City Directory as a separate organization, with the same business address as the pharmacy and Frank W.

Peterson as manager. The Sapphine line consisted of Sapphine Hair Tonic and Dandruff Cure, Sapphine Toilet Cream, Sapphine Toilet Soap and a number of other specialty items. Advertisements of the period claimed that Sapphine products were for sale by all barbers and druggists.
3043A . Clear; Style A2J (wide mouth)

3046   PHOENIX DRUG STORE
    501 Wash Ave So   1897-1901

3049   PIERSON, FRED G.
    253 Nic Av   1885-86
3049A **

3052   PIKE, EUGENE M.
    501 2nd Ave So   1885-88
    428 2nd Ave So   1889-1906
3052A **; 3052B Special

3055   PIKE DRUG CO.
    428 2nd Ave So   1907

[PIONEER DRUG STORE - See Pabody & Whitaker]

3061   PIONEER DRUG CO.
    2423 Central Ave   1904-06
    2430 Central Ave   1907-10

3064   PLYMOUTH DRUG CO.
    1121 Wash Ave No   1896

3067   POCAHONTAS PHARMACY
    2122 4th Avenue South   1907

3070   POMEROY, M. P.
    1223 S. 7th   1888-1907

3073   POOL, P. V. M.
    2424 Riverside Ave So   1884
    1220 N. E. Main   1885
    2401 E. Franklin Ave   1886-89, 83

3076 POOL & CO., P. V. M.
2401 Franklin Ave E.   1890-91

[POST OFFICE PHARMACY - See individual druggists for
bottles   1884-1914+
Even here in Minnesota, where collectors are often
more interested in the history of a bottle than in
its dollar value, few people get excited about
druggist bottles. Well, to each his own, but if
you look at one collector's "Best Shelf" you'll see
a little collection of bottles from the Post Office
Pharmacy. This is partly because he's a student of
North Side history, and partly just because he's
amazed that so many different bottle variants could
come from one store.

The store seems to have been built in 1884, at 1921
N. Washington, with its first occupants being
Edward Shumpik and John F. Danek. In 1890 Shumpik
died and Danek moved down the street to open his
own store. Shumpik's son, Edward Jr. took over the
store at 1921 Washington and ran it with mixed
fortunes for the next 9 years. For part of that
time he had a partner with the unfortunate name of
Myron L. Crapser. Edward Jr. was also a dentist,
but evidently not much of a businessman, as he was
in and out of bankruptcy court. Finally, in 1899,
Edward Jr.'s brother-in-law Chas. Robertson bought
into the business. It was about this time that the
store became known as the Post Office Pharmacy, for
the obvious reason that is was also Post Office
Substation #3, with Robertson in charge. Actually
this sort of thing was fairly common in the old
days. Some drug stores had post offices, libraries,
a jewelry store or even a bakery associated with
them. Anyway, Robertson (along with various
partners like F.J. Nagel 1900-1901) ran the store
until 1913, when Henry Knutson and John F. Dvoracek
purchased it. The next year Knutson dropped out
leaving Dvoracek, one of the numerous Bohemians
operating drug stores on the Northside, in full
ownership. An ad of this time called it "The
Leading Drug Store of North Minneapolis", and
described its elaborate fixtures and soda fountain.]

3082 PRESTON, C. W.
1600 Western Avenue   1908

3085 PRESTON & PRICE
1600 Western Avenue   1907

3088 PROCTOR & CO, P. R.
630 Hennepin Avenue   1892

3091 PROCTOR & DAVIDSON
630 Hennepin Avenue   1891

3097 RANDELL & CO, GEO. S.
603 - 6th Avenue South   1883

3100 RANUM, O. K.
224 E. 7th   1876-77

3103 RASCHE, D. E.
801 N. E. 2nd   1909

3106 RAUCH, HENRY
1228 N. E. Main   1893-1903
523 Plymouth Ave   1908-10
3106A **

3109 RAUCH & SCHMIDT
129 Nic Ave   1892
3109A **

3112 RECHE, HENRY C.
700 Western Ave   1887-88

3115 RED CROSS DRUG STORE
415 Wash Ave So   1889

3118 RED CROSS PHARMACY (See also S. J. Reynolds &
Edward Lambert)
717 3rd Ave So   1903-04
333 3rd Ave So, 1228 N. E. Main   1905
637 3rd Ave So, 1228 N. E. Main   1906-07
637 3rd Ave So   1908-09

3121 REEVES, FRED P.
300 S. E. 9th   1887-89

3122 REYNOLDS, S. J. (Red Cross Pharmacy)
717 3rd Ave So   1904

3124 REYNOLDS & CO.
1801 Washington Ave So   1887

3127 RIDGEWAY, JOSEPH
703 Wash Ave So   1879-81
603 Wash Ave So   1882

3130 RIEBETH, KATE G.
1109 6th Ave No   1887

3133 RIVIERE, TELESPHORE F.
701 N. E. Adams   1887
701 Adams & 429 4th Ave So   1888
701 Adams   1889

3136 ROBERTS, T. M.
508 & 719 Nic Ave   1896-97

3139 ROBERTS SUPPLY HOUSE, T. M.
717-721 Nic Ave   1898-1901

3142 ROBERTS SUPPLY CO, T. M.
717-721 Nic Ave   1903
717 Nic Ave   1904-05

3145 ROBERTS CO-OPERATIVE SUPPLY CO, T. M.
717 Nic Ave   1906-09

3148 ROBERTSON DRUG CO (Post Office Pharmacy)
1921 Washington Ave No   1902-09
3148A **; 3148B **

3151 ROBERTSON - CRAPSER DRUG CO.
1921 Washington Ave No   1899

3154 ROBERTSON - NAGLE DRUG CO. (Post Office Pharmacy)
1921 Washington Ave No   1900-01
3154A **; 3154B **

```
 _____
/  RAUCH & SCHMIDT          \
|      DRUGGISTS            |
|   129 NICOLLET AVE.      |
\      MINNEAPOLIS         /
 ---------------------------
```
(3109A)

```
 _____
/   HENRY RAUCH             \
|      DRUGGIST            |
|   523 PLYMOUTH AVE.     |
\      MINNEAPOLIS.        /
 ---------------------------
```
(3106A)

(3148A)

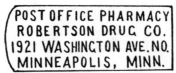

POST OFFICE PHARMACY
ROBERTSON DRUG CO.
1921 WASHINGTON AVE. NO.
MINNEAPOLIS, MINN.

(3148B)

ROBERTSON – NAGEL
POST OFFICE PHARMACY
MINNEAPOLIS, MINN.

(3154B)

C.A.ROBINSON
98 WESTERN AVE. COR. 12TH
MINNEAPOLIS

(3160A)

98 WESTERN AVE.

DR. JOY'S
TAR COUGH ELIXIR
MFG. BY C.A. ROBINSON

MINNEAPOLIS

(3160B)

C.A. ROBINSON
PHARMACIST
29TH AVE. N. & WASH.
MINNEAPOLIS

(3163A)

ROBERTSON
NAGEL
POST
OFFICE
PHARMACY
MINNEAPOLIS
MINN.

(3154A)

3157 ROBINSON BROS.
     701 N. E. Adams   1885

3160 ROBINSON, CHARLES A.
     1200 Western Ave   1887
     98 Western Ave   1888-95
3160A **;
3160B   Style A5H; Aqua; H7xL2-1/8xW1-1/4

3163 ROBINSON, CLARENCE A.
     2317 Washington Ave So   1888
     2829 Washington Ave So   1889-91
     2901 Washington Ave So   1892-94
3163A **; 3163B **

3166 ROBINSON, FRED C.
     2523 S. 25th   1883-92
     926 E. 24th   1893

3169 ROBINSON, FRED T.
     N.E. Summer & Adams   1886

3172 ROBINSON, GEO W.
     824 Western Ave   1887

3175 ROBINSON, H. W.
     66 W. 3rd   1876

3178 ROCKSTAD, ANFIN
     2900 Washington Ave No   1906-07
     2122 4th Ave So   1908-10

3184 ROSE & CO, A. H.
     208 Central (Nicollet House Block)   1878
     208 Central   1879-81
     208 Central, Main & Marshall   1882-83
     208 Central & 401 N. E. Main   1884
     102 & 208 Central   1885-90
3184A **; 3184B **; 3184C **

3190 ROSE DRUG CO., A. H.
     633 1st Ave So   1893-94

3193 ROSE, G. A.
     211 Central   1891-1900
     303 Central   1901-10
3193A **; 3193B **; 3193C **; 3193D Style A6G; Clear;
     H6-1/4 x D2-1/4 x W1-1/4; 3193E Dose glass;
     3193F Embossing on Baby Nurser

USE ROSE'S
GEO. A. ROSE
211 CENT. AVE.
COUGH BALSAM

(3193E)

GEO.A.ROSE Druggist
211 CENTRAL AVE.
MINNEAPOLIS

(3193A)

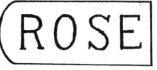

(3193B)

FROM ROSE'S

(3193C)

GEO. A. ROSE
DRUGGIST
303 CENT. AVE.

(3193F)

ROSE'S
COUGH BALSAM

(3193D)

A.H. ROSE & Co.
DRUGGISTS
MINNEAPOLIS

(3184A)

A.H. ROSE & Co.
MINNEAPOLIS
MINN.

(3184B)

A.H. ROSE & CO
DRUGGIST
MINNEAPOLIS, MINN.

(3184C)

ST. ANTHONY DRUG STORE
1402 N.E. MARSHALL ST.
MINNEAPOLIS

(3220A)

J.H.SANDBERG
PHARMACIST
501 CENTRAL AVE.
MINNEAPOLIS, MINN.

(3232A)

S.F. SANDERSON
PHARMACIST
MINNEAPOLIS

(3238A)

(3199A)

"SANDERSON'S PHARMACY"
MINNEAPOLIS, MINN.

(3244B)

Sanderson's
PHARMACY
MINNEAPOLIS, MINN.

(3244A)

(3229A)

C.A. SALMON & CO.
DISPENSING
CHEMISTS
MINNEAPOLIS

(3229B)

3223 ST LOUIS DRUG STORE
  203 Washington Ave No   1886
  501 Washington Ave So   1889, 92, 94
  501 Wash Ave So & 1543 Franklin Ave E   1890
  501 Wash Ave So & 402 Cedar Ave   1893
  633 1st Ave So   1895

3226 SALLS, J. H.
  1501 Hennepin Ave   1892-93

3229 SALMON & CO, G. A.
  253 Nic Ave   1880-82
3229A **; 3229B **

3232 SANDBERG, J. H.
  501 Central Ave   1888-1901
3232A **

3235 SANDBERG & MEUERER
  501 Central Ave   1903-05
  8 S. E. 4th   1906

3238 SANDERSON, S. F.
  828 Nic Ave   1888-90
3238A **

3241 SANDERSON, JOHN B.
  828 Nic Ave   1891-92

3244 SANDERSON'S PHARMACY
  828 Nic Ave   1893-1904
3244A **; 3244B **

3247 SANGER, H. A.
  928 Plymouth Ave   1906-08

3250 SAUNDERS, GEO.
  2101 Stevens Ave   1883
  2601 Stevens Ave   1884-89
  2603 Stevens Ave   1890-1902

3253 SAVAGE, W. D.
  3553 Nic Ave   1906
  3555 Nic Ave   1907-10

3256 SAVORY, E.
  Under Nicollet House   1865-67

3259 SAVORY, GEORGE A.
  253 Hennepin Ave   1875

3262 SAVORY, GEO. A. & JOHNSTON
  Wash Ave & Hennepin Ave   1869
  Johnston's Block opposite Nic. House   1871, 73

3265 SAVORY & WHITAKER (Nicollet Drug Store)
  Wash Ave & Hennepin Ave   1874
3265A **
An 1873 directory provided this story: "SAVORY &
JOHNSTON NICOLLET DRUG STORE, George A. Savory
claims to have been the first druggist in this
state to engage in business west of the Mississippi
River, having established his business in 1855.
The present partnership existed about three years,
Dr. George B. Johnston having purchased an interest

3196 ROSE & HICKS
  1533 Franklin Ave So   1883

3199 ROSE & MORGAN
  303 Central Ave   1908-09
3199A . Dose glass; Clear

3202 ROSE & SON
  333 Hennepin Avenue   1892

3205 ROSE & THOMPSON
  1632 N. E. Wash Ave. No.   1907-08

3208 ROUSSEAU, F. L.
  208 Central Ave   1893

3211 ROWLAND, W. H.
  3007 Hennepin Ave   1888

3214 RUSSELL & CASE
  208 Western Ave   1903-05

3217 RUUD & PETERSEN
  123 Washington Ave So   1892-96

3220 ST ANTHONY DRUG STORE
  1402 N.E. Marshall   1891
3220A **

SAVORY & WHITAKER DRUG STORE IN 1871,
PHOTO COURTESY OF MHS COLLECTIONS

(3265A)

in the business at that time. Their store is in
the fine stone block built by Mr. Johnston at the
corner at Washington and Hennepin Avenues. This
building is three stories high, 70 by 74 feet and
is an ornament to this city.

A comparison of bottles from the Pioneer and
Nicollet Drug Stores shows the obvious connection
between these two companies.

3268 SCANDIA DRUG STORE
  (See also Even Ousdahl & Sven Gjesdahl)
  1809 Riverside Ave   1890
  402 Cedar Ave   1896-1905
3268A **; 3268B **

3271 SCHEIF, E. F.
  1200 Western Ave   1888

3274 SCHELDRUP, M. A.
  800 E. 10th 1895-98
  2558 Lyndale Ave So   1908-09
3274A **

3277 SCHIEMER, JULIUS
  Land Office Bldg.   1859

3280 SCHMIDT, C. A.
  401 14th Ave So   1903

3283 SCHMITZ, L. M.
  316 Cedar Ave   1896-97

3286 SCHRODER & McNEAR
  600 Hennepin Avenue   1904-07

3289 SCHULTE, J. J.
  3801 4th Ave So   1909-10

3292 SCHULZE, W. J.
  1031 Hennepin Ave   1907

3295 SCHWEND & CO., G. W.
  517 14th Ave S. E.   1890-91

3298 SCHWEND, J.R.
  517 14th Ave S. E.   1892-96
  609 N. E. Marshall   1897-1900
  928 Plymouth Ave   1901

3301 SCOFIELD, F. H.
  2016 Cedar Ave   1882
  2122 4th Ave So   1887-91
3301A . Plain panels; Clear

3304 SCOFIELD & HANSON
  Cedar Ave & Franklin Ave   1881

3307 SCOFIELD & KNAPP
  2076 Cedar Ave   1883
  2201 4th Ave So   1884-86

3310 SCOTT & LASHER
  2 E Lake 1889-90

3313 SECURITY DRUG STORE (J. R. HOFFLIN)
  258 1st Ave So.   1883-94
3313A **

3316 SEGERSTROM, AUGUST A.
  33 S. 12th 1885
  1109 Wash Ave So   1891-93
  1223 Wash Ave So   1894-1910
3316A **

(3376A)

SIXTH AVE. PHARMACY
COR. LYNDALE & SIXTH AVES.
N. MINNEAPOLIS

(3376B)

SECURITY DRUG STORE AT CORNER OF 3RD ST & 1ST AVE S.
IN 1890, PHOTO COURTESY OF MHS COLLECTIONS

(3331B)

S. J. SHERMAN
DRUGGIST
424 NICOLLET AVE
MINNEAPOLIS, MINN.

(3331A)

(3334A)

E. SHUMPIK
PHARMACIST
MINNEAPOLIS

(3334B)

O. B. SKINNER
DRUGGIST
MINNEAPOLIS, MINN

(3355A)

3319 SEGERSTROM & CO.
33 S. 12th 1884

3322 SEIBERT, D. S.
1501 Hennepin Ave — 1889

3328 SHACKLEFORD, F. T.
1929 Washington Ave So — 1907

3331 SHERMAN, S. J.
424 Nicollet Ave — 1879-91
3331A **; 3331B **

3334 SHUMPIK, EDWARD S
1921 Washington Ave No — 1891-95, 97
3334A **; 3334B **

3337 SHUMPIK & CRAPSER
1921 Washington Ave No — 1896

3340 SHUMPIK - ROBERTSON DRUG CO.
1921 Wash Ave No & 1101 26th Ave No — 1908
1921 Washington Ave No — 1909-10

[SIXTH AVENUE PHARMACY - See H. A. SMITH]

3346 SIMMON, KARL
66 W. 3rd — 1877

3349 SJOBLOM, O. J. F.
1401 Wash Ave So — 1906-08

3352 SKINNER, CHAUNCEY M.
1426 Wash Ave So — 1883
1428 Wash Ave So — 1884-85
1428 Wash Ave So & 1718 4th Ave So — 1886-87
1718 4th Ave So — 1888
717 3rd Ave So — 1889-90

3355 SKINNER, OTIS B.
1st & 13th Ave No — 1878-79
1021 Wash Ave No — 1880
1121 Wash Ave No — 1881-2
2529 Wash Ave No — 1888
2531 Wash Ave No — 1889-95
2901 Wash Ave No — 1896-10
3355A **

3358 SKINNER & CO, O. B.
1121 Wash Ave No — 1883-86

3361 SLEMMONS, JOHN O.
89 Nic Ave — 1871-73

3364 SMETANA, W. S.
Hopkins 1898-1906

3367 SMITH, A. J.
631 Hennepin Ave — 1886-90

3370 SMITH, C.
128 Wash Ave So — 1874

3373 SMITH, JAMES A.
    314 Nicollet Ave   1875-78
    823 Nicollet Ave   1879-81

3376 SMITH, H. A. (Sixth Ave Pharmacy)
    642 6th Ave. No.   1894-1896
3376A **; 3376B **

3379 SMITH & KIMBALL
    314 Nicollet Ave   1874

3382 SORENSON, P. R.
    1929 Washington Ave So   1908
    928 Plymouth   1909-10

3385 SOUTH SIDE DRUG CO. (Same as Scandia Drug Store)
    402 Cedar Ave   1906

3388 SOUTHWORTH, E.
    Wensinger Block   1871

[SPINK & CO - See Medicine Mfg. section]

3395 SPRINGATE, J. L.
    930 Hennepin Ave   1884-85

3398 STANLEY DRUG CO.
    637 3rd Ave So   1915+
3398A **

3401 STAPLETON & CO, M. F.
    1543 Franklin Ave E.   1892

3404 STARK, T. F. (Homeopathic Pharmacy)
    426 Hennepin Ave   1879-82
    700 6th Ave No   1884-85
    700 6th Ave No, & 1301 6th Ave No 1886
    1320 6th Ave No   1887-88
    1326 6th Ave No   1889
    1306 6th Ave No   1890-92
3404A **; 3404B **

3407 STEINFELD, LOUIS
    928 Plymouth   1897

3410 STEININGER, J. A.
    941 Central Ave   1905-10

3413 STEVENSON, CARL
    2508 S. 8th 1901-06
    2500 Riverside Ave   1907-10

3416 STIERLE, ADOLPH
    200 E. 7th 1876-77

3419 STILES, J. E.
    St. Louis Park   1893-95

3422 STOCKING, L. D. (Druggist in charge at
    Noyes Bros. & Cutler)
    105 E. 3rd 1876

3425 STONE, J. R.
    823 Nicollet Ave   1882

3428 STORMS & CO., E. J.
    1320 6th Ave No   1906-10
3428A **

3431 STROHMEYER BROS.
    823 Nicollet Ave   1884-87, 91-92
3431A **

3434 STROHMEYER, H. L.
    823 Nicollet Ave   1888-90

3437 STROUT, W. P.
    2029 Central Ave   1900-04

3440 SUTTON, NELSON
    2451 Bloomington Ave   1884-88
    1515 E. Lake   1889
    127 Central Ave   1890-91
    2451 Bloomington Ave   1892-94

3443 SUTZIN, JACOB
    1323 Washington Ave So   1888

3446 SWEENY, R. O.
    7 W. 3rd 1876-77

3449 SWEET, E. P.
    1214 Western Ave   1881
    1200 Western Ave   1882-86
    100 Western Ave   1887-1895
    98 Western Ave   1896-1898
    208 Western Ave   1899-1901
    130 Western Ave   ?
3449A **; 3449B **; 3449C **; 3449D **; 3994E **

3452 SWEET & CO., E. P.
    5th & 11th Ave No   1885-88

Stanley PRESCRIPTION DRUGGISTS DRUG CO. COR. 3RD AVE SO. & 7TH ST. MINNEAPOLIS, MINN.

(3398A)

SWEET THE DRUGGIST 100 WESTERN AVE. MINNEAPOLIS

(3449A)

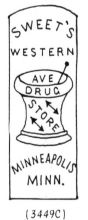

(3449C)

STARK'S PHARMACY MINNEAPOLIS

(3404A)

E.J. STORMS & CO 1320-6TH AVE NORTH MINNEAPOLIS, MINN.

(3428A)

STARK'S PHARMACY MINNEAPOLIS, MINN.

(3404B)

STROHMEYER BROS PHARMACISTS MINNEAPOLIS

(3431A)

(3449B)

E. P. SWEET
WESTERN AVE. & 12TH ST.
MINNEAPOLIS, MINN.
(3449D)

WM. H. SWEET
PHARMACIST
MINNEAPOLIS, MINN
(3455A)

WM. H. SWEET
PHARMACIST
MINNEAPOLIS, MINN.
(3455B)

SWEET & HAWTHORNE
COR. NICOLLET AVE. & 6TH ST.
MINNEAPOLIS
(3458A)

G. E. SWIFT
PHARMACIST
ROBBINSDALE MINN.
(3467A)

SYNDICATE BLOCK
PHARMACY
MINNEAPOLIS, MINN.
(3468A)

THOMPSON BROS.
PRESCRIPTION DRUGGISTS
COR. 26TH ST. & LYNDALE AVE. SO.
MINNEAPOLIS, MINN.
(3485A)

THOMPSON BROS.
DRUGGISTS
MINNEAPOLIS, MINN.
(3485B)

Syndicate Pharmacy
SYNDICATE ARCADE
ROOM 395
MINNEAPOLIS, MINN.
(3468B)

HIGHLAND PARK DRUG STORE
MINNEAPOLIS
(3503B)

HIGHLAND PARK
DRUG STORE
W. G. THOMPSON PROP.
(3503A)

THOMPSON'S
THROAT LOZENGES
A. D. THOMPSON
DRUG CO.
MINNEAPOLIS
MINN.
(3488A)

THOMPSON & SUMMER
5TH & HENNEPIN AVE.
MINNEAPOLIS
(3506A)

3455 SWEET, W. H.
   1731 Chicago Ave   1900-1910
3455A **; 3455B **

3458 SWEET & HAWTHORNE
   528 Nicollet Ave   1887-88
3458A **

3461 SWEET & HENRICHS
   5th & 11th Avenue No   1884

3464 SWEET & KISTLER
   642 6th Ave No   1887

3467 SWIFT GEO. E.
   1121 Wash Ave No   1887-89
   Parker Post Office - Robbinsdale 1890
   Robbinsdale 1891-95
   926 20th Ave No   1896-97
   Robbinsdale 1902-10
3467A **

3468 SYNDICATE BLOCK PHARMACY
   ?   ?
3468A **; 3468B **

3470 TALBERT - WHITE & CO.
   Main & Bay 1871
   105 Central Ave   1873-82

3473 TEELE, F. M.
   1533 Franklin Ave   1883

3476 TENNESON & CO.
   1500 Franklin Ave. E   1887

[TENTH AVENUE DRUG STORE - See Dow & Skinner]

3482 TENTH AVENUE PHARMACY
   926 E. 24th 1894

3485 THOMPSON BROS.
   2558 Lyndale Ave So   1892-95
3485A **; 3489B **

3488 THOMPSON DRUG CO., A. D. (Post Office Store)
   258 1st Ave So   1899-1903
   258 1st Ave So & 401 Nicollet Ave   1904-10
3488A . Square Tablet; Clear, H3-1/4x11-3/4xW1-1/4

3491 THOMPSON, E. R.
   308 Washington Ave No   1884
   531 Washington Ave No   1885

3493 THOMPSON, E. T.
   1339 Nicollet Ave   1896-97

3497 THOMPSON, F. L.
   1632 N. E. Washington   1909-10
3497A **

3500 THOMPSON, J. W.
   800 Washington Ave. S. E.   1893-1903

3503 THOMPSON, W. G. (Highland Park Drug Store)
   703 Washington Ave No   1884
   729 20th Ave No   1885-89
   929 20th Ave N. E.   1890-95
3503A **; 3503B **

3506 THOMPSON & SUMMERS
   501 Hennepin Ave   1883-84
3506A **

3509 THORKELSON, T. J.
   1337 Nicollet Avenue   1898

3512 TOEL, E. J.
    102 Central Ave   1891

3515 TONNING, MALTHE
    1323 Washington Ave So   1881

3518 TOWERS, A. C.
    2505 N. E. Harrison   1887

3521 TREDWAY & SONS
    333 Hennepin Ave   1890-91

3524 TREEN, R. T.
    1500 Hennepin Ave   1910

3527 TROW, G. O.
    3000 Minnehaha   1895-1901
    3001 Minnehaha   1902-1908
    2629 E. Lake   1909-10

3530 TRUMAN, H.D.
    St. Louis Park   1900

3533 TUFT, G. E.
    813 S. E. 4th   1904-1910

3536 TUPPER & CHAMBERLIN
    800 S. 10th 1899-1910
3536A **; 3536B **

3539 UNIVERSITY DRUG STORE
    401 14th Ave S.E.   1904-10
3539A **

3542 VANGIESON, EFFIE
    102 Central Ave   1897

3545 VANGIESON, MARCELLUS M.
    102 Central Ave   1898-1910
3545A **

3548 VEDELER, JOACHIM (Svane Apotheket)
    2000-2002 Riverside Ave   1885-89
    2200 Riverside Avenue   1890-1910
Joachim Vedeler was born in Oslo, Norway, in 1857 and immigrated to this country in 1886, where he opened a drugstore at 2000 Riverside Avenue in Minneapolis. This was in the middle of the heavily Scandinavian Cedar-Riverside neighborhood, so Joachim not only followed the old Norwegian custom of naming his store after an animal or bird, he also put up his products in bilingual bottles. In 1890 Vedeler moved up the street into a brand new red brick building at 2200 Riverside.

Since Riverside runs diagonally to the other streets, the store was built in the shape of a triangle. Vedeler settled into a long career, fifty years no less, of serving his community. He finally died in 1934, one of the last of the old time druggists. The store at 2200 Riverside was owned by a succession of men, and remained a drug store into the 1960's, when it became a community clinic (named Smiley's Point because of the building's unusual shape). The building still stands and is worth looking over, as it is probably the best preserved of the few Victorian era drugstores left standing in this city.
3548A **; 3548B **

3551 VOEGELI BROS
    2-4 Washington Ave So   1888-92
3551A **; 3551B **;
3554 VOEGELI BROS DRUG CO.
    2-4 Washington Ave So   1893-1903
    2-4 Washington Ave So & 628 Nicollet Ave   1904
    2-4 Washington Ave So & 628 Nicollet Ave,
      700 20th Ave No   1905-07
3554A **; 3554B **; 3554C Squat oblong, Clear, H3-1/2xL2-3/4xW1-1/2, threaded ground lip
3557 VOEGELI BROS. DRUG CO. (INC.)
    2-4 Washington Ave So & 628 Nicollet Ave,
      700 20th Ave No   1908
    2-4 Washington Ave So & 628 Nicollet Ave   1909
    2-4 Washington Ave So & 628 Nicollet Ave
      500-502 Hennepin Ave   1910
This firm, founded by Thomas & Fred Vogeli, had its start in LaMaure, N.D. in 1883. The two brothers came to Minneapolis and opened their shop on the corner of Washington and Hennepin, on November 1, 1887. Fred retired in 1892 and brother Henry took his place. That they did well is evidenced by the four branch stores they had in 1907. Natives of New Glarus, Wisconsin, they were very civically minded. Thomas, the senior partner, served as a member of the park board and at one time was also its President.

3560 VOGUE, F. S.
    249 Cedar Ave   1900

3563 WALLEN, A. J.
    2123 W. 21st   1908-09

FROM
University Drug Store
MINNEAPOLIS
(3539A)

TUPPER & CHAMBERLIN
DRUGGISTS
MINNEAPOLIS, MINN.
(3536A)

TUPPER & CHAMBERLIN
DRUGGISTS
MINNEAPOLIS, MINN.
(3536B)

VAN'S
QUICK
CURE
MMVanGieson
101 Central Ave
MINNEAPOLIS
MINN.
(3545A)

J. VEDELER
Svane Apotheket
The Swan Drug Store
MINNEAPOLIS, MINN.
(3548B)

J. VEDELER
THE SWAN DRUG STORE
2000 & 2002 RIVERSIDE AVE.
MINNEAPOLIS, MINN.
(3548A)

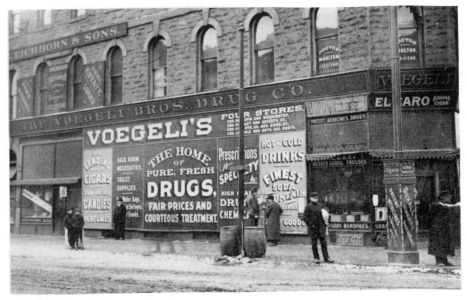

VOEGELI BROS. (3551A)
MINNEAPOLIS, MINN.

VOEGELI BROS. (3551B)
PRESCRIPTION DRUGGISTS
2&4 WASHINGTON AVE. COR. HENNEPIN
MINNEAPOLIS, MINN.

The Voegeli Bros.
Drug Co.
MINNEAPOLIS, MINN.
(3554B)

VOGELI BROS DRUG STORE IN THE "CENTER BLOCK" ON HENNEPIN AVE IN 1900, PHOTO COURTESY OF MHS PHOTO COLLECTIONS
(3554A)

THE VOEGELI BROS.
DRUG CO.
MINNEAPOLIS, MINN.

(3554C) Voegeli

MISS WANOUS
THE DRUGGIST
521½ NICOLLET AVE. 2ⁿᵈ FLOOR
MINNEAPOLIS
(3566A)

MISS WANOUS
THE DRUGGIST
720 NICOLLET AVE.
MINNEAPOLIS
(3566B)

WANOUS - DRUGS
MINNEAPOLIS
(3566C)

MISS JOSIE WANOUS.
2ⁿᵈ FLOOR 521 NICOLLET AVE.
MINNEAPOLIS, MINN.
(3566D)

WATKIN'S PHARMACY
PRESCRIPTIONS
2341 PENN. AVE. NO.
(3587A)

3566 WANOUS, J. A.
   7 Syndicate Block   1895-1901
   521 1/2 Nicollet Ave   1895-1901
   2nd Floor - Nicollet Block   1902
   720 Nicollet Avenue   1904-06
   705 Nicollet Avenue   1907-08
3566A **; 3566B **; 3566C **; 3566D Amber

3569 WAMPLER, A. J.
   40 Jackson   1876-77

3572 WAMPLER & CO.
   300 S. E. 9th   1891

3575 WASHBURN, M. E.
   3001 Hennepin Ave   1895-1910

3578 WASHBURN BROS.
   3001 Hennepin Ave   1894

[WASHINGTON SCHOOL DRUG STORE-See Crocker & Thompson]

3582 WASSER, (Nicollet Drug Store)
   828 Nicollet Ave E.   1909+

3584 WATERBURY, E. M.
   930 Hennepin Ave   1886

3587 WATKINS, CHARLES
   2341 Penn Ave No   1906-10
3587A **

3590 WEBBER, B. E.
   1120 26th Ave No   1903
3590A **; 3590B **

3593 WEBSTER & CHURCHILL (Nicollet House)
   15 Washington Ave So   1882-99
As early as 1867 a drug store was located in the Nicollet House. The city directory listings are as follows:
1867   E. Savory-Under Nicollet House
1879-80 Cable & Judd-3 Nicollet House Block
1881   F.M. Cable-15 Nicollet House Block
1882-99 Webster & Churchhill (Nicollet House)
       15 Washington S.
1900-91 Churchill & Scheldrup-15 Wash Av. S.
1902-10 C.S. Churchill-15 Wash Av. S.
The following 1902 article tells a good portion of this drug store story.
     "NICOLLET HOUSE DRUG STORE"
A drug store of which Minneapolis may feel justly proud is the Nicollet House Drug Store. Their commodious quarters cover 3,000 square feet of ground floor space area of a five-story brick building, better known as the Nicollet House located at Washington Avenue South. This store commands a very large trade throughout Minneapolis and vicinity, drawing a large transient trade however from the Nicollet Hotel. The house makes a speciality of high grade prescriptions work. They handle as specialties their own manufactured goods

111

and the Churchill "Quinine and Iron Tonic", Quinine Balsam", "Sarsaparilla" "Beef Iron and Wine", "Cod Liver Oil" etc.

Footnote:
For over 40 years the Nicollet House was the showplace hotel of Minnesota. It was the hotel where the rich tourists from the east stayed when they came up the Mississippi to see the West, the Indian, and Minnehaha Falls. Some historians have even said that the Nicollet Hotel was a major influence on the growth of Minneapolis at the expense of St. Anthony instead of the other way around.
3593A **; 3593B **; 3593C **; 3593D Sarsaparilla, Aqua; base "MCC"; 3594E Sarsaparilla shape; Aqua; H9; believed to be related to 3593D "Wheelers Sarsaparilla"

3596 WEINHOLD BROS (Family Drug Store)
1831 4th Ave So   1885-88
1829 4th Ave So   1889
1829 4th Ave So & 1329 Nicollet Ave   1890
1329 Nicollet Ave & 500 Hennepin Ave, &
1831 Hennepin Ave   1892
500 Hennepin Ave   1896-99
3596A **; 3596B **; 3596C **; 3596D **; 3596E **;
3596F Dose glass; 3596G Aqua; pat. med, shard, approx. 10" high; 3596H **; 3596J **

3599 WEINHOLD DRUG CO.
1329 Nicollet Ave, 500 Hennepin Ave &
2001 4th Ave So   1893
12-14 Washington Ave No, West Hotel,
2001-2003 4th Ave So   1894
3599A **

WEBBER DRUG CO.
DRUGGISTS
1120 TWENTY - SIXTH AVE N.
MINNEAPOLIS, MINN.
(3590B)

WEBBER DRUG CO.
DRUGGISTS
MINNEAPOLIS, MINN.
(3590A)

(3593A)

WEBSTER & CHURCHILL
PHARMACISTS
MINNEAPOLIS
(3593C)

WEBSTER & CHURCHILL
PHARMACISTS
UNDER NICOLLET HOUSE
MINNEAPOLIS
(3593B)

WEINHOLD DRUG CO.
LEADING PRESCRIPTION DRUGGISTS
MINNEAPOLIS, MINN.
(3599A)

WEINHOLD BROS.
FAMILY DRUG STORE
MINNEAPOLIS
(3596B)

(3593D-FRONT)

WEBSTER & CHURCHILL
DRUGGISTS   DRUGGISTS
MINNEAPOLIS
(3953D-BACK)

WEINHOLD BROS.
LEADING PRESCRIPTION DRUGGISTS
3 STORES
MINNEAPOLIS, MINN.
(3596A)

WEINHOLD BROS
FAMILY DRUGGISTS
MINNEAPOLIS, MINN
(3596C)

Weinhold Bros
WEST HOTEL
MINNEAPOLIS, MINN.
(3596E)

WEINHOLD
DRUGGIST
MINNEAPOLIS, MINN.
(3596F)

CASWELL'S BLOOD CLEANER
WEINHOLD BROS, AGENTS
(3596G)

WEINHOLD'S
PHARMACY
1831 4TH AVE S.
MINNEAPOLIS
(3596D)

WEINHOLD'S
PHARMACY
1831 4TH AVE. S.
COR. 19TH ST.
MINNEAPOLIS
(3596H)

WEINHOLD BROS
FAMILY DRUGGISTS
MINNEAPOLIS
(3596J)

3602 WEINHOLD BROS. & COOPER
(West Hotel) 500 Hennepin Ave   1895

3605 WEINHOLD, E. H.
528 Nicollet Ave   1897-1905
500 Hennepin Ave   1906-09
900 Nicollet Ave   1910
3605A **; 3605B ; 3605C **

3608 WEINHOLD, F. C.
500 Hennepin Avenue   1904-05
3608A **; 3608B **

3611 WELLER, J. H. (Metropolitan Pharmacy)
333 Hennepin Avenue   1882-89
528 Nicollet Avenue   1890
3611A **; 3611B **

3614 WENDT, S. M.
300 S. E. 9th   1893-94
1121 Washington Ave No   1895-96

3617 WEST, C. E.
2223 Harrison   1888

3620 WEST END PHARMACY
1229 Western Ave   1891-94

3623 WEST END DRUG STORE
924 Western Ave   1908

3626 WEST HOTEL DRUG STORE (Weinhold Bros)
500 Hennepin   1895, 1900-03
3626A **

3629 WESTERN AVENUE PHARMACY (See also E.P. Sweet)
4 Western Ave   1894

3635 WHITCOMB, S. O.
603 Washington Ave So   1879
505 Washington Ave So   1880-82
1501 Hennepin Ave So   1884-86
3635A **; 3635B **

3638 WHITAKER & HESLER
Washington Ave & Hennepin Ave   1875

3641 WILKES, A. P.
106 Fort (Seven Corners)   1877

3644 WILLIAMS, J. M.
102 Central Ave   1875

3647 WILLIAMS, J. W.
1211 E. Franklin   1885-1910
3647A **; 3647B **

3650 WILLIAMS DRUG CO.
26th & Emerson Ave No   1912-1915+
3650A **

(3605A)

(3605B)

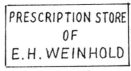
(3605C)

(3608A)

(3608B)

(3626A)

(3611B)

(3635A)

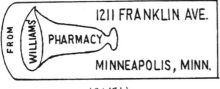
(3647A)

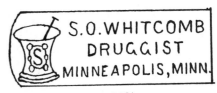
(3635B)

WILLIAMS DRUG CO.
COR.26TH ST.& EMERSON AVE. NO.
MINNEAPOLIS, MINN.
(3650A)

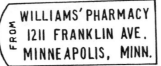
(3647B)

J.H. WELLER
DRUGGIST
MINNEAPOLIS MINN.
(3611A)

3653 WILLIAMS, R. E.
   1923 Franklin Ave So   1884-90

3656 WILLIAMS, U.G.
   603 Washington Ave So   1884-92

3659 WILSON BROS. (Forest Heights Drug Store)
   1514 20th Ave No   1891-92
   1500 20th Ave No   1893-95
   500 Crystal Lake Ave   1896
   1500 20th Ave No   1897-1902
   1500 Crysatal Lake Ave   1903
3659A **; 3659B **

3662 WILSON, E. B.
   1500 20th Ave No   1904-05

3665 WILSON, E. Y.
   929 - 20th Ave No   1896-98

3668 WILSON, S. J.
   1201 3rd Ave So   1891

3671 WINSLOW, N.A.
   4169 Wash Ave No   1901-1910

3674 WISHARD & HILL
   128 Wash Ave So   1875

3675 WITTICH, M. H.
   2451 Bloomington Ave   1895-99, 03-10
   1519 Franklin Ave E.
3675A **

3678 WITTICH & GLEASON
   1519 Franklin Ave E   1901-01

3581 WOLFRUM, MRS. CHARLES
   312 N. E. 5th   1882-85

3684 WOLFRUM, MRS. EMILY
   312 N. E. 5th   1886-87

3687 WOOSTER & LOY (Lion Drug Store)
   123 Washington Ave So   1879

3690 WORKMAN, H. A.
   Owatonna Road & Isabel   1877

3693 WORKMAN & PRIEDEMAN
   Owatonna Road & Isabel   1876

3696 YOST, FRANK C.
   2200 Hennepin Ave   1901-03

3699 YOUNG-PATTERSON & CO.
   44 Washington Ave So   1875-78

CHAS CIRKLER'S STORE AT 602 NICOLLET
IN 1900-MHS PHOTO COLLECTIONS

LATE ARRIVALS

FORD THOMPSON'S
DRUG STORE
MINNEAPOLIS, MINN.

(3497A)

(2422C)

(2812B)

(3133A)

PREPARED BY
MONS DE RAICHE
MINNEAPOLIS

(2028C)

(2686A)

HIGGIN'S PHARMACY
PRESCRIPTION DRUGGIST
26TH ST & NICOLLET AVE
MINNEAPOLIS, MINN

Lincoln & Gould
3000 Hennepin Ave.
Minneapolis

C. A. ROBINSON
DRUGGIST
MINNEAPOLIS

(3163B)

SWEET
THE DRUGGIST
MINNEAPOLIS

(3449E)

(3653A)

(3184D)

A. H. ROSE & CO.
DRUGGISTS
MINNEAPOLIS

(1966E)

WASHINGTON SCHOOL
DRUG STORE
MINNEAPOLIS

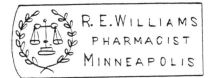

R. E. WILLIAMS
PHARMACIST
MINNEAPOLIS

(3554D)

(3554D ON BASE OF A HONEY
AMBER OINTMENT JAR WITH A
THREADED GLASS LID)

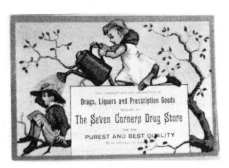

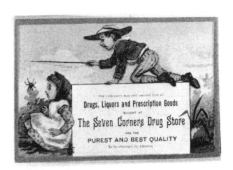

5
ST PAUL
DRUGGISTS

PHARMACY...IN THE GOOD OLD DAYS

The following excerpts are from a speech given in 1904 by A.J. Kline, a leading Minneapolis druggist, to the Pharmacy Class of the University of Minnesota.

"I remember well, when working in a drug store some years ago, when a customer called for a remedy for one or more reasons of various ills that effect mankind, it was our custom to take from the shelf some well-advertised patent medicine with a $2.00, $4.00" or $8.00 price attached and recommend it. There were some non-secret remedies to be sure, but the idea was rather new and the business was not pushed as it is now. Pharmaceuticals usually made by some manufacturing concern in the east were dispensed from pound bottles, with no thought of making them ourselves or buying in larger quantities to get better prices. Goods were displayed in low, cheap cases on high counters, instead of as now in beautiful plate glass floor cases. The patent medicine men, with their high priced and sensational methods of advertising were not nearly so numerous, as at the present time. The invariable sign of the drug store was the long row of shelf bottles on one side of the building and the colored show bottles in the windows.

As a future encroachment upon the legitimate business of pharmacy there hence came into existence in the last decade, numberless weird mysterous kind of faith cures, medical schools of all kinds, both regular and irregular, all of which known to us as drugless methods of cure and while these may be somewhat transitory in their nature, they have cut into the profits of the druggist. But the greatest departure from the professional side of pharmacy and that condition which has been added more than trouble to the retail pharmacist... that being the infinite variety of so called proprietary preparations sent out by manufacturing houses, with a mountain of literature setting the merits of their preparations and their superiority over all others of that class.

In spite of adverse business conditions-in spite of large capital against small, the corner drug store has come to stay. It is a public necessity. Who, I ask you, comes to the aid of the befuddled and belated wayfarer in search of his home, or the strangers within our gates in quest of the friend of his youth, Ole Olson or John Smith? Who carried messages to Mrs. Jones, 3 or 4 blocks away, telling her that Mr. Jones is unavoidably detained at his office, thus making his home-coming in the morning a little easier and more comfortable? Who answers the midnight call and cheerfully or otherwise, dispenses a dose of paragoric, thus adding another five cents to his yearly income? When sickness comes into family, to whom do they look for credit when the head of the family is temporarily out of employment? Who furnishes free phones, the directory and stamps? Who reads carefully the prescription of the old family physician, computing each dose so that the recording angel may not add to his list the name of an untimely arrival? Who, I say, but the accommodating corner druggist?

FOOTNOTES:

The "corner druggist" was soon to receive considerable relief from the "adverse conditions" that Mr. Kline referred to in his speech...because the next couple of years would see almost every state government and federal government enact powerful and sweeping legislation governing the quality, manufacture, advertising, and sale of drugs and medicines in the United States. Probably the most famous of these laws was the PURE FOOD AND DRUGS ACT OF JUNE 30, 1906.

PHARMACY IN THE EARLY DAYS
(by A.H. Rose From the Proceedings of the Minnesota State Pharmaceutical Association 1912)

Pharmacy in the '50's and '60's in Minnesota may have been somewhat crude, but yet I am inclined to the opinion that at that it was practiced perhaps more nearly as a profession, than at the present. In the early '50's there were few druggists in the state. In the late '50's druggists began to multiply especially in the river towns from Winona to St. Paul and from St. Paul to Mankato. In those days, the men in the drug business were looked upon and considered as professionals. Today, you are urged by your own men, to become merchants, and it seems that but little urging is required.

The early druggists for the conditions and time, I think, were men as capable as those of the present. They did their own compounding, pill making, made their own tinctures and sometimes fluid extracts, gathered roots and herbs, from the native gardens, ground and powdered their roots, herbs and other drugs. At that time there were no pharmaceutical houses trying to make us believe they could save us money by doing our work. There was less attention given to making the medicine pleasant to the taste than to its effectiveness. At that time there seemed to be no demand for the Pure Food and Drug Acts.

On account of the world wide advertising Minnesota did, many were induced this way and quite a large number of druggists located early in St. Paul. The earliest from '49 to '56 were W.H. Jarvis, L.C. Kinny, Thomas R. Foster, Dr. David Day, McDougal and Wren, Groff & McDougal, Morton & Pace, Wolf & Stover, Bond & Kellogg, Combs & Champlin (Champlin's Liquid Pearl), also a Mr. J.H. Schroeder.

I came to Minnesota May 1st 1861. The nearest railroad station to St. Paul at that time being La Crosse, I came from there via boat.

The druggists in St. Paul at that time, were Day & Jenks, Mr. H.W. Robinson, and Bath-Robe Miller, a German, so called on account of his continued wearing of a highly colored robe in his every day business. Dr. Miller was one of the druggists who was interested in horticulture, birds, fishes, etc., hence his store was quite a museum, and in those days one of the interesting features of the Capital of the state.

The other druggists in St. Paul were R.S. Combs, E.H. Biggs, R.T. Hand, R.O. Sweeny, J. Allen, later successor to R.S. Combs. Day & Jenks were the largest in the state, did quite a business supplying in a small way country merchants, with their castor oil, epsom salts, sulphur etc. Dr. Day after retiring from the drug business, went into politics, became a county commissioner and was chairman of the building committee, and superintended the building of the large beautiful courthouse still an ornament to St. Paul.

The St. Paul druggists at that time did a large business with the Indian traders. These traders came down annually with their buffalo hides, furs, etc. These were transported via ox-carts, a two-wheeled cart, being entirely made of wood even to the linch pin, being drawn by one ox. These conveyances numbered frequently 200 to 250 in one train. The creeking of the wheels which were never greased could be heard for miles.

The druggists in St. Anthony, St. Paul's rival city were S.L. Vawter, Talbert & White, Hemiup & Sims. Of course others had preceeded them---one was a Mr. Cahill in '56 who afterward became prominent in the milling business, also I believe a Mr. Crawford.

Before my day in Minneapolis, were in '56, Greely & Gray and in '58, Gray Bros., afterward T.K. Gray in '75. Another of the early ones was Thomas Gardiner who has been continuously in the business and is today, in Minneapolis. One of the interesting and peculiar things in connection with T.K. Gray was his continuing in business in one locality for over 50 years and the business still continuing in the same location as the T.K. Gray Drug Co., Mr. Gray having died a few years since. Mr. Gray was a man of great activity, one of the biggest advertisers in his day and a man of kindly qualities as demonstrated by the fact that many of his clerks remained from 8 to 12 years in his employ, and their embarking in the business on their own account in opposition to their old tutor and master, not seeming to ruffle Mr. Gray in the least. Mr.

George Savory was also one of the earlier druggists in Minneapolis.

In 1861 I entered the list of earlier druggists in Minneapolis. I visited Duluth in '63. The town was very small, a number of other ones in the state at that time being larger. I found there in the drug business a Mr. Trumbull and a Mr. C.E. Eyester. That you may have some kind of an idea as to the early Duluth, in '63 there was but one wheeled vehicle in the town, a spring wagon belonging to a hardware man. There may have been a baby wagon or two. And there was but about one mile of street navigable for any kind of a conveyance.

The early druggists in Winona were, Wickersham, Wieland, Chas. Benson, afterward Benson & Kendall, Mr. Edward, Dr. Weidle and 2 or 3 others, later in the '60's and early '70's Pelzer, A.O. Slade, Von Rohor.

Among the earlier in Stillwater, or perhaps the earliest were the Carli's, soon followed by H.M. Crandall and perhaps others.

At Owatonna a Mr. Bixby, (Bixby's death to Pain), and one other. In Mankato the first druggist was Geo. W. Cummings, 1853, then followed Wickersham Bros., later Frisbie & Shepherd in '61, followed by the Warners in '69 (Warners Minnesota Tonic).

The druggists in Shakopee were Mr. Lord, A Dr. Morrow, Mr. Howe and a Mr. Dutoit, later. Lord went into the insurance business and became a prominent state adjuster. Mr. Howe became the banker at Shakopee. Mr. Dutoit also went into politics, and is at present a member of the state legislature.

I knew most of these earlier druggists personally, from the fact that I was the first traveling man for the first wholesale drug house in the state. The wholesale business referred to through its successors, still continues as Noyes Bros. and Cutler.

The stocks carried in those days were not as varied, I am happy to say, as at the present time and differed somewhat in character, most stores handling aside from the ordinary drugs, patents and sundries, all kinds of brushes, paints, oils and glass, kerosene and lamps.

JOHN
BODEN

HENRY
RIETZKE

JOHN P.
JELINEK

C.T. HELLER

L.J. ABERWALD

The drug stores in the early days were the centers for the activities. The community met there to discuss politics, religion, etc. This was owing to the fact that the druggist was usually the best posted individual on all subjects in which the public was interested. They were generally the presidents and secretaries of all the institutions in the town for the betterment of the community. The men to whom I have referred came to this state not ostensibly for the purpose of adding to its ultimate greatness, or paving the way for future successes in their profession, but being honest in their endeavors, they unconsciously did that very thing, helping to make the great possibilities and opportunities which you, my fellow pharmacists, are now permitted to enjoy."

4044 AAMOTT, H. M.
   474 Wabasha   1903

4046 ABERWALD, L. J.
   Rice S.E. Cor. Iglehart   1902-1904
   303 Rice Cor. Iglehart   1905-1911
   301 Rice S.W. Cor. Iglehart   1912-1915
4046A **

4048 ADAMS, ALEXANDER
   110 Endicott Arcade   1902

4050 ADAMS, C. L.
   110 Endicott Arcade   1907-1910
   110 Endicott, Robert St. Bldg.   1911
4050A **; 4050B **; 4050C **

4052 ALLEN & CHAMPLIN
   Cor. Jackson & 7th   1867-1868

4054 ALLEN & CHASE
   323 3rd St.   1864-1866

4056 ALLEN & DORSEY
   Jackson S.W. Cor. 7th   1875-1878

4058 ALLEN, J. P.
   109 Jackson (Phoenix Drug Store) 1869-1874
   Jackson S.W. Cor. 7th   1879-1886
   414 Jackson   1887-1888
   161 E. 7th St.   1889-1911
4058A **; 4058B Round, Amber, H8-1/2 x D3-1/4, base embossed; 4058C Round, Clear.

4060 ANDERSON DRUG CO.
   77 1/2 W. 7th St.   1913
   77 W. 7th St.   1914-1915

4062 ANGIER, ALBERT F.
   106 Fort at Seven Corners   1873-1876

4064 ARCADE PHARMACY
   110 Endicott Arcade   1901-1902

4066 ARGAY, JOSEPH
   567 Broadway   1887-1889
   600 Jackson   1890-1897

4068 ARLINGTON PHARMACY
   954 Payne Ave.   1892-1893

4070 ARMSTRONG & SEARS
   Cor. 4th & Jackson   1867-1868

4072 ARONSOHN, D. M.
   685 Wabasha   1896

4074 ARZT, THEO. G. & CO.
   101 W. 3rd St.   1883-1885
4074A **

4076 BARNETT DRUG CO.
   382 N. Prior   1907-1908

4078 BARNETTS DRUG STORE
   430 Case   1914-1915

4080 BARTHOLOMEW & CO.
   527 Lafayette   1890

4082 BASTYR, T. W.
   118 S. Wabasha   1904
   546 Ohio   1905
   608 S. Smith   1908-1912

4084 BASTYR & GOTHMANN
   546 Ohio   1906

L.J. ABERWALD
DRUGGIST
ST. PAUL. MINN.
(4046A)

C.L. ADAMS
PHARMACIST
ST. PAUL
(4050B)

J. P. ALLEN
ST PAUL MINN
(4058A)

C.L. ADAMS
PHARMACIST
ST. PAUL
(4050C)

ALLEN'S
ULCERINE
SALVE
(4058C)

C. L. Adams
Pharmacist
St. Paul
(4050A)

THEO. ARZT & CO.
PHARMACISTS
ST. PAUL, MINN.
(4074A)

J. P. ALLEN SAINT PAUL MINN.
(4058B)

119

4086 BASTYR PHARMACY CO.
  608 S. Smith   1907

4088 BATELY, J. G. B.
  176 Concord   1912

4090 BATTO, JOHN A.
  219 Bates Ave.   1892
  828 E. 7th   1893-1895
  155 E. 3rd   1896-1897
  309 Jackson   1898-1903
  315 Jackson   1914
  671 N. Snelling   1915
4090A **; 4090B **

4092 BAZAR, THE
  147 E. 3rd St.   1908-1909

4094 BECKER, R. A. & CO.
  196 E. 7th St.   1874-1875
  161 E. 7th St.   1876-1881
  245 E. 7th   1882-1894
  241 E. 7th   1895-1903
4094A **; 4094B **; 4094C **; 4094D **; 4094E **

4096 BECKER, R. A. & SON
  5th N. E. Cor. Cedar   1904
  41 E. 5th St.   1905-1915
4096A **

4098 BEDFORD STREET PHARMACY
  640 Bedford   1908-1913

4100 BERGH, ROBERT
  227 E. 7th St.   1889-1890

EDWARD H. BIGGS
DRUGGIST
ST. PAUL MINN

(4102A)

THE HOSPITAL DRUG STORE
JOHN BODIN
ST. PAUL MINN.

(4106A)

JOHN BODIN & CO.
DRUGGISTS
ST. PAUL, MINN.

(4108A)

JOHN BODIN & CO.
DRUGGISTS
ST. PAUL, MINN.

(4108B)

4102 BIGGS, EDWARD H.
  3rd between Robert & Minnesota 1863-1865
  131 Third St.   1866-1868
  181 Third St.   1869-1870
  123 Third   1871-1879
  80 E. Third   1880-1881
  114 E. Third   1882-1884
4102A **

4104 BLAKEY, A. S.
  887 N. Snelling Ave.   1895

4106 BODIN, JOHN
  323 E. 7th St.   1882-1885
  329 E. 7th   1886-1894
4106A **

4108 BODIN, JOHN & CO.
  329 E. 7th & 856 Payne Ave. 1895-1899
  329 E. 7th & 881 Payne Ave. 1900-1906
4108A **; 4108B **

(4090A)

J. A. Batto
PHARMACIST
ST. PAUL, MINN.

(4090B)

R.A. BECKER
PHARMACIST
ST. PAUL, MINN.

(4094A)

WITCH OF ROSES
R. A. Becker
St. Paul

(4094B)

R. A. BECKER'S
PRESCRIPTION
DRUG STORE
ST. PAUL, MINN.

(4094E)

(4094C)

R. A. BECKER
PRESCRIPTION DRUGGIST
245 EAST SEVENTH ST.
ST. PAUL, MINN.

(4094D)

(4096A)

R. A. BECKER & SON
DRUGGISTS
ST. PAUL, MINN.

4110 BODIN - SUNDBERG DRUG CO.
   329 E. 7th, 881 Payne Ave.   1907
   329 E. 7th, 881 Payne, 879 Rice 1908-1910
   881 & 1110 Payne Ave, 879 Rice   1911-1912
     329 E. 7th, 249 E. 9th
   896 & 1110 Payne, 329 E. 7th,   1913-1915
     329 Rice, 249 E. 9th St.
4110A **; 4110B **; 4110C **

4112 BOND & KELLOGG
   3rd St. between Franklin & Washington 1851-1857

4114 BOND, J. W.
   3rd between Franklin & Washington 1858

4116 BORATH & ENGELKE
   481 Rice St.   1904

4118 BORK, A. W.
   548 Mississippi St.   1897-1901

4120 BORK, HENRY
   253 W. 3rd St.   1888-1890

4122 BOSTON & BEAL
   Dakota Ave. S.E. Cor. Isabel   1889

4124 BOSTON & STOVEN
   Cor. Bridge & Isabel   1880-1881
   S.E. Cor. Isabel & Dakota Ave. 1882
   20 E. Isabel   1883-1888

4126 BOTNER, RICHARD
   678 Grand Ave.   1900-1901

4128 BOURK, K. W.
   172 N. Snelling   1909-1910

4130 BOWDEN BROS.
   207 E. 7th St.   1880-1881
   315 E. 7th St.   1882
4130A **

4132 BOWDEN, JAMES W.
   980 E. 7th St.   1883-1886
   969 Fauguirer   1887-1892
   75 W. 3rd St.   1893-1895

4134 BRACKETT, R. A.
   858 Selby   1896-1898
4134A **

4136 BRACKETT & SON
   858 Selby Ave.   1895

4138 BRILL, W. S.
   483 Broadway   1886-1890

4140 BROOME, J. H.
   127 Martin   1883-1885
   137 Martin   1886-1888
   139 Martin   1889-1890
   769 Wabasha   1891-1892

4142 BROTCHER, H. M.
   618 Rondo   1910-1915

4144 BRUNHOFF, FRED & CO.
   180 W. 3rd St.   1884-1885

4146 BULL, EMIL
   678 Grand Ave.   1895-1900
4146A **

4148 BURKE, MARY A.
   707 E. 3rd St.   1886

4150 BUTLER, M. J.
   171 N. Dale Cor. Selby   1911-1912

4152 CAMPBELL, A. A.
   235 Rondo   1895-1910
4152A **; 4152B **

Bodin Sundberg Drug Co. ST. PAUL, MINN. (4110A)

BODIN - SUNDBERG DRUG CO 881 PAYNE AVE ST. PAUL, MINN. (4110B)

BODIN - SUNDBERG DRUG CO. ST. PAUL MINN. (4110C)

A.A. CAMPBELL RONDO ST. PHARMACY 235 RONDO ST. ST. PAUL, MINN. (4152A)

BOWDEN BROS DRUGGISTS ST PAUL, MINN. (4130A)

A.A. CAMPBELL 235 RONDO ST ST. PAUL, MINN. (4152B)

(4134A)

Robt. A. Brackett Pharmacist St. Paul, Minn.

(4146A)

CROCUS HILL PHARMACY EMIL BULL

4154 CAMPBELL BROS.
  858 Selby Avenue Cor. Victoria   1899
  858 Selby, 740 Grand & 238 Rondo   1900
  858 Selby, 740 Grand   1901-1903
  858 Selby, 678 & 740 Grand   1904-1906
  858 & 920 Selby, 678 & 740 Grand   1907-1908
  678 & 740 Grand, 920 Selby   1909-1912
  740 Grand Ave.   1913-1915
4154A **

4156 CAMPBELL BROS. & ST. CLAIR
  678 Grand Ave.   1912-1913

4158 CAMPBELL, D. R.
  118 S. Wabasha   1899

4160 CAMPBELL, J. E.
  N.S. Grand Ave. 2 E. of 1st   S.S.P.   1902

4162 CANNON, C. H. & CO.
  216 E. 7th St.   1882

4164 CAPITAL DRUG CO.
  481 Rice   1904-1915
4164A **

4166 CAPPELL, JOHN F.
  741 Mississippi   1893

4168 CARROTHERS, W. H.
  495 Bradley   1884-1885
  Hewitt Ave. 1 E. of Snelling   1888-1890
  759 Snelling   1892

4170 CENTRAL DRUG STORE
  125 W. Central   1914

4172 CENTRAL PHARMACY
  529 Wabasha   1897-1899

4174 CHAPIN & HARTFIELD
  798 E. 7th   1888-1889
  Concord Ave   2 S. of Grand   S.S.P.   1890-1891

4176 CHARENDON DRUG CO.
  396 Wabasha   1896-1898

4178 CITY DRUG STORE
  E. S. Concord 7 S. of Grand Ave.   1908

4180 CITY DRUG STORE
  6-8 W. 6th St.   1906-1907
  8 W. 6th   1908-1911, 1914-1915
  8 W. 6th, 175 N. Concord   1912
  8 W. 6th, 161 N. Concord   1913

4182 CLARK & FROST
  N.W. Cor. Third & Robert   1882-1888
4182A **; 4182B **; 4182C **; 4182D **

4184 CLOUGH, C. F.
  858 Selby   1909-1915

4186 COAN, M.E.
  396 Wabasha   1899-1900
  395 Wabasha   1901-1905
  391 N. Prior   1910-1914

4188 COLBERG & PAEHLER
  541 Mississippi St.   1909-1910

4190 COLLIER, W. K.
  199 E. 7th   1892-1905
  193 E. 7th   1906-1910
4190A **

4192 COMB, RICHARD F.
  Cor. 9th & Jackson   1863-1866

4194 CONDIT, A. D.
  2 W. Third St.   1880-1881
  567 Broadway   1884-1886

[CONDIT & LAMBIE - SEE LAMBIE & CONDIT]

4196 CONGER, F. A.
  349 University Ave.   1886

Capitol Drug Co.
St. Paul

(4164A)

(4182A)

CLARK & FROST
PHARMACISTS
ST. PAUL
MINN.

(4182B)

For The
HAIR
Clark & Frost's
RUM
AND
QUININE
ST. PAUL
MINN.

CAMPBELL BROS.
PHARMACISTS
ST. PAUL. MINN.

(4154A)

CLARK & FROST
CHEMISTS
ST. PAUL.
MINN.

(4182C)

(4190A)

W. K. COLLIER
DRUGGIST
ST. PAUL. MINN.

CLARK & FROST
PHARMACISTS
ST. PAUL, MINN.

(4182D)

4198 CONGER BROS.

THE CONGERS
by Benjamin Backnumber
from THE DAILY NEWS, September 10, 1911.

"At the risk of incarceration in a United States Penitentiary, I'm going to be a coiner; not of $5, $10 or $20 gold pieces, but of words--at least one word. Triamese, it is. How does it strike you? We used to hear lots about the Siamese twins. Now I shall tell you something of the Triamese twins--the old retail drug firm of Conger Bros. There were of course, three of them or they wouldn't be Triamese-- Fred A., Stephen B. and Joseph J. until the last one withdrew.

Joe it was who first of the three had the pleasant pleasure and ecstatic ecstasy to say nothing of the honorable honor of forming my acquaintance 30 years ago. It was when he ran one of the firms three stores at Selby Ave. and St. Albans St. It was opened there in 1893 and there he remained until 1909 when he disposed of it and ceased being a Triamese.

(4198A)

(4198B)

(4198C)

(4198G)

(4198D)

(4198E)

(4198F)

Steve had personally administered the affairs of the branch at University and Virginia Aves. ever since it was planted there in 1885. It is the oldest drug store under one continuous management and at the same stand in Saint Paul.

The third powder and pill joint of Conger Bros. has all along been in the hands of Fred who dispensed his potions at Mackubin St. and Laurel Avenue at Makubin and Selby. It may be asserted without fear of challenge that Fred Conger has the largest personal acquaintance of any name in St. Paul. He has a finger in the pies of numerous activities, business and civic, besides drugging. His shop is unique among all the lurking places of apothocaries in or out of Christiandom. It is St. Anthony Hill's grand intrepot of merry anecdotes and grin-hatching jests. Everyone knows that Phred's famaccutical truck ain't wuth a durn for anything except for to kill people off; but the beauty of it is, he promptly brings them back to life again with his jokes.

The Conger family is French, having originated in Alsace. The name then was Congre. The first Conger to land in America was John, a civil engineer, who laid out the site of Rahwas N.J. in 1667. Afterward he went to Canada and settled at Picton, on the north shore of Lake Ontario. That has been the seat of the Congers ever since. The old homestead still stands in as good a condition as ever and which continues in possession of the family. It was built by Stephen, John's grandson, in 1786 and that is where the St. Paul brothers travel to at vacation time."

349 University Ave.	1887-1888
497 Laurel Ave., 349 University	1889-1892
497 Laurel, 349 University & 680 Selby	1893
499-680 Selby Ave., 349 W. University	1894-1905
501 & 680 Selby Ave., 349 University	1906-1907
501-503 & 680 Selby, 349 University	1908
503 Selby, 349 University	1909
501 Selby, 349 University	1910-1915

4198A **; 4198B Pat. Med. Aqua; 4198C **; 4198D **; 4198E **; 4198F **; 4198G **

4200 COOK & NOBLE
302 Rice St.   1886-1888

(4212A)

DAVENPORT
PHARMACIST
ST. PAUL, MINN

(4212B)

DAYTONS BLUFF
PHARMACY
ST PAUL, MINN.

(4222A)

4202 COURTNEY PHARMACY
39 S. Cleveland | 1915

4204 CRANDALL & BAKER
161 N. Concord   S.S.P. | 1914-1915

4206 CROCUS HILLS PHARMACY
678 Grand Ave. | 1910-1915

4208 DAHL, HANS
1135 Rice | 1912-1913

4210 DALE STREET PHARMACY
621 University Ave. | 1908-1910

4212 DAVENPORT, GEORGE C.
76 Wabasha | 1880-1881
404 Wabasha | 1882-1883
640 Mississippi | 1884-1888
1012 E. 7th St. | 1889-1890
973 E. 7th | 1891-1900, 1902-1906
971 1/2 & 973 E. 7th | 1901, 1907
4212A . Amber; 4212B Amber; 4212C Amber

4214 DAVENPORT & SCHOELL
973 E. 7th St. | 1908-1915

4216 DAVIDSON, F. P.
235 Rondo | 1889
581 E. 7th St. | 1890

4218 DAY, J. H. & CO.
188 Concord | 1886
176 Concord | 1887-1888
194 Concord | 1889

4220 DAY & JENKS
Cor. 3rd & Cedar | 1858-1866

4222 DAYTONS BLUFF PHARMACY
940 E. 7th St. | 1914-1915
4222A **

4224 DETTLOFF, F. E.
1160 Selby | 1908-1915

4226 DIBB, T. J.
600 Jackson | 1886-1889

4228 DICKMAN BROS.
1039 Grand | 1913

4230 DICKMAN, G. A.
799 Grand Ave. | 1910-1912
870 Grand Ave. | 1913
800 & 1039 Grand Ave. | 1914
1039 Grand Ave. | 1915

4232 DICKMAN, H. W.
969 Fauquier | 1893-1901
830 E. 7th St. | 1902-1911
1039 Grand | 1912

4234 DINWOOD & WYLLIE
561 Broadway | 1883-1884

4236 DORIS, J. J.
609 Pittsburgh Bldg. | 1910

4238 DOUGLAS, R. H.
541 Ohio | 1893-1899

4240 DRECHSLER, F. X.
1105 W. 7th St. | 1911
1105 W. 7th, 130 W. Winifred | 1912-1913
1105 W. 7th, 129 W. Winifred | 1914
1105 W. 7th, 127 W. Winifred | 1915

4242 DREIS, P. J.
S.W. Cor. 9th & St. Peter | 1883
465 St. Peter St. | 1884-1915
4242A **; 4242B **

4244 DREIS & MESSING
296 Sibley | 1905-1913
296 & 206 E. 3rd | 1914-1915

4246 DREIS & MITSCH
114 St. Peter St. | 1874-1881
429 St. Peter St. | 1882
4246A **; 4246B **

P. J. DREIS
DRUGGIST.
ST. PAUL

(4242A)

P. J. DREIS
DRUGGIST
ST. PAUL

(4242B)

DREIS & MITSCH
DRUGGISTS
COR 9TH & ST. PETER STS.
ST. PAUL

(4246A)

DREIS & MITSCH
DRUGGISTS
Cor. 9TH & St PETER STS
St PAUL

(4246B)

4248 EAGLE DRUG STORE
   441 Univerity Ave.   1900

4250 ECLIPSE DRUG CO.
   118 S. Robert   1893-1895
4250A . (Bottle Pieces)

4252 EDWARDS, E. H.
   1949 St. Anthony Ave.   1907

4254 EGBERT, H. G.
   621 University   1914-1915

4256 ELMQUIST, ALDOR
   University N.W. Cor. Snelling   1913

4258 ELMQUIST DRUG CO.
   1581 University Ave.   1914-1915

4260 ELMQUIST, J. G.
   172 N. Snelling   1911-1915

4262 EMMERT, L. Z.
   35 W. 4th St.   1901-1902
4262A **

4264 EMPRESS DRUG STORE
   476 Wabasha   1913

4266 ENDICOTT PHARMACY
   110 Endicott Arcade   1912-1915

4268 ENGLUND, D. C.
   621 W. University Ave.   1901
4268A **

4270 ENTRUP, L. F.
   529 Wabasha   1898-1899

4272 ENTRUP & SELLS
   529 Wabasha   1897

4274 ERDMAN, WILLIAM
   541 Decatur   1887

4276 ERNST, O. A.
   361 Earl   1914

4278 EVENSON, C. H.
   2262 W. Como   1912-1915

4280 EWING, W. B.
   398 Robert   1886-1889
4280A **

4282 EXPO PHARMACY
   2389 University   1911

4284 FABER, F. W. & CO.
   428 Wabasha   1890-1892
   400 Wabasha   1894
4284A **

4286 FABER, F. W.
   529 Wabasha   1895-1896
   309 Jackson   1905-1912

4288 FABER & BROWN
   Wabasha N.E. Cor. 6th   1893

4290 FARBER, A.
   581 Robert   1886

4292 FERTE, JOSEPH E.
   6 Mississippi St.   1874-1876
   59 Mississippi   1877-1878
   294 Rice St.   1882

4293 FIELD, SCHLICK & CO.
   Wabasha & 4th   1897-1898
4293A **

4294 FIESELER, K. L.
   936 Raymond   1899-1902
   930 Raymond   1903-1905
   930 Raymond, 2190 N. Raymond   1906-1909
   930 Raymond   1910-1911
   930 Raymond, 2389 University   1912-1914
   2389 University   1915

4296 FISHER, W. F.
   144 E. 7th St.   1879
   216 E. 7th St.   1883-1884

4298 FLANAGAN, W. T.
   608 S. Smith   1913-1915

4300 FOLTY, G. F.
   N.E. Cor. Ohio & George   1884-1885

4302 FREY, G. R.
   425 W. 7th   1890

4304 FRIEDMANN, F. C.
   St. Peter N.W. Cor. 7th   1902-1905
   429 St. Peter St.   1906-1908
   429 St. Peter, 499 Grand   1909
   429 St. Peter St.   1910-1915
4304A **;

(4268A)

DAVID C. ENGLUND
COR UNIVERSITY AVE & DALE ST.
ST. PAUL, MINN.

F. W. FABER & CO.
MARKET HOUSE PHARMACY
ST. PAUL, MINN.   (4284A)

L. Z. EMMERT
PHARMACIST
COR. 4TH & ST PETER STS
ST. PAUL MINN.
(4262A)

FIELD, SCHEICK & CO.
ST. PAUL, MINN.
(4293A)

(4304A)

"FROM
EWING'S
DRUG STORE
SAINT PAUL"
(4280A)

7TH & ST. PETER STS.
Friedmann's
Drug Stores
GRAND AVE. & AVON

(4305A)

FROST & BROWN
PHARMACISTS
ST. PAUL. MINN.

(4308B)

W. A. FROST & CO.
PHARMACISTS
ST. PAUL, MINN.

(4310A)

W. A. Frost & Co.
St. Paul

(4310C)

(4310B)

(4308A)

(4310E)

FROST'S
ROSE
AMANDINE
CREAM

(4310G)

FROSTS
RUM
&
QUININE
LOTION
FOR THE
HAIR

(4310H)

4305 FROST & AKERS
  ?
4305A **   ?

4306 FROST & CO.
  380-382 Dayton Ave.   1882

4308 FROST & BROWN
  119 E. 3rd St.   1889
  119 E. 3rd, 378 Selby   1890-1891
4308A **; 4308A2 Emerald Green; 4308B **

4310 FROST, W. A. & CO.
  W. A. Frost was born in St. Hohn, New Brunswick, in
  1854. At age 16 he moved to New York to work in a
  drug store and attend the College of Pharmacy. Upon
  graduating, in 1878, he moved to Willmar, Minnesota,
  where he ran a drug store in partnership with a man
  named Clark. When their store burned down in 1880,
  the two men moved to St. Paul and started a new
  store. Clark was replaced for a few years by a man

named Brown, but for most of his career Frost was
sole proprietor of his store, which, incidently,
still stands and has been converted to a popular
eatery.
119 E. 3rd, Selby Ave. S.E. Cor. Western 1892-1893
6th S. E. Cor. Minnesota,
    Selby S. E. Cor. Western   1894-1896
378 Selby S. E. Cor. Western   1897-1905
378 Western Ave.   1906-1909
378 Selby Ave.   1910-1915
4310A **; 4310A2 Amber; 4310B Round, Aqua, H7-3/4 x
D2-3/4; 4310C Style A1E, Teal Green, H5; 4310E **;
4310E2 Amber; 4310G Shoulder Seal; 4310H Style
unknown; 4310J Dose Glass; 4310K Aqua, Style Unknown

4312 FRY, CHRISTIAN
  527 Lafayette Ave.   1886-1887

4314 FUCHS, ANTHONY
  798 E. 7th   1890-1898
4314A **

4315 FUCHS, ANTHONY & SON
  798 E. 7th   1899

4316 FUCHS, E. J.
  798 E. 7th St.   1900-1915
4316A **

4318 GERICKE, J. T. DRUG CO.
  190 Concord   1914-1915

W. A. FROST

A. FUCHS
PEOPLES PHARMACY
ST. PAUL.

(4314A)

E. G. Fuchs
Druggist
798 E. 7TH ST.
ST. PAUL

(4316A)

W.S.GETTY
PHARMACIST
ST. PAUL, MINN.

(4324A)

(4341A)

W.S.GETTY
THE HAND PHARMACY
ST.PAUL.MINN.

(4324B)

(4341B)

W.S.GETTY
PHARMACIST
ST PAUL, MINN.

(4324D)

(4344A)

FROM THE GOLDENRULE
DRUG DEPARTMENT
ST. PAUL,

GOLDEN RULE
DRUG DEPARTMENT
ST. PAUL

GUERNSEY'S PHARMACY
COR. DALE & SELBY
ST. PAUL , MINN.

A.T. GUERNSEY
DRUGGIST
ST. PAUL

(4344B)

A.T. GUERNSEY & SON
DRUGGISTS
ST. PAUL. MINN.

(4345A)

CY-DO-LINE
A.T. GUERNSEY & SON
ST. PAUL

(4345B)

(4350A)

(4350B)

COMPLIMENTS
OF
W.S.GETTY
PHARMACIST
ST. PAUL

(4324E)

F. H. HAINERT
DRUGGIST
ST. PAUL,MINN.

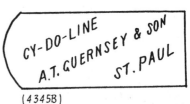

F.H.HAINERT
DRUGGIST
374 DAYTON AVENUE
ST. PAUL, MINN.

4320 GEISENHEYNER, WM. O. & CO.
 961 W. 7th St.   1886

4322 GEISERT, T. B.
 640 Bedford   1907-1915

4324 GETTY, W. S.
 139 W. 3rd St.   1884-1891
 348 Robert St.   1892-1899
 110 Endicott Arcade   1900-1901
4324A **; 4324B **; 4324B2 Amber; 4324D **; 4324E
Dose Glass

4326 GETTY'S ARCADE PHARMACY
 110 Endicott Arcade   1902-1906

4328 GIFFORD, HENRY
 476 Wabasha   1908-1911

4330 GOLDBERG - KEILBRON CO.
 92-102 E. 7th St.   1910

4341 GOLDEN RULE
 E. 7th St   1897-1898
4341A **; 4341B **

4332 GONNIEA, G. D. W.
 3rd Junction of 5th   1912-1914
 4th Junction of 5th   1915

4334 GOTWALD, G. A.
 N. W. Cor. 13th & L, Orient   1884-1886
 862 Payne Ave.   1887-1890

4336 GRABEN DRUG CO.
 548 Mississippi St.   1902-1904

4338 GRABEN, O. H.
 190 Concord   1905

4340 GRAND AVE. PHARMACY CO.
 799 Grand   1905-1906 & 1909

4342 GRISWOLD & CO.
 144 E. 7th St.   1880-1881

4344 GUERNSEY, A. T.
 171 Dale St.   1889-1892, 1900-1902
4344A **; 4344B **

4345 GUERNSEY, A. T. & SON
 171 Dale St.   1893-1899
4345A **; 4345B **

4346 HAASE DRUG CO.
 1135 Rice St.   1911

4348 HAGAN & GENTSCH
 40 1/2 Jackson   1874-1875

4350 HAINERT, F. H.
 374 Dayton Ave.   1884-1886
 173 Western Ave. N.   1887
 The Albino   1888-1891
4350A **; 4350B **

4352 HALL, A. T.
 428 Dakota Ave.   1887-1890
 428 S. Wabasha   1891-1893
 362 St. Peter St., 428 S. Wabasha   1894-1896
 362 St. Peter St.   1897-1907
 362 St. Peter Cor. 5th   1908-1912
4352A **; 4352B **; 4352C **; 4352C2 Amber; 4352D **

(4352D)

A.T.HALL
DRUGGIST
ST. PAUL
MINN.

(4352A)

(4352B)

(4352C)

(4354A)

(4370A)

(4357A)

4354 HALL & KRAFT
  428 S. Wabasha   1897-1903
4354A **

4356 HALL & GEISSEL
  428 S. Wabasha   1904-1915

4357 HALL, W. W.
  91 S. Robert   ?
Probably same as Siegler Mnfg. Co.   1887-1889
4357A **

4358 HALSEY BROS. CO.
  109 E. 7th   1900-1908
  388 Minnesota   1909-1915
4358A . French Square, Amber; 4358B French Square,
       Amber

4360 HAMLINE SUPPLY CO.
  761 N. Snelling Ave.   1889

4362 HAND, RICHARD T.
  375 3rd St.   1867-1870
  324 3rd   1871-1873
  122 W. 3rd   1874-1876

4364 HARMS, F. J.
  930 Raymond   1915

4366 HAUPT, C. H.
  Dale N.E. Cor. laurel Ave.   1889-1890
  136 N. Dale   1891-1892

4368 HAZEL MNFG. CO.
  152 Charles   1899

4370 HEBERHART, C. E.
  295 W. 7th St.   1884-1892
4370A **

4372 HEINZEL, HENRY
  751 N. Snelling Ave.   1907-1911
  1152 E. 7th St.   1912-1915

4374 HEITZMAN, FRANK
  8 W. 6th St.   1912

4376 HELLER, C. T.
  528 St. Peter St.   1888-1893
  10th N. E. Cor. St. Peter   1894-1899
  10th N. E. Cor. St. Peter, Wabasha
    N. W. Cor. 10th   1900
  33 W. 10th, Wabasha S. W. Cor. 10th   1901
  10th N. E. Cor. St. Peter, 529 Wabasha 1902-1903
  529 Wabasha, 33 W. 10th   1904-1908
  529 Wabasha, 31 W. 10th   1909
  529 Wabasha, 33 W. 10th   1910
  484-486 Wabasha, 33 W. 10th   1911-1915
4376A **; 4376B **

4378 HENDRICKS, W. E.
  161 E. 7th   1913-1915

4380 HENING, J. C.
  678 Grand   1902-1903

4382 HERBERT BROS.
  430 Case   1903

4383 HERBERT & CO.
  430 Case   1904

4384 HIGHOUSE, J. C.
  315 E. 7th St.   1882-1883
  170 Dakota Ave.   1884-1887
  361 Dakota Ave.   1888-1889
  361 S. Wabasha St.   1890-1891

4386 HIPPLER & COLLIER
  199 E. 7th St.   1886-1891

4388 HIRSCHNER, V. A.
  235 Rondo   1890-1894

(4358A)

(4376A)

(4358B)

(4376B)

J.P. JELINEK'S STORE IN 1908

4390 HOLCOMB, F. A.
954 Payne Ave.   1902-1905
190 Concord, 960 Payne Ave.   1906
960 Payne Ave.   1907-1915
4390A **

4392 HOLCOMB & MAGNUSON
954 Payne Ave.   1900-1901
4392A **

4394 HORRIGAN & MCCOLL
640 Mississippi St.   1889-1891

4396 HOSKINS, C. A.
E. S. Concord 7 S. of Grand   S.S.P.   1908-1909
160 Concord   S.S.P.   1910-1911
Snelling Ave. N. E. Cor. Grand   1912-1913
4396A **

4398 HOVORKA, W. J.
1028 W. 7th St.   1886-1914
4398A . Amber

4400 ITALIA DRUG CO.
441 E. 7th St.   1915

4402 JELINEK, J. P. & CO.
John P. Jeninek was born in Prague, Austria, on June 19th, 1870. He came to America with his family in 1879 and settled in New Prague, Minnesota. In 1880 the family moved to St. Paul. John was educated in the public schools in St. Paul and while still a boy, in 1886, having finished his education, he entered the drug business. In four years, by constant application to work, he found himself ready to take up the business himself. He was admitted to practice pharmacy in Minnesota in 1890 and in 1898 opened up a store at 961 West 7th St. In 1898 he bought another store at the corner of West 7th and Sherman Streets and conducted a successful business at both establishments.
961 W. 7th St.   1899-1900
959-961 W. 7th   1901-1903
295 & 959 W. 7th St.   1904-1909
295 & 961 W. 7th St.   1910-1915
4402A **; 4402B **

4404 JENKS & BIRD
Corner 3rd & Cedar   1858-1868
175 3rd St   1869-1873
132 E. 3rd St   1874-1875
First listed in directories in 1858, but an 1872 ad states "The oldest Drug house in Minnesota, Est. 1849"
4404A **

4406 JENKS & GORDON
Cor. 3rd & Cedar   1867-1868
175 3rd St.   1869-1870

4408 JENKS, J. R.
175 3rd St.   1871-1873
32 E. 3rd   1874-1875
13 W. 3rd   1876

4410 JENSEN, H. P.
741 Mississippi   1894

4412 JOHNSON, H. MARTIN DRUG CO.
4th N. W. Cor. St. Peter St.   1915
4412A **

(4390A) *Frank A. Holcomb*
DRUGGIST
ST. PAUL, MINN.

(4392A) *Holcomb & Magnuson*
DRUGGISTS
ST. PAUL. MINN.

(4396A) CITY DRUG STORE
C. A. HOSKINS
SO. ST. PAUL, MINN.

(4402B) *J. P. Jelinek*
DRUGGIST
295 W. 7TH ST. COR SHERMAN
961 W. 7TH ST. COR. JAMES

(4402A) *J. P. Jelinek*
DRUGGIST
ST. PAUL, MINN.

(4404A) JENKS. & BIRD
SAINT PAUL

(4398A) SYRUP
WILD CHERRY
COMPOUND
MANUFACTURED
BY
W. J. HOVORKA
FAMILY DRUGGIST

(4412A) *H. Martin Johnson* DRUG Co.
4TH & ST. PETER STS. ST. PAUL. MINN.

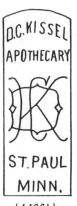

(4422A)

(4439A)

(4440A)

"MEDICAL HALL"
COR. THIRD & WABASHA STS.
SAINT. PAUL, MINN.
LAMBIE & BETHUNE

(4442A)

(4444A)

4414 KARRAS DRUG CO.	
740 Rondo	1915
4416 KEPIER, E. E.	
450 S. Robert	1899-1907
458 S. Robert	1908-1909
123 W. 7th St.	1910-1913
4418 KELLAN, A. B.	
920 Selby	1913-1915
4420 KENYON, E. S. & CO.	
300 Maria Ave.	1884-1887
298 Maria Ave.	1888-1889
4422 KISSEL, DANIEL C.	
315 & 317 Fort	1882
315 W. 7th St.	1883-1894
315 & 317 W. 7th	1895-1896
Kent N. W. Cor. Thomas	1897-1898
561 Thomas	1899-1905
619 Blair	1906-1909
125 W. Central Ave.	1910-1914
4422A **	
4424 KNICKERBOCKER DRUG CO.	
679 Wabasha	1906
126 W. Central	1907-1908
4426 KNOX DRUG CO.	
61 E. 3rd	1889
4428 KNUDSEN, JAS.	
722 N. Hamline Ave.	1915
4430 KREGEL, W. C.	
481 Rice St.	1910
4432 KREYCHIE, J. L.	
619 W. University Ave.	1890
4434 KULT, FREDERICK	
440 Wabasha	1884-1897
4436 KURTH, A. F.	
722 N. Hamline Ave.	1914
4438 LAMBERT, GEORGE M.	
Jackson between 5th & 6th St.	1867-1868

4439 LAMBIE	
4439A **	?
4440 LAMBIE & BACON	
N. W. Cor. 3rd & Wabasha	1879-1881
4440A **	
4442 LAMBIE & BETHUNE	
N. W. Cor. Third & Wabasha	1882-1886
311 Wabasha	1887
4442A **	
4444 LAMBIE & CONDIT	
70 Wabasha Cor. 6th	1874-1875
2 W. 3rd St.	1876
4444A **	
4446 LAWSON, A. A.	
1581 University	1907-1911
1563 University	1912-1915
4448 LEE, OLOF	
910 Payne Ave.	1890-1904
908 Payne Ave.	1905
966 Arcade, 908 Payne Ave.	1906-1915
4448A **; 4448B **	
4450 LEE, WM.	
114 E. 3rd St.	1887
4452 LEHMANN, J. A.	
Grand N. E. Cor. Snelling	1914
4454 LEHMANN, J. H.	
1579 Grand	1915
4456 LEVY, HENRY	
1949 University	1915
4458 LIBBY, CHARLES H.	
315 E. 7th St.	1884-1885
4460 LIDDELL, M. B.	
497 Laurel Ave.	1884-1886
4460A **	
4462 LILLIS, M. A. & CO.	
499 W. 7th St.	1909-1915
4464 LILLYBECK, P. L.	
392 E. 7th St.	1886-1890

OLAF LEE
PHARMACIST
ST. PAUL, MINN.

(4448A)

OLAF LEE
DRUGGIST
908 PAYNE AVE. ST. PAUL

(4448B)

M. B. LIDDELL'S
LAUREL AVENUE PHARMACY
ST. PAUL, MINN.

(4460A)

L.J. ABERWALD'S STORE AT GRAND & FAIRVIEW

SEVER WESTBY'S STORE AT 3RD & MARIA AVE

F. B. SCHULTZ'S STORE AT SELBY & FAIRVIEW

J.V. RITSCHELL'S STORE IN THE HAMLINE DISTRICT

C.T. HELLER'S STORE ON WABASHA

4466 LINDBERG, C. V.
75 1 N. Snelling — 1904-1905

[LION DRUG STORE - SEE O. O. WOLD, LUNELL & SEARLE])

4468 LONDON DRUG CO.
190 Concord — 1912-1913

4470 LOEW, WM. E.
Robert S. W. Cor. 12th — 1889-1890
583 Robert — 1891-1892
Robert S. W. Cor. 12th — 1893-1899
581 Robert — 1900
583 Robert — 1901-1904

4472 LUDINGTON, T. E.
302 Rice St. — 1895

4474 LUEDERS & CO.
849 Rice — 1889

4476 LUEDERS, L. H.
849 Rice, 599 Dale — 1890-1892
Rice S. W. Cor. Milford — 1893
879 Rice — 1894-1907
4476A **; 4476B **

4478 LUEDERS, G. H.
599 N. Dale — 1893

4480 LUEDERS, MRS. SUSAN
751 Mississippi — 1897-1902
956 Gaultier — 1903-1904

4482 LUNELL & SEARLE (LION DRUG STORE)
227 E. 7th St. — 1887
4482A **

4484 LUNKENHEIMER, P. T.
1682 Grand — 1914-1915

4486 LUTZ, PETER C.
394 Wabasha — 1882-1883
368 Wabasha — 1884-1889
364 Wabasha — 1890-1897
4486A **

4487 LYONS, ADAM
298 Maria Ave. — 1890
41 E. 4th St — 1893-1894
621 W. University — 1895-1898
4487A **

4488 LYONS & HAWLEY
41 E. 4th St. — 1891-1892
4488A **

4489 LYONS & TICKNOR
707 E. 3rd St. — 1887-1890

4490 MACALESTER PHARMACY
Grand Ave. N. E. Cor. Snelling — 1913

4492 MACRAY DRUG CO.
751 N. Snelling Ave. — 1906-1910

4494 MADSON, HANS & CO.
176 Concord — 1889-1911
4th N. W. Cor. St. Peter — 1912-1914
4494A **; 4494B **

4495 MAGNUSON, E. C.
190 Concord — ?
4495A **

4496 MAGNUSON, F. A.
190 Concord — 1907-1909
4496A **; 4496B **

(4476A) L. H. LUEDERS DRUGGIST ST. PAUL, MINN.

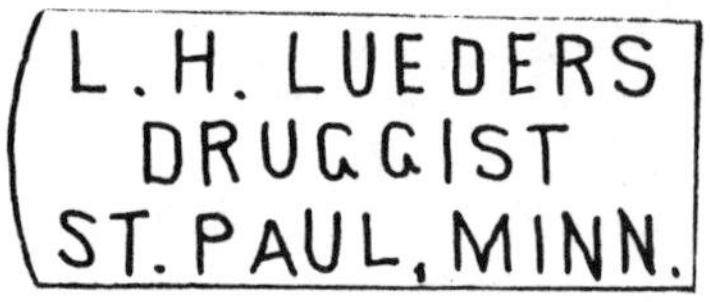

(4482A) LUNELL & SEARLE LION DRUG STORE 227 E 7TH ST ST. PAUL. MINN.

(4486A) P. C. LUTZ. DRUGGIST ST. PAUL, MINN.

(4488A) L. H. LUEDERS PRESCRIPTION DRUGGIST ST. PAUL, MINN. (4476B)

(4487A) LYONS DISPENSING PHARMACY ST. PAUL MINN.

(4488A) LYONS & HAWLEY ST. PAUL, MINN.

(4494A) HANS MADSON DRUGGIST ST. PAUL, MINN.

(4496A) F. A. MAGNUSON, DRUGGIST 190 EAST CONCORD, ST. PAUL

(4495A) E. C. MAGNUSON DRUGGIST 190 EAST CONCORD ST. ST PAUL

(4494B) H. Madson Chemist St. Paul, Minn.

(4496B) F. A. MAGNUSON. DRUGGIST 190 EAST CONCORD, ST. PAUL

(4500A) MAGNUSON DRUG CO. DRUGGISTS ST. PAUL, MINN.

(4500B) MAGNUSON DRUG CO. PRESCRIPTION DRUGGISTS ST PAUL, MINN.

GEO. MARTI
PHARMACIST
ST. PAUL. MINN.

WEST SIDE

(4516A)

George Marti
PHARMACIST
ST. Paul, Minn.

(4516B)

GEO. MARTI
PHARMACIST
ST. PAUL MINN.

(4516C)

(4524A)

McCOLL DRUGGIST ST. PAUL

(4530A)

McMASTERS & GETTY
PHARMACISTS
ST. PAUL, MINN.

(4532A)

S. R. McMASTERS
APOTHECARY
ST. PAUL, MINN.

MERRIAN PARK PHARMACY
PRIOR & ST ANTHONY AVES
ST PAUL, MINN.

(4536A)

4498 MAGNUSON PHARMACY
190 Concord — 1910

4500 MAGNUSON DRUG CO.
190 Concord — 1911
4500A **; 4500B **

4502 MANSUR DRUG CO.
7th S. W. Cor. Robert — 1905-1914
102 E. 7th — 1915

4504 MANWARING, J. J.
116 Jackson — 1873-1875

4506 MARELIUS & BECKER
640 Bedford — 1890-1892

4508 MARELIUS, C. R.
640 Bedford — 1893-1904
640 Bedford, 430 Case — 1905-1906

4510 MARELIUS, MRS. A. C.
430 Case — 1907-1913

4512 MARSDEN, C. B.
950 Jackson — 1892

4514 MARK, JOSEPH
851 Payne Ave. — 1902

4516 MARTI, GEORGE
110 Dakota Ave. — 1882-1885
118 Dakota Ave. — 1886-1889
118 S. Wabasha — 1890-1898
4516A **; 4516B **; 4516C **

4518 MARTI, JOHN
Robert N. E. Co. Congress — 1895
450 S. Robert — 1896-1898

4520 MATTHEW, D. J.
741 Mississippi St. — 1891-1892

4522 MAXWELL, H. A.
694 St. Peter St. — 1911-1915

4524 MCCOLL, HENRY
640 Mississippi — 1892-1895
483 Broadway — 1896-1909

483 Broadway, Moore Bldg. 7 Cors. — 1910-1911
175 W. 7th 7 corners — 1912-1915
4524A **; 4524B ** Etched Dose Glass

4526 MCDONALD PHARMACY
Marshal S. E. Cor. Cleveland — 1912-1913
2058 Marshal Ave. — 1914-1915

4528 MCLAUGHLIN, A.
527 Lafayette Ave. — 1891-1892
685 Wabasha — 1896

4530 MCMASTERS & GETTY
94 Wabasha — 1880-1881
428 Wabasha — 1882
428 Wabasha, 139 W. 3rd — 1883-1884
4530A **

4532 MCMASTERS, S. RUSSELL
122 W. Third — 1877-1881
139 W. Third — 1882
428 Wabasha (Market House Pharmacy) — 1884-1887
7th Cor. Wabasha — 1888-1889
4532A **

4534 MERCHANTS PHARMACY
309 Jackson — 1909-1913

4536 MERRIAN PARK PHARMACY
391 N. Prior — 1906-1915
4536A **

4538 MIERKE, E. A.
309 Jackson — 1904
680 Selby — 1909-1914
681 Selby — 1915

4540 MIDDENTS, P. H.
466 Wabasha — 1890-1901
472 Wabasha — 1902-1906
476 Wabasha — 1907

4542 MILLER, W. H.
Cor. 3rd & Exchange & Fort — 1858-1863
368 3rd St. — 1864-1873
Cor. 4th & Exchange — 1880-1881
331 Exchange — 1882
333 N. Exchange — 1883-1884

4544 MILLER, WILLIAM H. & SON
164 W. 3rd — 1874-1875
Exchange Cor. 4th — 1876-1879

4546 MILNE, H. J.
458 S. Robert — 1910-1915

4548 MINNESOTA TRANSFER DRUG CO.
1910 University — 1912-1915

GEO. J. MITSCH & Co.
DRUGGISTS
ST. PAUL.
(4552A)

WALTER NELSON
DRUGGIST
ST. PAUL
(4582A)

(4568A)
L. MUSSETTER
DRUGGIST
ST. PAUL

Summit Pharmacy
F. A. MUNCH
ST. PAUL, MINN.
(4566A)

(4574A)
NEFF & ROSENQUIST
PHARMACISTS
152 E. 7TH ST. ST. PAUL

4550 MISSISSIPPI PHARMACY
   548 Mississippi St.   1912-1915

4552 MITSCH, GEO. J. & CO.   HOMEOPATHIC MED
   N. W. Cor. 7th & St. Peter   1883-1885
   429 St. Peter, 574 Rice   1886-1892
   7th N. W. Cor. St. Peter   1893-1900
4552A **

4554 MOHL, FRED
   161 E. 7th   1912

4556 MOREY, A. L.
   936 Raymond Ave.   1892-1894

4558 MORGAN, F. M.
   1931 University   1907

4560 MORRISON, FRANK
   430 Case   1890-1891

4562 MORTON, W. H.
   Jackson between 5th & 6th St.   1856-1859

4564 MULLER, E. J.
   961 W. 7th St.   1889-1898

4566 MUNCH, F. A. (SUMMIT PHARMACY)
   751 Mississippi St.   1903
   Rice S. E. Cor. Summit Ave.   1904
   284 Rice St.   1905-1909
   282 Rice St.   1910-1915
4566A **

4568 MUSSETTER, LATHROP
   330 Wabasha & 3rd & Wabasha   1887-1888
   Wabasha S. E. Cor. 4th   1889-1893
4568A **

4570 MUSSETTER, L. & W. A.
   3rd N. W. Cor. Wabasha   1889-1890

4572 MUSSETTER, W. A.
   330 Wabasha   1894-1896

4574 NEFF & ROSENQUIST
   152 E. 7th St.   1888-1896
   7th S.W. Cor. Jackson   1887-1899
   158-160 E. 7th St.   1900-1915
4574A **

4576 NELSON & ENGELKA
   481 Rice St.   1905

4578 NELSON, G. W.
   603 Wabasha   1914-1915

4580 NELSON, J. W.
   621 W. University   1902-1905
   561 W. University   1906-1915

4582 NELSON, WALTER
   887 Rice St.   1886-1887
   954 Payne, 887 Rice   1888
   954 Payne, 887 Rice, 741 Mississippi 1889-1890
   890 Rice   1891-1894
   890 Rice, 936 Raymond   1895-1897
   481 & 890 Rice, 936 Raymond   1898
   481 & 896 Rice, 1185 Wabasha   1899-1900
   303-481 & 896 Rice, 379 Carroll 1901
   481 & 896 Rice, 379 Carroll   1902
   896 - 481 & 284 Rice   1903
   1946 W. University, 896 Rice   1904
   897 Rice   1905 & 1907 & 1908
4582A . Amber

4584 NELSON WALTER PHARMACY
   897 Rice St.   1909-1910

4586 NELSON, MRS. JENNIE
   897 Rice   1911-1914

4588 NEWELL, E. L. & CO.
   Raymond Ave N. E. Cor. Hampden   1889
   936 Raymond   1890-1891

4590 NOBLES & COOK
   136 Dale St.   1888

4592 NOBLE & FARWELL
   35 W. 7th St.   1896
   35 W. 4th St.   1897

4594 NOBLE & FRENCH
   529 St. Peter St.   1882

4596 NOBLE, W. W.
   35 W. 4th St.   1898-1900
4596A **

[NOYES BROS. & CUTLER - SEE HOUSEHOLD SECTION]

[N. W. DRUG CO. - SEE MED. MFGRS.]

(4596A)
W. W. Noble
PHARMACIST
COR. 4TH & ST. PETER STS.

```
┌─────────────────────┐      ╭──────────────────────╮      ╭──────────────────────╮
│   F. M. Parker      │      │    F. M. PARKER      │      │    F. M. PARKER      │
│     DRUGGIST        │      │  364 WABASHA ST.     │      │  5TH & WABASHA ST.   │
│ 5TH & WABASHA, ST.PAUL,MINN.│ │   ST. PAUL, MINN.    │      │   ST. PAUL, MINN.    │
└─────────────────────┘      ╰──────────────────────╯      ╰──────────────────────╯
       (4610A)                      (4610B)                       (4610C)
```

```
            (4610D)                                              (4612A)
╭──────────────────────╮                              ╭──────────────────────╮
│   F. M. Parker       │                              │ F. M. PARKER & CO.   │
│       DRUGGIST       │                              │ 5TH & WABASHA STS.   │
│        ST. PAUL, MINN.│                              │   ST. PAUL, MINN.    │
╰──────────────────────╯                              ╰──────────────────────╯
```

```
   (4616A)                                              (4626A)
┌──────────────────────┐                              ┌──────────────────────┐
│  PEOPLE'S PHARMACY   │                              │  PORTLAND PHARMACY   │
│   ST. PAUL,  MINN.   │                              │  9TH AND BROADWAY    │
└──────────────────────┘                              │   ST. PAUL, MINN.    │
                                                      └──────────────────────┘
```

```
       (4630A)                    (4638B)                       (4638A)
┌──────────────────────┐    ╭─────────────────────╮     ┌──────────────────────┐
│ GEORGE PRESLEY'S     │    │   S. H. REEVES      │     │    S. H. REEVES      │
│    PHARMACY          │    │   CORN CURE         │     │     DRUGGIST         │
│ ST. PAUL, MINN.      │    │   ST. PAUL          │     │ 7 CORNERS, ST. PAUL  │
└──────────────────────┘    ╰─────────────────────╯     └──────────────────────┘
```

4602 OHDE, L. A.
  572 Kent   1910-1915

4604 OLSON, A. H.
  912 S. Robert   1915

4606 OTTO, E. A.
  361 Earl St. (cor Hastings Ave.)   1908-1915

4608 PAEGEL, GEORGE R.
  75 W. 3rd St.   1889-1892

4610 PARKER, F. M.
  364 Wabasha
4610A **; 4610B **; 4610C Style unknown, Aqua;
4610D **

4612 PARKER, F. M. & CO.
  964 Arcade   1901
  751 N. Snelling   1902-1903
  364 Wabasha   1909
4612A **

4614 PARKER & WESTBY
  679 E. 3rd St.   1891-1893
4614A **

4616 PEOPLES DRUG CO.
  W. 3rd Junction of 5th   1909-1914
4616A **

4618 PETTERSEN, P. G.
  236 E. 7th   1892-1894
  436 Sibley   1895

4620 PETTIGREW, H. P.
  302 Rice   1888-1890

4622 PIERCE, EUGENE
  235 Rondo   1911
  237 Rondo   1912

4624 POETZ, F. H.
  548 Mississippi St.   1906-1915

4626 PORTLAND PHARMACY
  483 Broadway   1912-1915
4626A **

4628 POTTS, W. S.
  Between Wabasha & St. Peter   1862-1863

4629 POTTS, W. S.
  211 3rd   1864-1865

4630 PRESLEY, GEORGE
  640 Bedford   1887-1889
4630A **

4632 PRUSSIAN REMEDY CO.
  20 E. Chicago   1910

4634 PURPLE, W. L.
  600 Jackson   1883-1885

4636 RANUM, O. K.
  224 E. 7th St.   1876-1878

4638 REEVES, S. H.
  500 W. 7th   1886-1887
  499 W. 7th   1888
  Defiel Blk - Seven Cors.   1889-1892
  Defiel Blk - 7 Corners, 175 W. 7th   1893-1902
  175 W. 7th, Defiel Blk., 4 N. E. Cor. 3rd   1903
  175 W. 7th, Defiel Blk.   1904-1905
  175 W. 7th St.   1906-1909
4638A **; 4638B Style unknown

4640 REIMER, A. T.
  312 Rice   1886

4642 RICE, C. A.
  751 N. Snelling Ave.   1901

A.T. HALL'S STORE IN THE LOWERY BLDG

The First Prescription Filled in the St. Anthony Hill
Section of St. Paul. This Prescription was filled by
Herman Reitzke in 1881.

HERMAN RIETZKE'S STORE AT SELBY & WESTERN

DRIES & MESSING PHARMACY AT 296 SELBY

(4650F)

(4650A)

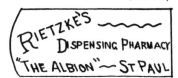

(4650C)

(4650B)

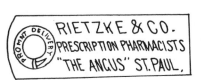

(4650D)

(4650G)

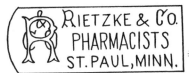

(4650E)

	380 Dayton, 499 Selby	1890-1892
	Selby Ave. S. W. Cor. Western	1893-1908
	380 Selby	1909-1915

4650A . Aqua; 4650B **; 4650C **; 4650D **; 4650E **; 4650F **; 4650G **; 4650H Embossed Baby bottle, examples unavailable

4652 RITSCHEL, J. V.
761 N. Snelling Ave.   1910-1915

4654 ROBBINS, J. B.
440 Wabasha   1883-1884

4656 ROBINSON, HENRY W.
3rd between Franklin & Washington   1862-1863
323 3rd St.   1864-1866
227 3rd   1867
66 W. 3rd   1873-1879
88 W. 3rd   1880-1881
101 W. 3rd   1882
4656A **; 4656B **

4658 ROGERS & TEACHOUT
500 W. 7th   1883-1884

4660 ROHRBECK, W. F.
1135 Rice   1915

4661 ROLLINS, E. B.
329 W. 7th St   1906

4662 ROLLINS, E. B. & CO.
295 W. 7th St.   1897-1902

4663 ROLLINS, R. M. & CO.
295 W. 7th St.   1895-1896

4664 ROMAN & ROHRBECK
Wabasha S. E. Cor. 4th   1897-1898
330 Wabasha   1899-1900
333 Wabasha   1901-1912

4666 ROSE, A. H.
46 Jackson   1869-1870
Cor. 3rd & Jackson   1871

4668 ROSS, WM. M.
527 Wabasha   1893
525 Wabasha   1894

4670 RUTHERFORD, C. F.
35 W. 4th St.   1902
35 & 39 W. 4th   1903-1904
35 W. 4th   1905, 1907-1911
4670A **; 4670B **

4672 RUTHERFORD, W. C.
77 W. 7th   1912

4674 SANSBY BROS.
498 Thomas   1912
800 University   1913-1915

4676 SCHELDRUP & WOLD
151 E. 7th St.   1879-1881

4644 RICE STREET PHARMACY
302 Rice St.   1896-1900

4646 RIDER, O. C.
1026 W. 7th   1909-1911
1013 W. 7th   1912-1915

4648 RIEGER, PAUL
3rd between Exchange & Franklin   1862-1863
342 3rd   1864-1866
344 3rd   1867-1868
295 3rd   1869-1870
309 3rd   1871

4650 RIETZKE & CO.
368 Dayton Ave.   1883-1885
380 Dayton Ave.   1886-1889

H. W. ROBINSON
ST . PAUL

(4656A)

(4656B)

H.W. ROBINSON
ST. PAUL, MINN.

(4670A)

C.F. RUTHERFORD
DRUGGIST
COR 4TH & ST. PETER STS.

(4670B)

OPEN ALL NIGHT
C.F. RUTHERFORD
DRUGGIST
COR 4TH & ST. PETER STS.

4678 SCHIFFMANN & LYONS
  679 E. 3rd St.   1889-1890

4679 SCHIFFMANN & SON
  679 E. 3rd St.   1890

4680 SCHIVEDER, J. N.
  Cor. 5th & Jackson   1856-1862
  3rd between Franklin & Washington   1863
  310 3rd St.   1864-1865

4682 SCHOTT, HARRY A.
  Ohio & Winifred   1884-1885
  Ohio N. W. Cor. Alice   1886
  495 Ohio   1887
  188 Concord   1888

4684 SCHULTZ, F. B.
  1818-1820 Selby Ave.   1911-1913
  1820 Selby Ave.   1914-1915

4685 SCHUMACHER & CO.
  548 Mississippi   1892-1893
  543 Mississippi   1894

4686 SCHUMACHER'S PHARMACY
  499 W. 7th   1889-1891

4687 SCHUMACHER, A. & G. A.
  499 W. 7th, 954 Payne   1892-1899

4688 SCHUMACHER, A. J.
  499 W. 7th   1900-1908

4689 SCHUNEMAN & EVANS
  6th & Wabasha   1897-1898
4689A **

4690 SCHWANKI, HENRY
  897 Rice   1915

4692 SEARS, W. H.
  176 Concord   1913-1915
4692A **

4693 SELBY DRUG CO.
  171 N. Dale Cor. Selby   1906-1915
4693A **

4694 SEITER, O. E. & A. T. (BROS)
  828 E. 7th St.   1892
  190 Concord   1893-1896

4695 SEITER, O. E.
  190 Concord   1897-1904
4695A **

4696 SEMMER BROS.
  500 W. 7th   1884-1885

4698 SEYMOUR, J. T.
  1931 University Ave.   1905-1906

4700 SHERWIN & NOBLE
  529 St. Peter St.   1883-1885

4702 SIGLER, WM. H.
  104 Wabasha   1880-1881
  440 Wabasha   1882
  764 Wabasha   1895
  104 S. Robert   1896
  764 Wabasha   1897-1898
  679 Wabasha   1905
  1810 University   1913

4704 SIGLER MNFG. CO.
  91 S. Robert   1887-1889
  1188 S. Robert   1893-1894
  679 Wabasha   1902

4706 SIMMON, KARL
  66 W. 3rd St.   1877-1881
  N. W. Cor. 3rd, Market   1882
  Cor. 4th & Jackson, 3rd & Market   1883-1884
  331 Jackson, 3rd & Market   1885
  331 Jackson, 75 W. 3rd St.   1886-1887
  198 E. 7th, 75 W. 3rd   1888
  200 E. 7th St.   1889-1891
4706A **

4708 SIMPSON, MRS. M. A.
  Cor. 3rd & Bates Ave.   1884-1885

4710 SLEEPER, J. H.
  328 Sibley   1888-1890

4712 SLEEPER, O. A.
  North St. Paul   1899

4714 SMETANA, F. W.
  583 Robert   1905-1910
  579 Robert   1911-1915
4714A **

4716 SMITH, F. A.
  1135 Rice   1914
  860 University   1915

4718 SMITH, J. W.
  112 S. Robert   1909-1915

4720 SMITH, W. N.
  527 Lafayette Ave.   1889

Schuneman Evans Drug Dept.

(4689A)

W. H. SEARS
PRESCRIPTION DRUGGIST
COR. STATE & CONCORD, ST PAUL

(4692A)

SELBY DRUG CO, INC
DALE & SELBY
ST. PAUL

(4693A)

(4695A)

O. E. SEITER
—DRUGGIST—
ST. PAUL, MINN.

(4706A)

KARL SIMMON'S
METROPOLITAN
DRUG STORE
ST. PAUL

(4714A)

F. W. Smetana
PHARMACIST
ST. PAUL, MINN.

A.W. SONNEN & CO.
PHARMACISTS
ST. PAUL, MINN.

(4722A)

St.Paul Drug Co.
St. Paul, Minn.

(4732A)

TRITURATION
FROM
ST.PAUL HOMEOPATHIC PHARMACY
ST. PAUL, MINN.

(4734A)

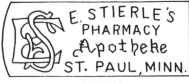
E. STIERLE'S
PHARMACY
Apotheke
ST. PAUL, MINN.

(4742A)

STIERLE'S
PHARMACY
ST. PAUL, MINN.

(4742B)

A.T. SUNDBERG
COR. DALE & SELBY
ST. PAUL, MINN.

(4754A)

4722 SONNEN, A. W. & CO.	
574 Rice	1890-1906
574 Rice, 799 Grand	1907-1908
574 Rice	1909-1915
4722A **	
4724 SORBY, H. O.	
759 N. Snelling Ave.	1893-1894
4726 SPIES, C. F.	
769 Wabasha	1889
4728 SPRAGUE & LIBBY	
S. W. Cor. Rice & Charles	1883-1884
4730 SPRAGUE, J. W.	
401 Rice	1884-1885
481 Rice	1886-1897
4732 ST PAUL DRUG CO.	
5th S. E. Cor. St. Peter,	1913-1915
& 4th N. W. Cor. Wabasha	
4732A **	
4734 ST PAUL HOMEOPATHIC PHARMACY	
109 E. 7th St.	1899-1900
107 E. 7th	1901
4734A **; 4734A2. Amber	
4736 ST PAUL RETAIL DRUG CO.	
253 W. 3rd St.	1886
4738 STEIN, GOTTLEIB	
52 E. 7th St.	1871-1872
4740 STELLA DRUG CO.	
440 Wabasha	1896-1897
4742 STIERLE, ADOLPH E.	
181 E. 7th St.	1874-1875
200 E. 7th	1876-1881
302 E. 7th	1882-1894
4742A **; 4742B **	

4743 STIERLE, ADOLPH, Jr.	
302 E. 7th	1895-1911
4744 STILES, DANIEL L.	
235 Grove	1882
N. W. Cor. 13th & L'Orient	1883-1884
4746 STRAIGHT BROS.	
Grotto S. W. Cor. Rondo	1891-1895
740 Rondo	1896-1903
740 Rondo & S.S.P.	1904-1910
740 N. Concord S.S.P.	1911
E. S. Concord 2 S of Grand S.S.P.	1912
740 Rondo,	
Concord S. W. Cor. Grand S.S.P.	1913-1914
162 N. Concord Cor. Grand S.S.P.	1915
4748 STROUTS DRUG STORE	
237 Rondo	1913-1915
4750 STROUT E. S. & CO.	
497 Laurel Ave.	1887-1888
4752 STUART & LUTZ	
S. E. Cor. Wabasha & 6th St.	1880-1881
4754 SUNDBERG, A. T.	
171 N. Dale Cor. Selby	1903-1905
4754A **	
4756 SWABODA, OSCAR	
476 Wabasha	1914-1915
4758 SWEENEY, R. O. & CO.	
211 3rd St.	1864-1873
7 W. 3rd St.	1874-1881
10 W. 3rd St.	1882-1886
9 W. 3rd St.	1887-1889
4759 TAPPER, RANAL F.	
207 Bates	1883-1884
4760 TAYLOR & MYERS	
109 E. 7th St.	1886-1899

4760A . Amber; 4760B . Amber; 4760C . Amber; 4760C2**;
4760E . Style unknown, Amber; 4760F . Style unknown,
Amber; 4760G . Amber; Ground Stopper

COCA-CALISAYA TONIC
TAYLOR & MYERS PHARMACY CO.
109 E. 7TH STREET
ST. PAUL, MINN.

(4760F)

GLYCOID
TAYLOR & MYERS PHAR. CO.
ST. PAUL, MINN.

(4760E)

TAYLOR & MYERS
PHARMACY CO.
109 E. 7TH ST.
ST. PAUL, MINN.

(4760B)

PHARMACY CO
109 E 7TH ST.
ST PAUL MINN.

(4760C)

TAYLOR & MYERS
PHARMACY CO.
ST. PAUL

(4760A)

4788 WABASHA DRUG STORE	
118 S. Wabasha	1903
4790 WAGNER, ANTON	
961 W. 7th	1888
4792 WALTHERS, DR. E.	
84 E. 7th	1871-1872
4794 WAMPLER, A. J.	
40 Jackson	1876-1879
S. W. Cor. Jackson & 4th	1880-1882
4794A **; 4794B **; 4794C Teal Green	
4796 WAMPLER & MUSSETTER	
330 Wabasha	1886
4798 WATHNE, OSCAR	
799 Grand	1908
4800 WAY, J. R.	
253 W. 3rd St.	1887
4802 WEBB, J. W.	
13 Leech	1887
4804 WECHSLER, HYMAN	
Bridge near 5th	1878-1879

4762 THOMAS, DORR.	
91 S. Robert	1889-1892
118 S. Robert	1893-1903
4764 THOMAS & SMITH	
118 S. Robert	1904-1906
112 S. Robert	1907-1908
4765 TICKNOR, GEORGE	
?	?
4765A **	
4766 TICHNOR & JAGGER	
Hotel Ryan - 398 Robert	1890-1892
404 Robert	1893-1910
4766A **	
4768 TRUDGEN, R. C. & CO.	
993 W. 7th	1897
1028 W. 7th	1898-1900
4770 TYRRELL BROS.	
110 Endicott Arcade	1912-1914
4772 UMLAND, G. F.	
459 Rice	1887
441 University	1888-1901
4773 UMLAND, A. C.	
441 W. University	1902-1907
438 University Ave.	1908-1915
4774 VAN DUYNE, F. & CO.	
826 E. 7th	1884-1886
828 E. 7th	1887-1891
4774A **	
4776 VAUGHAN, E. A.	
185 W. 6th	1911-1913
4778 VAWTER & ROSE	
111 3rd St.	1864-1366
4780 VAWTER, ROSE & ETTER	
111 3rd St.	1867-1868
4782 VERNON, P. C.	
622 Como Boul.	1913
4784 VERNON, MRS. E. M.	
622 Como	1914-1915
4786 VENVE, CHARLES & CO.	
761 W. 7th St.	1884-1885
550 Robert	1886-1888
629 Mississippi	1889

(4794A)

A.J. WAMPLER
PRESCRIPTION
DRUGGIST
SAINT PAUL. MINN.

A.J. WAMPLER
DRUGGIST
ST. PAUL, MINN.

(4794B)

GEORGE TICKNOR
DRUGGIST
HOTEL RYAN
ST. PAUL

(4765A)

TICKNOR & JAGGER
DRUGGISTS
HOTEL RYAN
ST. PAUL

(4766A)

A.J.W.
cor. Jackson &
Druggist
ST. PAUL, M.

(4794C)

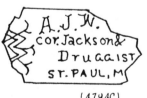

F. VANDUYNE
ST. PAUL MINN.

(4774A)

SEVER WESTBY
MARIA AVE & 3RD ST
ST. PAUL, MINN.

(4812A)

A.P. WILKES
DRUGGIST
SEVEN CORNERS
ST. PAUL MINN.

(4820B)

WEST SIDE PHARMACY
Deutsche Apotheke
WIN FRED & BIDWELL STS.

(4814A)

(4828B)

Willmert Drug Co
541 Mississippi St.
St. Paul. Minn.

(4824A)

A. P. WILKES
DRUGGIST
ST. PAUL, MINN.

(4820A)

WILLMERT DRUG CO
641 MISSISSIPPI ST.
ST. PAUL, MINN.

(4824B)

B. J. WITTE
RICE PARK PHARMACY
SAINT PAUL

B. J. WITTE
RICE PARK PHARMACY
ST. PAUL, MINN.

(4828A)

4806 WEITER, F. W.
   621 W. University   1906-1913

4808 WELLS, J. C.
   Merrian Park   1886
   2055 St. Anthony Ave.   1887-1888

4810 WEST END PHARMACY
   7th N. W. Cor. Bay   1910-1911
   1105 W. 7th St.   1912-1913

4812 WESTBY, SEVER
   679 E. 3rd   1894-1915
4812A **

4814 WEST SIDE PHARMACY
   130 W. Winifred   1909-1913
4814A **

4816 WHITE HOUSE DEPARTMENT STORE
   7th & Cedar   1906-1907

4818 WICKS, W. G.
   318 Jackson   1888
   309 Jackson   1889-1894

4820 WILKES, A. P.
   106 Fort near 7 Corners   1877-1881
   7 Corners, 372 Dayton   1882-1883
   7 Corners   1884-1886
   959 W. 7th   1887
   7 Corners   1888-1890
   Selby Ave. S. E. Cor. Victoria 1892-1894
4820A **; 4820B **

4822 WILLIAMS & STAPLETON
   430 - 432 Case   1896-1900
   430 Case   1901-1902

4824 WILLMERT, G. A. DRUG CO.
   541 Mississippi   1906-1908
4824A **; 4824B **

4826 WINCOTT, R. T.
   302 Rice   1892

4827 WINCOTT, R. T. & CO.
   302 Rice   1893-1894

4828 WITTE, B. J. & CO.
   Market S. E. Cor. 5th   1888
   360 Market   1889
   360 Market, 527 Lafayette 1890
   360 Market   1891-1894
   29 E. 7th   1895
4828A **; 4828B **

4830 WOERNER, CAROLINE
   640 Bedford   1886

4832 WOLD, OSCAR, O. (LION DRUG STORE)
   227 E. 7th   1882-1886
4832A **; 4832B **

4834 WOLFT, W. H.
   3rd near Wabasha   1856-1860

4836 WOLFRUM, G. A.
   597 N. Dale   1894
   599 Dale   1895-1900
   572 Kent   1901-1909

4838 WOOLSEY, A. L.
   1947 St. Anthony Ave.   1888-1889 & 91 & 92
   Woodruff Blk.   1890 & 1893-1894
   391 N. Prior   1895-1896 & 1900-1904
   St. Anthony N. W. Cor. Prior 1897-1898 & 1899
4838A **

4840 WOOLSEY - PRINCELL CO.
   391 N. Prior Ave.   1905

4842 WORKMANN & PRIEDEMANN
   Owatonna Rd. Cor. Isabel 1876

4844 WORKMANN, H. A.
   Owatonna Rd. Cor. Isabel 1877-1878

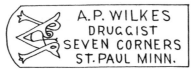

O.O.WOLD
DRUG STORE
ST. PAUL
MINN

(4832A)

O. O. WOLD
DRUG STORE
ST. PAUL, MINN.

(4832B)

A. L. WOOLSEY
DRUGGIST
MERRIAM PARK, MINN.

(4838A)

```
4846 WYETH, JNO & BRO. (INC)
     233 E. 4th St.                        1910

4848 YERXA, F. R. & CO.
     7th S. W. Cor. Cedar                  1902
4848A .**

4850 YOST, FRANK
     621 University Ave.                   1899-1900

4852 YOUND & TUCKER
     432 Case                             1892

4854 ZIMMERMANN, B. & E.
     307 Jackson                          1883
     318 Jackson                          1884-1887
4856 ZIMMERMANN, E. & CO.
     529 St. Peter                        1886
     Wabasha S. W. Cor. 10th              1887-1890

4857 ZIMMERMANN, EMIL (CAPITOL PHARMACY)
     527 Wabasha                          1891-1892
4857A **
```

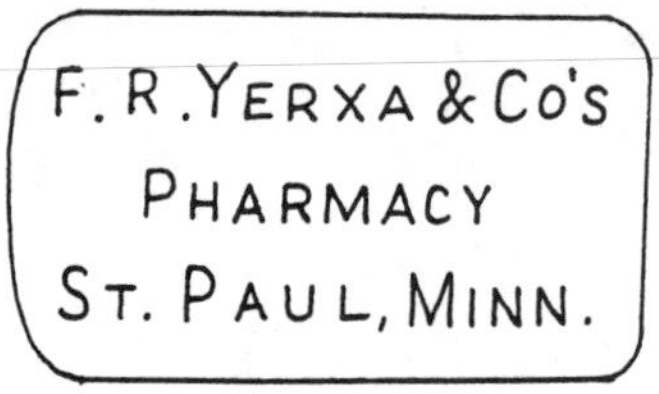

F. R. YERXA & CO'S
PHARMACY
ST. PAUL, MINN.

(4848A)

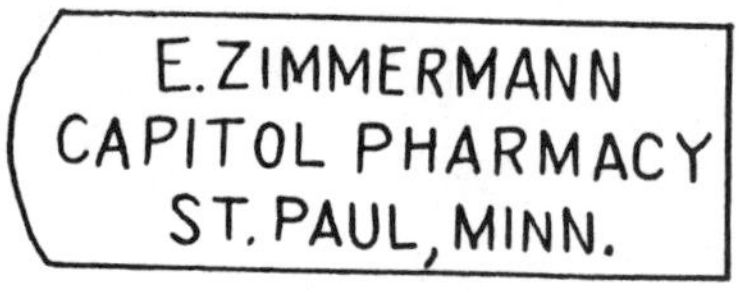

E. ZIMMERMANN
CAPITOL PHARMACY
ST. PAUL, MINN.

(4857A)

LATE ARRIVALS

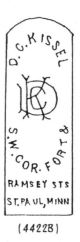

D. C. KISSEL
S. W. COR. FORT &
RAMSEY STS
ST. PAUL, MINN

(4422B)

6
MINNESOTA
DRUGGISTS
(EXCLUDING MINNEAPOLIS & ST PAUL)

F. M. CABLE & CO.
PHARMACISTS
BRAINERD, MINN.

From
Southwestern Minnesota Hospital
Heron Lake, Minnesota

Research for this section of the book has not yet begun. However, a cursory check of the state business directories shows that there were hundreds of druggists in business in the small towns of Minnesota prior to 1910. Colleecting bottles from these companies is a wide open and inexpensive field for the beginning collector. A few embossings are shown to give the reader a hint at the variety of bottles that can be found.

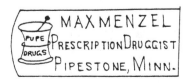

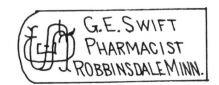

KELLY & HAMRE
DRUGGISTS
NORTHFIELD, MINN.

J. E. KYLLO
PHARMACIST
RED WING, MINN.

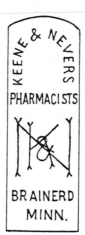

KEENE & NEVERS
PHARMACISTS
BRAINERD
MINN.

CITY PHARMACY
WORTHINGTON, MINN.

OLSON & ELLINGSON
DRUGGISTS
RED WING, MINN.

MAX WIRTH'S
PHARMACY
Deutsche
Apotheke
DULUTH
MINN.

R.L. MORLAND
WORTHINGTON
MINN.

A. GUEVLI
DRUGS AND GEN'L MDSE
WINDOM, MINN.

WEBER & HEINTZ CO
DRUGGISTS
ROCHESTER
MINN.

CITY HOSPITAL
DRS. WIEDOW & MORK
WORTHINGTON, MINN.

JOHN VON ROHR
WINONA, MINN.

7

MINNEAPOLIS

PATENT MEDICINES

By all accounts the patent medicine era, which had its heyday in this country between 1800 and 1906, must have been one of the most colorful pageants in American history. It was a time when the rapidly growing population suffered the scourges of tuberculosis, typhoid, yellow fever and cholera as well as all the lesser aches, pains and afflications to which the human body (and imagination!) is vulnerable. Physicians had few really effective medicines to offer; in any event doctors were few and scattered, and many were frauds or incompetent.

Into this gap stepped the patent medicine vendors, each proclaiming the merits of his particular boon to mankind. Estimates as to just how many different patent nostrums were sold in this country run to over 100,000! These medical saviors waged an endless fight for the customer's dollar, with the weapons being the newspaper advertisement, the testimonial, the medicine show and sometimes outright counterfeiting of other successful products.

The term patent medicine is actually a misnomer, dating back to 18th century England where "patents of royal favour" were granted to some medicine manufacturers. In fact, very few patent medicines were registered with the United States Patent office since to do so would have required disclosure of their contents. Trademarks and distinctive bottle designs, however, often were patented.

In the early part of the Twentieth Century there came a series of revelations which destroyed the public's faith in patent medicines. The most famous of these was the 1905 series of articles in Collier's magazine by Samuel Hopkins Adams. Imagine the indignation when people learned that "Wm Radum's Microbe Killer" consisted of very dilute red wine; that "Colden's Liquid Beef Tonic" (recommended for treatment of alcohol habit) contained 26.5% alcohol; that "Kaufman's Sulphur Bitters" ("contains no alcohol") in fact, contained 20.5% alcohol and no sulphur! Worse still, many of the medicines contained hefty amounts of morphine, cocaine or even heroin. No doubt there were many cases of addiction or even fatal overdose, especially in children.

In the matter of a few years the robust patent medicine industry collapsed, the victim of public distrust and legislation such as the 1906 Pure Food and Drug Act. Some of the better advertised remedies, or those which actually had some therapeutic merits, were able to survive in the new era. Indeed, a few still are hanging on today, but the rapid advances of medical science soon made them nothing more than quaint anachronisms with their ingredients and advertising claims both considerably watered down.

Throughout the patent medicine era Minnesotans seemed to prefer medicines made by large "out east" companies. Thus, "Kilmer's Swamp Root" and the various Dr. Pierce's medicines are the commonest ones dug hereabouts. There was, however, a modest local medicine industry which had its origins in the early days of Twin Cities settlement.

The first to put up special herbs and potions in the 1860's and 70's were druggists such as J.P. Allen of St. Paul, and T.K. Gray and James Murison of Minneapolis. Some druggists continued to bottle their own remedies clear through to the end of the patent medicine era despite pronounce- ments from their professional societies that patent medicines were unsafe, unethical and bad for their prescription trade.

Another group of companies who put up medicines were the various "stock food" (that is to say, veterinary product) companies acting on the general theory of "good for man and beast". Some of these firms got their start with veterinary remedies and later added medicines for human consumption, while other firms did the reverse, starting with patent medicines and then switching to "stock food" to find refuge from the Pure Food and Drug Act.

But the most varied and fascinating group of medicine men were the many small time operators, the ones who never failed to bill themselves as "Doctor" or "Professor," the ones who lived in the back of their shops and peddled the more outrageous cures, oils, balsams, remedies and liniments. Often little is known about them, and it is here that the imagination can play. For instance, a certain Dr. Maymore is known only from an ad in an 1870's Minneapolis newspaper which describes his "Egyptian Stomach Bitters and Oils of the Holy Land" and tells a story of how he was maligned and looked down on by the regular medical establishment until the testimonials from customers started rolling in. That's all that is known about him, but one can almost see the mustachioed old

charlatan, operating out of a storefront with a short term lease, his carpetbags packed and waiting by the back door ready to skip town when the bills come due or when the word gets around that his nostrums, like most of the others, cannot cure the genuinely ill.

The patent medicine era is over, and it is getting increasingly difficult to find old-timers who can remember taking "Kilmer's" or "Pinkham's Compound."

It is for the best, of course, considering all the benefits of modern medicine, but who can look back without fascination and perhaps a bit of longing on a time when people were innocent enough to put their faith in "Bixby's Death to Pain", or "Van's Quick Cure?"

GUIDE TO PATENT MEDICINE BOTTLE STYLES

Patent medicine bottles were made in a variety of body shapes with a variety of mouth finishes and neck shapes. Some bottles had flat sides, some indented side panels, and some a combination of both. This BOTTLE STYLE GUIDE illustrates some of the more common bottle types. Thruout this section of the book the medicine bottles will be described by style number as follows:

BODY SHAPE + INDENTED PANELS + MOUTH FINISH

For example, a bottle described as STYLE E6H would have a type E body shape, would be indented on all 4 sides, and would have a type H mouth finish. Below is a list of some bottle styles and the associated name that various bottle manufactures assigned that style in their order catalogues. In some cases the authors have invented names for a particular style not found in a catalogue.

BOTTLE STYLE NAMES

A5A-PLAIN THREE SIDE PANEL (AQUA);
    MISSOURI PANEL (AQUA); IOWA
    PANEL (AQUA); MADISON PANEL
    (FLINT); FRUIT SYRUP PANELS
    (FLINT)
A5H-LONG NECKED PANELS (AQUA);
    CASTOR OIL PANELS (FLINT)
A6A-SHORT NECK PANELS (AQUA);
    WISCONSIN PANEL (AQUA);
    MICHIGAN PANEL (AQUA)
A6C-SHORT BALL NECK PANELS (FLINT);
A6D-ARGYLE PANELS (FLINT); TALL
    BALL NECK PANELS (AQUA & FLINT)
A6G-EDWARDS PANEL (AQUA)
A6H-ALABAMA PANELS (AQUA); ARKAN-
    SAS PANEL (AQUA); MISSISSIPPI
    OIL PANEL (FLINT); ROWE PANEL
    (AQUA); CASTOR OIL PANEL (AQUA)

B6A-WARRANTED PURE PANEL (AQUA)

C5A-FULL MEASURE EXTRACT PANELS
    (FLINT)
C6D-ROUND SHOULDERED BALL NECK
    (FLINT)

D5A-"X" PANEL (AQUA)

E5A-PLAIN OVAL PANELS (AQUA &
    FLINT); HART PANELS (FLINT)
E6H-TENNESSEE PANELS (AQUA)

F1A-FLAT EXTRACT (FLINT)
F1K-TAPER NECK EXTRACT (FLINT)
F4A-SHORT NECKED PANEL-FLAT (FLINT)

G6A-DIXIE PANELS (FLINT & AQUA)

H6A-TAPER PANELS (FLINT)

J5A-EMULSION PANELS (AQUA)
J5G-BELVING PANELS (AQUA)

K5G-SARSAPARILLA PANELS (AQUA)
K6G-GEORGIA PANELS (FLINT)

L5H-SPINK PANELS (AQUA); COD
    LIVER OIL PANELS (AQUA)

BODY SHAPES

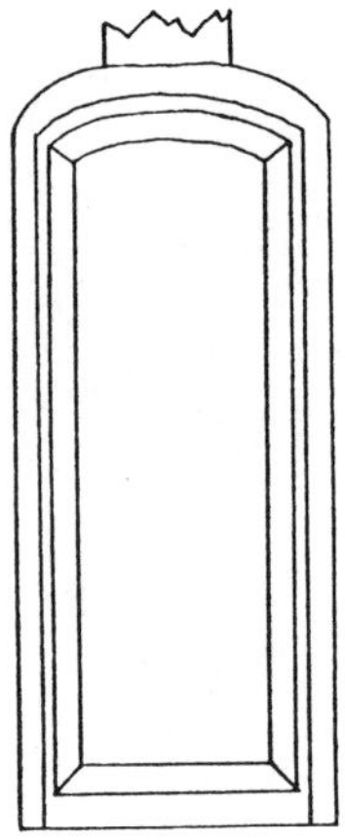

A

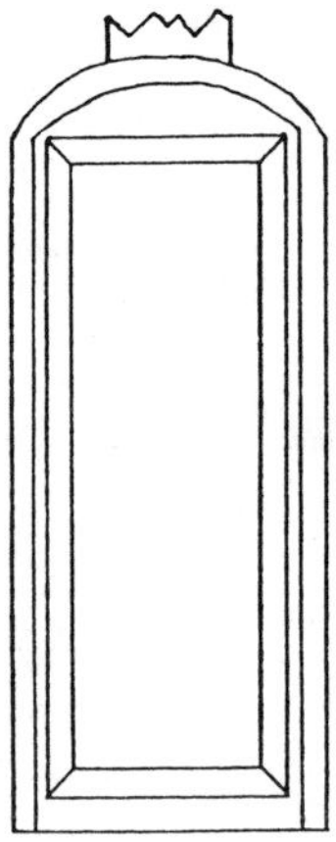

B

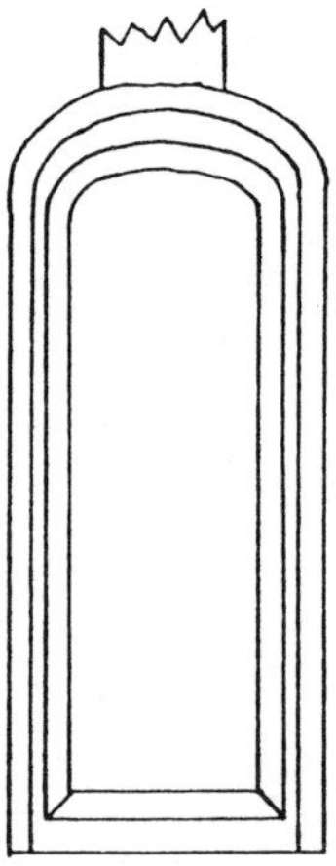

C

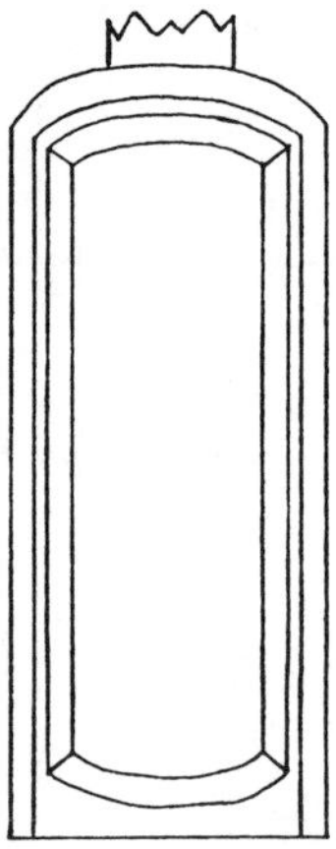

D

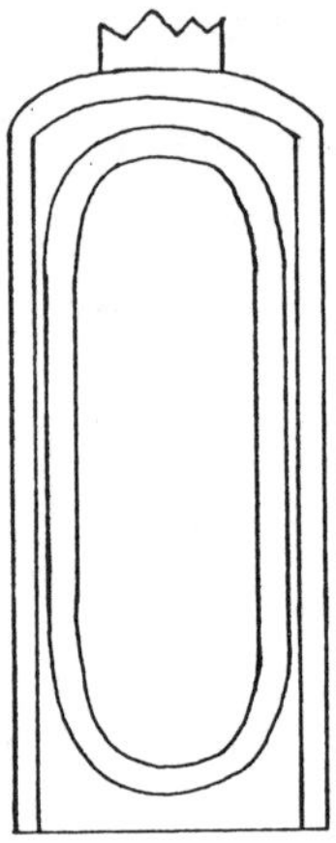

E

F

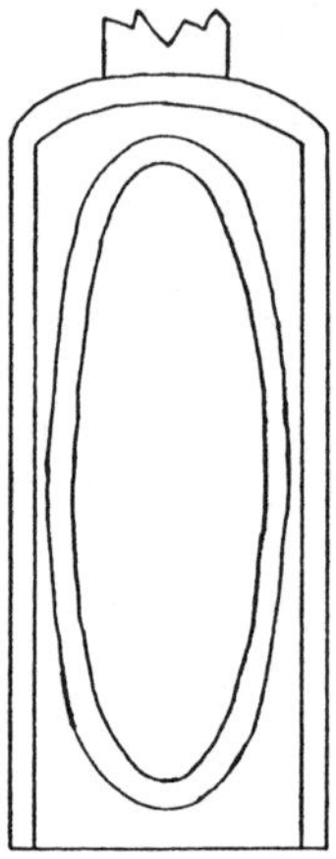

G

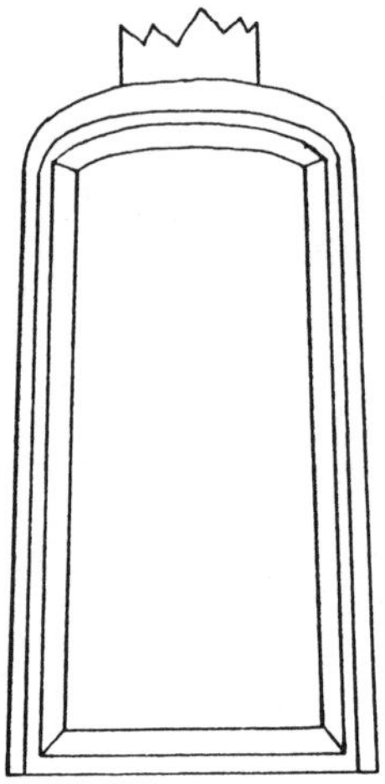

H

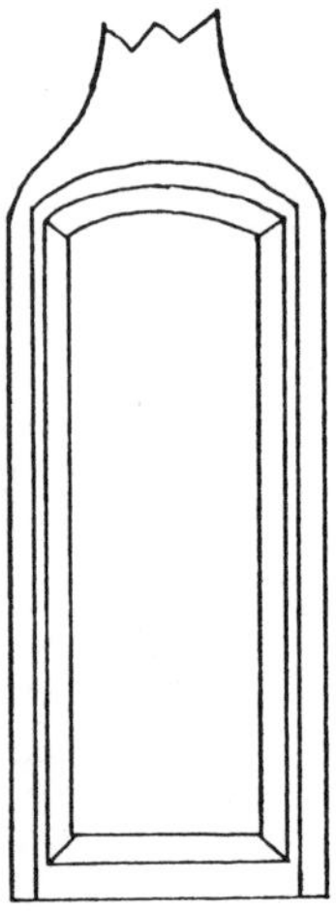

J

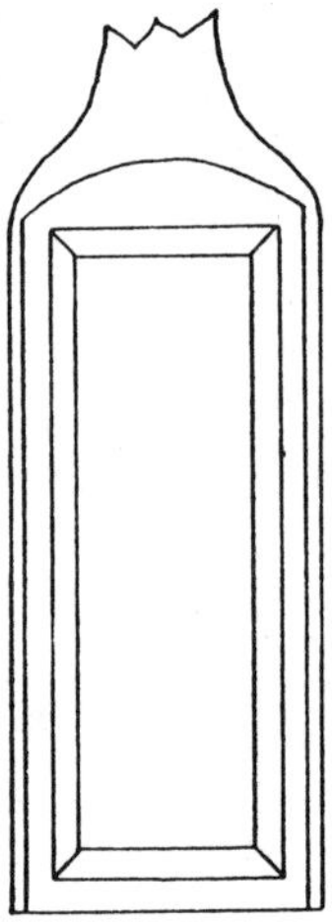

K

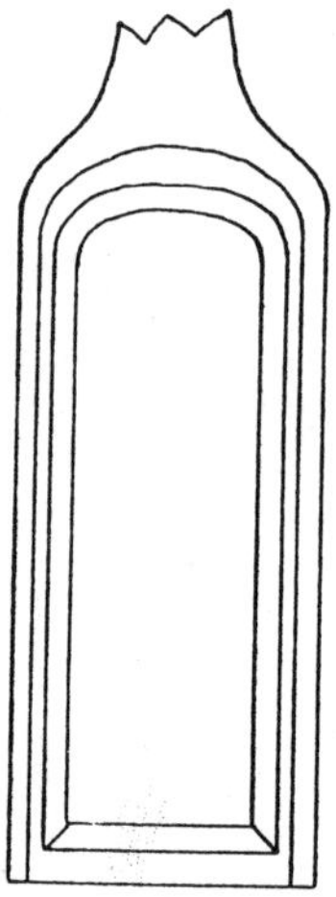

L

PANELED SIDES - FLAT SIDES CODE

1. FLAT ON ALL 4 SIDES

2. FLAT ON 3 SIDES &
   PANELED FRONT

3. FLAT EDGES & PANELED FRONT &
   PANELED BACK

4. FLAT FRONT & FLAT BACK &
   PANELED EDGES

5. FLAT BACK & PANELED FRONT &
   PANELED EDGES

6. PANELED ON ALL 4 SIDES

MOUTH FINISHES & NECK STYLES

A-EXTRACT OR PATENT LIP

B-PACKER OR DEEP LIP

C-SHORT BALL NECK

D-TALL BALL NECK

E-PRESCRIPTION LIP

F-RING OR BEAD LIP

G-DOUBLE RING LIP

H-OIL FINISH

J-SQUAT NECK

K-FLARE LIP

L-TAPER NECK

M-BRANDY OR WINE FINISH

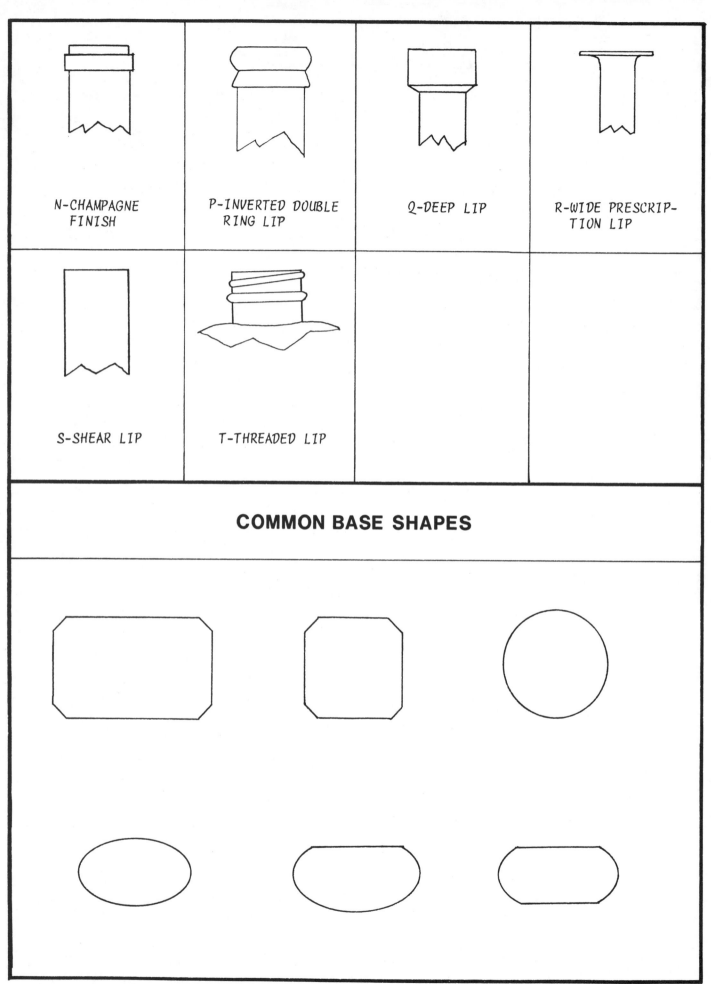

N-CHAMPAGNE
FINISH

P-INVERTED DOUBLE
RING LIP

Q-DEEP LIP

R-WIDE PRESCRIP-
TION LIP

S-SHEAR LIP

T-THREADED LIP

COMMON BASE SHAPES

ALLEN BROS.
TOILET CREAM
1020 HENNEPIN AVE.
MINNEAPOLIS, MINN.

(1603A)

ALLEN BROS.
MINNEAPOLIS

(1603C)

BARBOUR'S FLAVORING EXTRACTS.
DOCTOR DUNLAP'S
ANCHOR BITTERS
TRADE MARK REGISTERED
SILVER SPOON
BAKING POWDER
ARCTIC PURE GROUND SPICES, &c.
ARCTIC READY PREPARED FLOUR.
TERMS:

DR. DUNLAP'S
ANCHOR BITTERS

ARCTIC MANUFACTURNIC CO
MINNEAPOLIS

(3728A)

ARCTIC
MANUFACTURING Co.
MINNEAPOLIS, MINN.

(3728B)

UNCLE JOSH'S
RHEUMATIC CURE
MRS. DR. MARY BARKER
MINNEAPOLIS, MINN.

(3733A)

AUSTIN'S ANTISEPTIC
DANDRUFF DESTROYER
AND NEW HAIR GROWER
MINNEAPOLIS, MINN.

(3730A)

ANTI-CHAP
MINNEAPOLIS PHARMACY Co.
BABENDRIER & VAN NEST
MINNEAPOLIS, MINN.

(2830B)

3710 ADAMS MFG. CO.   1902

3712 AHWAGO SPECIFIC CO.   1907

[ALLEN BROS - See Druggist section]

3714 ALLEN, W. J.   1888-1905

3716 ALLEN, W. S.   1902

[ANDERSON & CO, ALFRED - See Household Products section - The paper label on bottle 1350C reads "BORTHENS Cod Liver Oil"]

3720 AMBOR MFG. CO.   1892

3722 AMERICAN COMPOUND CELERY CO.   1898

3724 AMERICAN HERB CO.   1901-1910

3726 AMERICAN STANDARD STOCK FOOD CO.   1898

3728 ARCTIC MFG. CO.   1879-1888
The Arctic Manufacturing Company was a partnership of R.A. Stolz and L.A. Barbour. They manufactured specialty items for druggists and grocers. In addition to Dr. Dunlap's Anchor Bitters, they made flavoring extracts, spices, crackers, baking powder, soaps and perfumes. The company symbol was a polar bear.

The company name changed to Arctic Cracker and Spice Company in 1882 and sales invoices indicate that they were still selling Dr. Dunlap's Anchor Bitters in 1885.
3728A . Plain Schnapps; amber; H8-3/4xW2-3/4xL2-3/4
3728B . Tall long neck cylinder; Clear, H4-1/4xD1-1/2

3730 AUSTIN, J. H.   1898-1900
John H. Austin was a classic medicine man. Preferring to call himself "Professor" J.H. Austin, he drifted into town sometime in the late 1890's. Upon arrival, he set up an office on the 5th floor of the Syndicate Building. Claiming to be a Dermatologist, he ran a number of advertisements in the local newspapers. Appearing in all of Austin's ads was a rather ferocious-looking "microbe", which was his trademark. Perhaps the thought of a bug like that crawling around on your head was enough to make you run out and buy a bottle of the preparation.

Austin operated in Minneapolis for only three years (1898-1900), which accounts in part for the rarity of the bottle. In 1901 he moved to Chicago, where he remained for at least 15 years. He wore many hats, billing himself as a Dermatologist, a Bacteriologist, and a mail-order operator. Since the Pure Food and Drug act of 1906 did not cover medicines for external use, it is likely that he continued selling his dandruff destroyer long after other medicine men were forced out of business.
3730A Premier Oval; Clear; H6-3/4

3732 BALLARD, S. W.   1887

3733 BARKER, DR. MARY
3733A

3734 BARTHOLOMEW, S.   ?

3736 BELDING MEDICINE CO., DR.   1908-1915
Marion Willis (Will) Savage was born in Marleborough, Ohio in 1859. While he was a young boy, his family moved to Iowa. From his father, a

THE CAPTION ON THIS PHOTO READ: "OUR CHEMICAL LABORATORY WHERE THE DR. BELDING REMEDIES ARE MANUFACTURED. THE ABOVE ENGRAVING SHOWS PART OF OUR CHEMICAL LABORATORY WHICH IS ONE OF THE VERY BEST EQUIPPED LABORATORIES IN THE COUNTRY. WE EMPLOY THE HIGHEST CHEMICAL SKILL IN TESTING AND COMPOUNDING ALL OF OUR DIFFERENT PREPARATIONS AND GUARANTEE THEM STRICTLTY HIGH CLASS. THE DR. BELDING MEDICINE CO.. MINNEAPOLIS, MINN."

physician and druggist, Savage developed an interest in medicine. At the age of 22, Savage married and bought a farm. Unfortunately, the following year a flash flood destroyed his crops, land and home. Undaunted, Savage moved to Dubuque and opened a stock food business. Misfortune struck once again when Will's partner disappeared with all the company profits.

Savage moved to Minneapolis in 1886 and opened a small business in the wholesale district where he began manufacturing stock foods. Two years later he purchased the 1887 Minneapolis Exposition Building, a move which marked his business with prominence.

Savage's business grew rapidly and soon became the largest of its kind in the world. The business was named the International Stock Food Company. Savage had a knack for words and was well known as an advertising wizard. His slogan "Three Feeds For One Cent" was known all over the world.

By 1893, Savage was well on his way to becoming a millionaire. In 1896 he made a move that would make the Savage name even more famous. Savage purchased 750 acres of land on the outskirts of Minneapolis and started a horse stable. His collection of championship pacers was soon the talk of the horse racing world. When the world heard that Savage had purchased a beautiful mahogany bay named Dan Patch his stock food business skyrocketed.

The horse was exhibited and raced across the country and traveled in its' own private railroad car. On September 8, 1906 at the Minnesota State Fair Dan Patch ran a 1:55 mile breaking the world record.

Sometime during this whirlwind of activity, Savage branched into the people medicine business and in 1908 he started the Dr. Belding's Medicine Company which was located at 121 1st Ave North. The business ended with the death of Savage on July 12, 1916. Will Savage died just 32 hours after the death of his beloved horse Dan Patch. Savage's sons cotinued to operate the International Stock Food Company.

3736A . Style J5G and Style J5A; Aqua; H7-1/2xW2-3/8 xL1-1/4;
3736B . Style J5G; Aqua; H7-1/2xW2-3/8xL1-1/4;
3736C . Style J5G; Aqua; H7-1/2xW2-3/8xL1-1/4;

3738 BELLAIRE BROS   1900-1901

3740 BERG, EMIL   1893

3742 BENNESON, F. J.   1896

3744 BEST EVER CHEMICAL CO.   1902-1904

3746 BISHOP & GWEN   1888
   3747 Bixby, L.   ?
   Luther Bixby was born in Vermont. In 1864 he moved to Owatonna, Minnesota to take the job of County Surveyor. He soon entered the drug store business and some time in the 1870's concocted his BIXBY'S DEATH TO PAIN. In 1880 he moved to Minneapolis and began publishing the Minneapolis Temperance Review. He also continued to sell his Death to Pain. In 1886 he moved to Chicago. He died August 7, 1895.

3747A . Style A6G; Aqua

3748 BLAISDELL MEDICINE CO.   1909

MINNEAPOLIS, MINN.
(3736A) DR. BELDING'S SIX PRAIRIE HERBS COUGH AND LUNG REMEDY
DR. BELDING MEDICINE CO.

MINNEAPOLIS, MINN.
DR. BELDING' SKIN REMEDY (3736B)
DR. BELDING MEDICINE CO.

DR. BELDING MEDICINE CO.
(3736C) DR. BELDINGS WILD CHERRY SARSAPARILLA
MINNEAPOLIS, MINN.

(3747A) BIXBY'S DEATH TO PAIN

3750 BLANCHARD, JOSEPH   1900-1906

3752 BRAZILIAN ASTHMA CURE   1900-1902

3754 BURLING, JAMES   1902

3756 CALIFORNIA CHEMICAL CO.   1903-1910

3758 CAMDON TONIC CO, MADAM   1894

3760 CANNON DIGESTIVE JUICE   1905-06

3762 CARDINAL REMEDY CO.   1903-05

3764 CHENEY, I. L.   1907

3766 CHIEF MOUNTAIN ASH   1896

CIRKLER'S
BENZOATED CREAM   (1901D)

(1901E)   CIRKLER'S
BORATED CREAM

CIRKLER'S
ORIENTAL BALM   (1901F)

Clevenger's INDIAN Hair Balsam

For sale by all druggists, or sent by us to any address on receipt of price. $1.00 per bottle.

Contracts for restoring hair taken under guaranty at any agency of this Company.

Clevenger Hair Balsam Co.,
PROPRIETORS.
Citizens Bank Building, 416 Nicollet Ave., Minneapolis.

[CIRKLER, C. H. - See Druggist section]

3768 CLASON, J. J.   1891

3770 CLAYTON & CO., M. A.   1904

3772 CLEVENGER, WM. - Indian Hair Balsam   1893-94

3774 CLOUGH, L. H.   1910

3776 COLE, DANFORTH   1896

3778 CRESCENT FAMILY REMEDY & SUPPLY CO.   1896-99

[CROCKER & THOMPSON - See Druggist section]

3780 CUBAN MEDICINE CO.   1905

[DANEK, JOHN - See Druggist section]

3782 DAVIDSON, J. P.   1904, 1908

3784 DAYOLHEASALE, CHIEF   1909

WASHINGTON LOTION
(1966B)   CROCKER & THOMPSON MFR'S
MINNEAPOLIS, MINN.

3786 DEAD SHOT REMEDY CO.   1901-1904

3787 DENTORIS   1909-1915
3787A . Private mold; Clear; H2-3/4xW1xD1-1/4; base
         embossing

3788 DIME REMEDY CO.   ?
3788A . Jug

3789 DORAN, J. E.   1909

3791 DUKES, J. B.   1902

3792 DURHAM, G. H.   1894-98

3794 EATON CHEMICAL CO.   1908

3796 EATON & CO., R. D.   1902-1904
"Good for Man or Beast" was a claim made by many
patent medicine hawkers, probably including Roderick
Dhu Eaton. Eaton at least knew about the second
half of the saying, for he was a veterinarian.

Dr. Eaton was born in 1859 in Whitewater, Wisconsin, and practiced the vet trade in Hastings and
Fergus Falls before coming to Minneapolis in 1889.
His business and home addresses changed every few
years after that, but were mostly on the north side
of town.   Throughout the 1890's he was listed in
the City directories as a veterinary surgeon;
sometimes in private practice, and sometimes working
for the Minneapolis Brewing Company (probably taking
care of their draft horses).   Then, in 1903, he was
listed as the president and general manager of the
Removine Chemical Co., which manufactured Removine,
"a remedy for bunches, lameness, aches and pains and
rheumatism."   This company was only around until
1905 or '06, although Eaton remained in the medicine
business, on and off, until his death in 1917. Some
of his later endeavors included "The R.D. Eaton

DR.
R.D. EATON'S
REMOVINE
MINNEAPOLIS
MINN.
(3796A)

DANEK'S
PERFECTION HAND LOTION

(1993D)

DANEK'S
WILD CHERRY
COUGH BALSAM

(1993B)

DENTORIS
MINNEAPOLIS

(3687A)

Chemical Company, Proprietors of Eaton's Family and Veterinary Remedies, Extracts, Spices and toilet articles," (1908-13); and the Peerless Medical Company (1913).
3796A . Private mold; Aqua; H7-1/4xW2-1/4

3798 EDWARDS, D. E.   1866-1890
David Edwards was born March 19, 1816 in Franklin County Pa. After living in Ohio, Missouri and Pennsylvania, where he engaged in milling and farming until 1854, he moved to St. Anthony, Minnesota with his wife and four daughters. At this early date there were only twelve houses on the West Side, and nothing whatever in the way of improvements.

St. Anthony was a typical frontier lumbering town, where everything in the building line was constructed from lumber manufactured at the original saw-mills No. 1 and No. 2.

Edwards, who was called Colonel Edwards, was an exceptional philanthropist. Many early settlers received unselfish and timely aid from Edwards and were actually saved from hunger and suffering. As one biography states, "He was a man always bubbling over with mirth, one who basked in the sunshine of life and was ever on the alert to dispel those clouds that cast their shadows over the lives of the struggling but sturdy pioneers."

Edwards' hall was known far and wide as an ideal place for dances, concerts, festivals, political gatherings and overflow justice court meetings.

For many years Colonel Edwards was also known as Doctor Edwards as a result of his inventing EDWARD'S MONITOR LINIMENT in 1866. The product was very popular and to a great extent replaced Johnson's ANODYNE LINIMENT a "down east remedy that every Maineite would swear by".

Edwards died in September of 1890.
3798A . Style A6G; Aqua; H5-3/4xL2xW1-1/4

3799 ERNST, MRS. J. A.   1895

3800 ESTERLY MEDICINE MFG. CO.   1909
The 1909 Northwestern Druggist advertised this company as the manufacturer of Dr. Koehl's German Throat and Lung Balsam.
3800A . Style A6A; Clear; H5-3/4xW1-7/8xL1;
3800B . Style A6A; Clear; H5-3/4xW1-7/8xL1;

3801 FEELY, MARY & CROCKER, FRED
     (Hair products)   1895-1915+
3801A .

3802 FISCHER, R. E.   1899, 1908-1910

MONITOR
LINIMENT
———————
D. EDWARD'S
ST ANTHONY MINN.
(3798A)

Dr. KOEHL'S GERMAN
THROAT AND LUNG
BALSAM
(3800A)

(3800B)
Dr. KOEHL'S GERMAN
THROAT AND LNUG
BALSAM

DERMOLA
GERMAN MEDICINES
MINNEAPOLIS, MINN.
(3808A)

(3808B)
MINNEAPOLIS, MINN.
———————
SAVAGE'S COLORLESS
SKIN REMEDY
———————
THE GERMAN MFG. CO.

(3801A)
FEELY AND CROCKER
SYNDICATE HAIR STORE
15 NICOLLET MINNEAPOLIS
MINN.

Colonel Edwards, being a philanthropist, was desirous of using his capital where it would to the most good and benefit the greatest number. Therefore he decided to engage in "general merchandise."

As there was no building suited to his requirements, he decided to erect one of limestone. It was the first stone building in town and was three stories high.

This pioneer store contained the largest stock of general merchandise in the state, and the fact that its wholesouled proprietor had not the heart to refuse credit to any who lacked the ready cash, naturally brought him some financial discomfort.

3804 FORD, T. F.   1906-07

3806 FORTIER, MRS. N.C.   1907

3808 GERMAN MEDICINE CO.   1888-1903
3808A . Short blake, Clear; H5xL2xW1-1/2
3808B . Style unknown; Aqua; H7xL2-1/8xW1-1/4

3810 GIRRBACH, G. F.   1895-96

3812 GOODWIN & CO., THURSTON   1884

3814 GRANBERG, MARTIN   1902-09

THE GENUINE
LIEBIG'S CORN CURE
GRAY & HOFFLIN

(2273B)

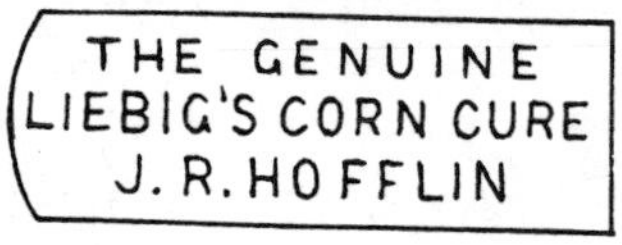

THE GENUINE
LIEBIG'S CORN CURE
J. R. HOFFLIN

(2437D)

(2449B)

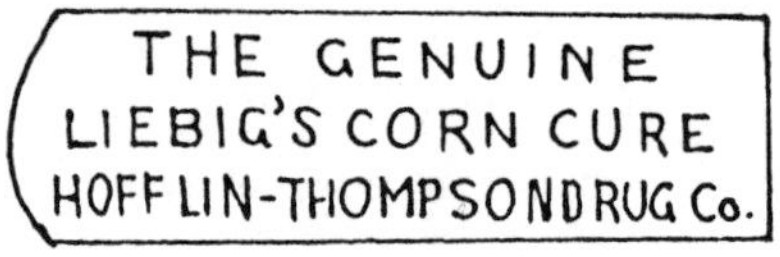

THE GENUINE
LIEBIG'S CORN CURE
HOFFLIN-THOMPSON DRUG Co.

J. R. HOFFLIN & CO.
PRESCRIPTION
101 WASHINGTON AVE. SO.
DRUGGISTS
MINNEAPOLIS

(2443C)

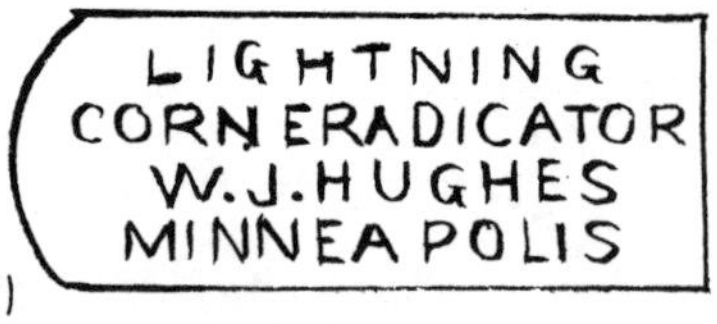

LIGHTNING
CORN ERADICATOR
W. J. HUGHES
MINNEAPOLIS

(2479G)

3816 GRATTON, TIMOTHY	1901-02
[GRAY, T. K. - See Druggist Section]	
[GRAY & HOFFLIN - See Druggist section]	
3818 GRAY, ORRIN	1890
3820 GUARANTY MORPHINE CURE CO	1898-99
3822 HAMBURG MEDICINE CO.	1889-91
3823 HAMERSLEY & CO., MRS. M	1394
3824 HARDING MEDICINE CO., MFGR of "DR HARDING'S CELEBRATED CATARRH CURE	?
3825 HEAL DRUG CO. 3825A . Style A6D; Aqua; H6-1/2xL2-1/4xW1-1/4	?
3826 HENDRICKSON, F. C.	1908-10
3828 HIGMAN, L. F.	1902

[HOFFLIN, J.R. - See Druggist section]

3830 HORTENBACH, F. J.   1897-1911
  Manufacturer of Dr. F. J. Hortenbach Life Bitters

3832 HOWARD CHEMICAL CO.   1906

3834 HUFFMAN HANSEN DRUG CO.   1903

3836 HUGHES, L. G.   1903

[HUGHES, W. J. - See Druggist section]

3838 HYGENOL CO.   1906-1930
The story of the Hygenol Company is first related in a 1906 edition of the Northwestern Druggist, which states that the firm had recently been organized for the purpose of "preparing for the drug trade certain toilet articles manufactured according to the formulae of Dr. Carel," who was a professor in the University of Minnesota Medical

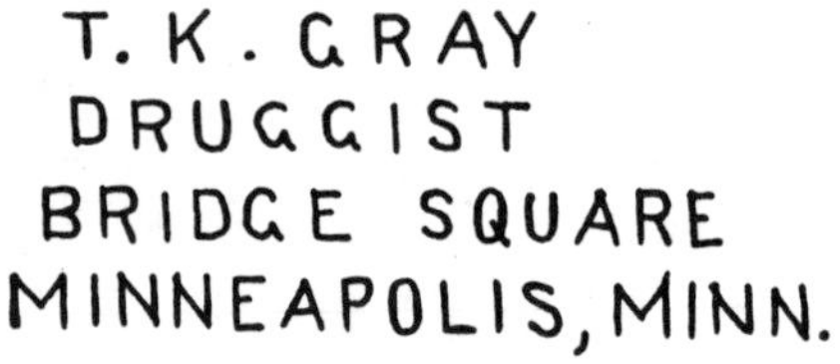

T. K. GRAY
DRUGGIST
BRIDGE SQUARE
MINNEAPOLIS, MINN.

(2267B)

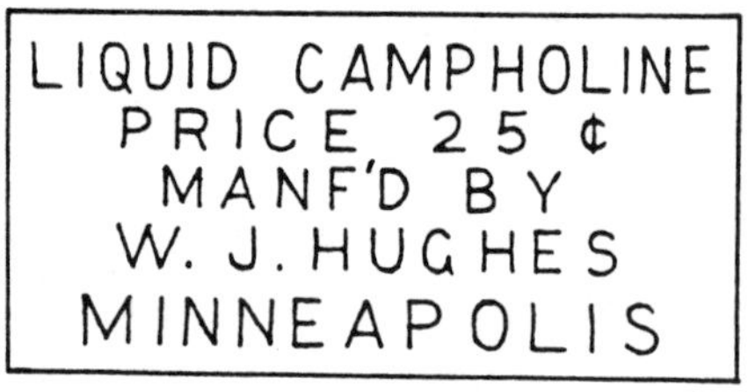

(2267C)

T. K. GRAY & CO.
DRUGGISTS
108 BRIDGE SQUARE
MINNEAPOLIS

HUGHES
ANODYNE
OIL
W. J. HUGHES
MANUFACTURER
MINNEAPOLIS, MINN.

(2479E)

LIQUID CAMPHOLINE
PRICE 25 ¢
MANF'D BY
W. J. HUGHES
MINNEAPOLIS

(2479D)

(2479F)

HEAL DRUG CO.
MINNEAPOLIS

(3825A)

LIQUID CAMPHOLINE
W. J. HUGHES MAN.F.R.
MINNEAPOLIS, MINN.

(3838B)

THE
HYGENOL CO
HYGENOL
TRADEMARK
MINNEAPOLIS
MINN.

(3838E)

THE HYGENOL COMPANY
HYGENOL
TRADEMARK
MINNEAPOLIS

(3838C)

HYGENOL CO
HYGENOL
TRADEMARK
MINNEAPOLIS
MINN

(3838A)

(3838D)

INTERNATIONAL FOOD CO
SILVER PINE
HEALING OIL
MINNEAPOLIS, MINN.

(3839A)

(3853A)

DR. HOOPERS
PENETRATING
A.J. KLINE & CO.
MINNEAPOLIS, MINN.

(2572E)

School. Dr. Carel supposedly discovered these formulae for hair and scalp products, then turned them over to the campus barber. The barber, a Mr. Sam Reynolds, tested the products for several years on the heads of students, professors, and deans. The results were said to be good, with baldness being "cured" in some instances.

Products manufactured included a 3-in-1 treatment containing a one oz. box of scalp ointment, a 3 oz. tin of cream shampoo, and an 8 oz. bottle of Hygenol Hair and Scalp Tonic. This kit sold for one dollar. Another bottled product was Hygenol Liquid Green Soap. The Hygenol Company went to some lengths to claim that no injurious chemicals were contained in their products, emphasizing that no animal oils, mercury, wood alcohol, or lead were to be found in them.

At the time of its organization in 1906, the company was located on campus, at 319 Washington Ave. S.E. H.C. Carel was president and consulting chemist, Sam Reynolds was vice president, R.C. Thompson, secretary and manager and C.R. Thompson, treasurer. Within a few years the two Thompsons took over the business and moved to 2839 Hennepin Ave. So. The company survived well into the 1920's.

3838A . Private mold; Clear; H3-1/2
3838B . Cherub pomade; Milk glass; base & side embossing
3838C . Private mold; Clear; H5-1/2 x D2
3838D . Private mold; Clear
3838E . Private mold; Clear

3839 INTERNATIONAL FOOD CO.	1890-1900

3839A . Style J5G; Clear; H6xL2xW1-1/8, H8-1/4xW2-1/2xL1-1/2;
3839A2. Style J5G; Aqua; H6xL2xW1-1/8, H8-1/4xW2-1/2xL1-1/2;

3841 JACOBS, MRS. MARY	1893
3842 JAMES, J. P. R.	1893
3844 JANSEN MEDICINE CO., DR.	1904-09
3846 JENNER, BERNHARD	1888-1896
3848 JENNER, B-ESSENCE OF LIFE	1887
3850 KAMI-KU-R1 MEDICINE CO.	1904-07
3852 KEABER, H. P.	1898
3853 KENNEDY, SUFFEL & ANDREWS	1904-1905

3853A . Tall Seal Brandy; Clear; H10 x D2-3/8

3854 KENNY, R. A.	1901
3856 KENYON, T. N.	1901-10
3858 KIRKPATRICK & BOURQUIN	1899

[KLINE, A. J. - See Druggist section]

3860 KLUNGS MFG CO.	1898-1905
3862 KNAPP & CO.	1885

GOPHER
MANUFACTURED ONLY BY
J. L. KOLL
MINNEAPOLIS, MINN.

(3863A)

DR. G. F. LA PAUL
PHYSICIAN & SURGEON
RHEUMATISM & CHRONIC DISEASES
A SPECIALTY
MINNEAPOLIS, MINN.

LIGHTNING OIL
COMPANY
MINNEAPOLIS, MINN.

(3882A)

3863 KOLL, J. L.   1908-1917+
3863A . Private mold; Clear; H8-1/4

3864 KONDON MFG. CO.   ?
  In 1885 Thomas Kenyon went on the road as a
  traveling saleman, handling drug specialties for
  Frederick F. Ingram of Detroit, Michigan. Soon
  after, he established the Kondon Manufacturing Co.
  and was the originator of Kondon's Catarrhal
  Jelly. At first he distributed free samples
  everywhere. This was followed by very strong
  letters to dealers telling them the value of
  Kondon's Catarrhal Jelly. The basement of his home
  was used for the manufacture of the product, but
  soon this became too small. In 1907 he advertised
  in newspapers in the west and his business
  continued to grow.
3864A . Salve tin

(3864A)

3868 LAMB, MRS. L. M.   1899

3870 LANDSFELDT MEDICAL SKIN TONIC   1891

3872 LANDSFELDT MEDICAL WASH CO.   1890

[LA PAUL, DR. G. F. - See Druggist section]

3874 LAVORIS CHEMICAL CO.   1904-1906
3874A . Private mold; Round; Clear; H4-3/4xD1-3/4;
        base and shoulder embossing

3876 LEE, J. D.   1889

3878 LEWIS, G. H.   1896

3880 LIFE WONDER CO.   1903-06

3882 LIGHTNING OIL CO.   1909-1910
3882A . Style A5A; Clear; H6-3/8xW2

3884 LUCAS, A. C.   1898

3886 LYFE'S ONE-DER CO   1905

3888 MAGNETIC PAIN KILLER CO.   1906

3890 MANUFACTURING PHARMACIST CO.   1898-99

3892 McCURDY, G H.   1900

3894 McCLUSKEY, F. A.   1897-1901

3896 MEDICATED VAPOR CO.   1893

3898 METZGER MEDICINE CO   1888-1893

[MEURER - See Druggist Section]

3900 MIDDLETON & CO., J.E.   1896

3901 MINNEAPOLIS DRUG CO   1907-1950
3901A . Jug
3901B . Watch Fob
3901C . Jug

LAVORIS

(3874A)

(3874A)

(3901B)

(3901A)

(3901C)

ANTI-CHAP
MINNEAPOLIS PHARMACY Co.
BABENDRIER & VAN NEST
MINNEAPOLIS, MINN.

(2830B)

MINN. OIL OF LIFE CO.

MINNEAPOLIS

(3907A)

MEURER'S
CARNATION CREAM
MINNEAPOLIS

(2812B)

JAS MURISON & Co
NORTH STAR
LUNG & THROAT
BALSAM
MINNEAPOLIS, MINN.

(2866A)

CURRAN'S HERB BITTERS
PEPSINIZED

THE NAPA VALLEY WINE CO.
MINNEAPOLIS, MINN.

(996C)

FRISCO COUGH SYRUP
MANUFACTURED BY
NORGREN MEDICINE CO.
MINNEAPOLIS.

(3921A)

FRISCO COUGH SYRUP   NORGREN
MEDICINE Co
MINNEAPOLIS

(3921B)

(P320A)   FRISCO COUGH SYRUP   C. E. NORGREN
MANUFACTURED
SHERBURN, MINN

3902 MINNEAPOLIS MEDICINE CO.   1910

[MINNEAPOLIS PHARMACY CO - See Druggist section]

3904 MINNEAPOLIS VIAVI CO   1906-10

3906 MINNESOTA MEDICAL CO.   1897-1910

3907 MINNESOTA OIL OF LIFE CO.   ?
3907A . Style A5H; Aqua; H7; MCC on Base

3908 MINNESOTA STATE VETERINARIAN REMEDY CO   1904-06

3910 MINNESOTA VIAVI CO   1893-1905

3912 MINNESOTA VIMEDIA CO   1910

3914 MONARCH MEDICINE CO.   1898-1907

3916 MOUNTAIN PANTHER, CHIEF   1896

[MURISON, JAS - See Druggist Section]

3918 NATIONAL HERB CO.   1903-05

3920 NELSON, J. T.   1903-10

3921 NORGREN MEDICINE CO.   1907-1965
Throughout the patent medicine era the various
nostrums, potions, and pills always enjoyed greater
acceptance in rural areas than here in the Twin
Cities. Quite a number of small medicine companies
sprang up in smaller communities, and a few, such
as the Norgren Medicine Co., were successful enough
to move to the "Cities" and take their shot at a
bigger market.

The Frisco Cough Syrup story begins in the small
southern Minnesota town of Sherburn, near Fairmont,
in 1882. That was the year that a forty year old
Swedish immigrant named Charles Norgren established
a drug store there. Like many early drug stores it
was a community center, being at times used for
dances.

It is difficult to say exactly when Norgren began
putting up his own medicines, although this
newspaper bit from 1893 may provide a clue.
    "Bring on your heavy corn. Mr. Norgren hasn't
    enough seed corn yet, but offers another
    prize. Carl Sivert of Fox Lake won the first
    bottle."

Two of Norgren's products were analyzed by the State
of Minnesota in the early 1900's. One, Norgren's
Sure Cure Headache Capsules contained acetanilid
caffiene and sodium bicarbonate, while the Frisco
Cough Syrup was likewise a rather benign mixture of
6% alcohol, 2.9 drops chloroform per ounce, sugar,
and tar.

Charles Norgren and his son George P. Norgren,
moved to Minneapolis in June of 1908, setting up
shop at 401 W. Lake Street. A Mr. G.H. Lambert was
also involved in the company, which sometimes
advertised as "druggists", other times as "Norgren
Medicine Co., drugs, chemicals and sundries, manufacturers of Frisco Cough Syrup and Old Country
Liniment."

The Norgren Medicine Co. never prospered, but it
certainly perservered. It survived Charles
Norgren's death in the 1920's and continued on
through the 30's...and 40's...and 50's. Somewhere

E. M. PIKE
MINNEAPOLIS, MINN.

(3052B)

98 WESTERN AVE.

DR. JOY'S
TAR COUGH ELIXIR
MFG.ᴰBY C.A. ROBINSON

(3160B)

MINNEAPOLIS

SAPPHINE

(3043A, 3970A)

along the line George Norgren left the medicine trade, dealing in buttons and notions instead. By the mid 1950's Helmer and Elanor Johnson ran the company, then located at 211 1st Avenue North. They were able to keep the firm afloat until 1965, the last year it is listed in the City Directory.
3921A . Style A5A; Clear; H7xL2-1/4xW1-1/4
3921B . Style A5A; Clear; H6-1/2xL2-1/4xW1-1/4

3922 NORTHERN VIMEDIA CO   1907

3924 NORTHWESTERN WINE CO   1894

3926 OZOFORM CO.   1909

3928 PARMENTER, H. M.   1898

3930 PATTY, C. S.   1905-09

3932 PEERLESS CO.   1906

3934 PERKINS AMERICAN HERBS   1904

3936 PERSIAN TOILET CO.   1899

3938 PETERSON, H. M.   1906

3940 PETTIT MEDICINE CO.   1906-09

3942 PHIPHER MEDICINE CO.   1891-94

[PIKE, E. M. - See Druggist section]

3944 POTTER CHEMICAL CO.   1897-1908

3946 RADAMS MICROBE KILLER   1890-1900

3948 REAS BROS & CO   1900-04

3950 REGAN & GIFFORD MFG. CO   1898

3952 RED CROSS CHEMICAL CO.   1905

[REMOVINE CHEMICAL CO. - See R. D. Eaton]

3956 RHODES & CO, Dr. D.   1902

3958 RHOADES, J. C.   1896

[ROBINSON, C. A. - See Druggist section]

3959 ROCKOLEAN MFG. CO.   1898

3960 ROGERS, MRS. MARGARETTE   1896

3962 ROGLER , JOHN   1898

[ROSE, G. A. - See Druggist section]

3964 RUBLOFF, HARRY   1902

3966 SAINT CLOUD, C. F.   1898-1900

3968 SANDER CHEMICAL CO.   1895-1909
3968A . Philadelphia Oval; milk glass; H3-3/4

3970 SAPPHINE CHEMICAL CO.   1906-1918+
3970A . Clear; Style A2J (wide mouth)

3972 SCOTT, MRS. J. E.   1891

3974 SECURITY REMEDY CO.   1903
3974A . Style J5G; Aqua; H8-3/8 x L2-3/4 x
         W1-1/2;
3974B . Style J5G; Aqua; H6xL2xW1-1/8
3974C . Style J5G; Clear; H5-1/2xL1-7/8xW7/8
3974D . Salve Tin

3976 SHEPARD MEDICINE CO., DR. BERTHA   1895

3973 SIMCOX, E. G.   1900

3980 SMITH, J. H.   1894-1907

(3974D)

ROSE'S
COUGH BALSAM

(3193D)

USE ROSE'S
GEO. A. ROSE
211 CENT. AVE.
COUGH BALSAM

(3193F)

Sanders Chemical Co
Minneapolis.
Minn.

(3968A)

ANTISEPTIC HEALER 25 CENTS	ANTISEPTIC HEALER $1.00	RHEUMATIC LINIMENT 25 CTS
SECURITY REMEDY CO.	SECURITY REMEDY CO	SECURITY REMEDY CO.
MINNEAPOLIS, MINN.	MINNEAPOLIS, MINN.	MINNEAPOLIS, MINN.
(3974C)	ANTISEPTIC HEALER $1.00	(3974B)
	(3974A)	

3982 SODERGREN, H. A.	1902	3986 SOULE, M. L.	1893, 1899-1902
3983 SODERGREN BROS.	1898-1907	3988 SPENCER, J. DeW.	1906-09
3983A . Style unknown; Clear; H5-3/4xW1-3/4		3990 SPENCER, J. H.	1894-95
3983B . Style A6D; Aqua; H5-5/8xL1-7/8xW1		3992 SPENCER MEDICINE CO.	1897-1905
3984 SODERGREN & CO.	?	3994 SPENCERIAN MEDICINE CO.	1888, 1896
3984A . Style A6D; Aqua; H5xL1-3/4xW1			
3985 SOULE MEDICINE CO.	1903-1910		

ANTENIA
SODERGREN BROS
MANUFACTURING CHEMIST
MINNEAPOLIS, MINN.
(3983A)

SODERGREN BROS
MINNEAPOLIS, MINN.
(3983B)

SODERGREN & CO
MINNEAPOLIS, MINN.
(3984A)

3996 SPINK & CO.   1880-1888

The Scotch Bitters story begins way back in 1867 when James Murison opened up his "Model Drug Store" in the Merchants Block of Minneapolis. Murison and Co. stayed in business until 1875, by which time they were located at 44 So. Washington, in Westphal's Block. Working as clerks for Murison were 3 men who would figure prominently in the later history of Dr. Gregory's; James Spink, Levi Patterson and Hugh Young. In 1875 or '76 two of these clerks bought out their employer, the new firm being called Young, Patterson and Co. It was also around this time that Gregory's Scotch Bitters was first made, although we shall probably never know whether Murison or Young, Patterson first marketed it.

Like many 19th century businesses Young, Patterson put out a yearly almanac, one of which (1878) has survived. This little booklet contains a wealth of information including several ads and testimonials for Gregory's Bitters. Among other things, we learn that Young, Patterson was the sole manufacturer of the bitters in the U.S., having purchased

SPINK & Co. (3996A)
NICHOLL'S BALSAM
OF BLACKBERRY
MINNEAPOLIS, MINN.

(3996B) SPINK & Co.
NICHOLL'S SYRUP
OF BLACKBERRY
MINNEAPOLIS, MINN.

SPINK & Co. (3996D)
MINNEAPOLIS

SPINK & COMPANY STORE 1881-PHOTO COURTESY OF MHS

TWO VERSIONS OF DR GREGORY'S SCOTCH BITTERS, BY SPINK & KEYES AND BY NICHOL'S MEDICINE COMPANY

the formula at a "large price." According to their ads it was "The greatest tonic and BLOOD PURIFIER of the age, from the formula of Dr. GREGORY, the noted Edinburgh Physician." This Edinburgh physician was James Gregory, who lived from 1753-1821. Besides being an eminant surgeon he was a University professor and "first physician to his Majesty in Scotland." It is highly unlikely he really had anything to do with the bitters that borrowed his name. But that didn't bother Young and Patterson, they sold 500 dozen bottles in 1877, and expected to double that in '78. At a dollar a bottle this was probably one of their biggest money makers. According to various claims made in the almanac Gregory's Bitters were beneficial for Dyspepsia, Loss of Appetite, Biliousness, Lassitude, General Debility, Weakness of the stomach, liver, kidneys or spleen, Bad Humors, Morning Headache, Mountain Fever etc., etc., etc. In addition to specific information about Scotch Bitters, the almanac tells much about Young, Patterson in general; their merchandise included flavoring extracts, bottled castor, olive, machine and illuminating oils, as well as Gregory's Bitters, Hammon's Quinque, Camphor Ice with Glycerine, North Star Lung and Throat Balsam, The Great Persian Healer, Glycerine Cream and Young's Ext. Jamaica Ginger.

Nonetheless, Young, Patterson fell upon hard times, and by 1880 had sold the business back to James Spink, who had spent the late 1870's selling plumbing supplies and operating the Minneapolis Harvester Works near Lake Street. Spink kept the old store, as well as Young and Patterson as employees, for a year or so, moving to 716 South 6th St. in 1884. While written sources on Spink and Co. are hard to come by, they did leave several embossed bottles, including North Star Lung and Throat Balsam, Nicholl's Balsam of Blackberry, and Nicholl's Syrup of Blackberry. There are strong indicators that it was Spink who put out the embossed Doctor Gregory's.

In 1888 Spink again changed his address (to 204 Washington Ave. No.) and added a partner, Charles Keyes. Little is known about the new firm, Spink and Keyes, except that they retained the rights to Dr. Gregory's, which they put up in a paper label bottle. This partnership lasted until 1896, after which time Spink left town, eventually ending up in Big Lake Minnesota as a salesman for the Leslie Paper Company.

The next company to bottle the Scotch Bitters seems to have been the Nichols Medicine Company of St. Paul, again in a paper label only bottle. Although they didn't advertise in the City Directory, it seems safe to assume this company was around in the late 1890's, having bought the rights to Spink and Keyes products and probably adding a few of their own. The name of the company is very interesting, being so similar to the name Nicholls that shows up on several Spink and Co. bottles. Just what the connection was, or for that matter who Nicols (Nicholls) was is unknown. In any event, the 1897 Lyman-Eliel Drug Company catalog lists a number of products attributable to the Nichols Company: Nichol's Peruvian Bark and Iron, Nichol's Number 12, Nichol's Carbolic Salve, Nichol's Blackberry Cordial, North Star Lung and Throat Balsam, and of course, Gregory's Scotch Bitters, which wholesaled for a paltry $3.00 a dozen.

It is rumored that yet one more individual marketed the bitters after the turn of the century; a Mr. Andrew J. Kline, a druggist at 2600 Bloomington Ave. So., Minneapolis.

Of the several Gregory's variants the paper label Nichols Medicine Co. version is the most common. It has a picture of some fellow in a kilt, probably Dr. Gregory, as well as the usual stuff about Bilious Attacks, Purifier of the Blood etc. The embossed Gregory's is quite scarce.

Our famous Dr. GREGORY,
SCOTCH BITTERS well hath made;
And thereby human misery
And sickness hath allayed.

They cleanse and PURIFY THE BLOOD
Of all that's in it foul;
They give the cheek its youthful glow
And life unto the soul.

(3996E) DOCTOR GREGORY'S
SCOTCH BITTERS

SPINK & Co.   (3996F)
KNOWLTON'S LINIMENT
MINNEAPOLIS, MINN.

SPINK & CO.
NORTH STAR
LUNG & THROAT
BALSAM
(3996C)   MINNEAPOLIS

DYSPEPSIA'S dull and gnawing pain
Here finds a sure relief;
And health and strength come back again,
When ordered by their chief.

THE KIDNEYS by its action gain
Their customary ways,
And hope and vigor come again
With many happy days.
--From the Young, Patterson & Co. Almanac 1878.--

3996A . Style F4G; Aqua; H5;
3996B . Style unknown; Aqua; H5-1/4xL2xW1-1/4,
     extract lip
3996C Style L5H; Aqua; H6xL2-1/4xW1-1/4;
   Base "I.G. Co."
3996C2 Style C5G; Aqua; H6
3996D Style unknown
3996E Plain schnapps; amber; H9-1/4xL2-3/4xW2-3/4;
     Base "I.G. Co."
3996F Style A5H; Aqua; H7-1/2xL2-1/4xW1-3/4;
3996A2 Style A5A; Aqua; H5-1/4xL1-5/8xW7/8;

3997 SPINK & KEYES   1888-1896

3998 SPRINGSTEEN MEDICINE CO.   1893-1895

4000 STAEDE, E. I. P.   1906

4002 STANDARD CELERY COMPOUND CO.   1897-98

4004 STATE ELECTRO-MEDICAL INSTITUTE   1901

4006 STERLING CHEMICAL CO   1905-06

4008 SVR MEDICINE CO.   1905

4010 SWANSON, C.W.   1901

4012 SWEDISH SPECIFIC CO.   1905

[THOMPSON, A. D. - See Druggist section]

4014 TWIN CITY REMEDY CO   1902

4016 UNION CHEMICAL WORKS   1898-1902

TYPICAL PATENT MEDICINE BOTTLE STYLES

THOMPSON'S
THROAT LOZENGES
A.D.THOMPSON
DRUG CO.
MINNEAPOLIS
MINN.

(3488A)

(3545A)

U.S. DISPENSARY CO.
MINNEAPOLIS, MINN.

(4018A)

Voegeli

(3554C)

4018 UNITED STATES DISPENSARY CO   1889-1894
   The motto of this company was "Que Prosunt
Omnibus", which translates loosely to "that which
is beneficial to all". Among their numerous
products were U.S.D. Turkish Cough Syrup, U.S.D.
Lung Ointment and U.S.D. Woman's Friend. Probably
the use of the U.S.D. initials was an attempt to
hoodwink the public, as U.S.P. (United States
Pharmacopia) were the letters used to signify that
a product was recognized as safe and legitimate.
This seal of approval would never have been given
to a patent medicine.

The embossed U.S.D. bottles probably held either
the Lung Ointment or Thomas' Catarrh Cure, as these
were the major products of the company.
4018A . Private mold

4020 UNIVERSAL STOCK CABINET CO.   1908-1910

[VAN GIESON, M. M. - See Druggist section]

4022 VEYRAC, J. M.   1905-1908

4024 VIVIDUS CO.   1895-1900

163 [VOGELI - See Druggist Section]

(4028A)

4028 VOLK REMEDY CO.   **1895-1906**

One of the many patent medicine companies doing business in Minneapolis during the golden age of patent medicines was the Volk Remedy Company. This company first appeared in 1895, with Mrs. Louisa M. Volk (who was also listed in the directory for that year as a music teacher) as president.

The next year the name was changed to Volk & Co., Medicine Manufacturers, with Caleb Johnson and Walter J. Hughes in charge. Mrs. Volk was never again associated with the company. By 1899 Volk & Co. appears to have been temporarily out of business, and Mr. Johnson had moved to Long Beach, California.

In 1900 the company reappeared, again as the Volk Remedy Co., with E.T. Fischer as president. The company advertised that they had been incorporated in 1892, which is only a "little fib" compared to some of the patent medicine "hype" of that age. Their ads went on to say that they were "Manufacturers and Dealers in Proprietary Medicines. Sole agents for Hindoo Oil, and proprietors of Eureka Catarrh Cure."

Despite claiming to cure nearly every disease and injury known, the company lasted only seven more years, disappearing after 1907, apparently "done in" by the Pure Food and Drug Law. R.E. Fischer stayed in the medicine business until 1912, but no link between him and any specific medicine company has been found for those later years.

4028A . Private mold; milk glass; 8 sides, base embossed

4030 WA HOO REMEDY CO		1902
4032 WALLS, Mrs. G.		?
4034 WARDE, A. G.		1902-1908
[WEINHOLD BROS. - See Druggist section]		
[WEBSTER & CHURCHILL - See Druggist section]		
4036 WILLIAMS, R. S.		1889
4038 WORLD MEDICAL CO.		1910
4040 WRIGHT MEDICINE CO.		1896-1902

CASWELL'S BLOOD CLEANER
WEINHOLD BROS, AGENTS

(3596G)

WEBSTER & CHURCHILL
MINNEAPOLIS

(3593D BACK)

WHEELERS
SARSA
PARILLA

(3593D FRONT)

8
ST PAUL
PATENT MEDICINES

[ABERLE, WESTHEIMER CO - See Whiskey section]

4900 ADLERIKA, THE CO.   1910-1913

4902 ALLEN, J. P. MEDICINE CO.   1905-1913

[ALLEN, J. P. - See also Druggist section]

4904 AMERICAN MEDICINE CO.   1895-1897

4906 ARTZ MEDICAL CO.   1906-1913

4908 AYES ONE DAY CURE   1898

4910 BALL, WM. H. & CO.   1898

4912 BAVARIAN MEDICINE CO.   1905-1908

[BECKER, R. A. - See Druggist section]

[BENZ, GEORGE & SONS - See Whiskey section]

4914 BLACKFORD, SAMUEL   1877-1888
  (In 1877 Blackford advertised as agent for Dr. E. B.
  Halliday's St. Paul Blood Purifier
4914A . Style unknown

ST. AUGUSTINE BITTERS

ABERLE, WESTHEIMER CO.

SOLE PROPRIETORS

ST. PAUL, MINN.

(1204B)

(4058B)

(1210N)

(1210Q)

ALLEN'S
ULCERINE
SALVE
(4058C)

S. BLACKFORD PROPRIETOR
SAINT PAUL. Minn.

(4914A)

DIGESTINE
◇ 3 ◇
BITTERS
P.J. BOWLIN & SON
SOLE PROPRIETORS
ST. PAUL MINN.

(1214A)

DIGESTINE
◇ 3 ◇
BITTERS
P.J. BOWLIN LIQUOR CO.
SOLE PROPRIETORS
ST. PAUL MINN.

(1213F)

DIGESTINE
◇ ⊙ ◇
BITTERS

(1213G)

GOLDEN OIL
RHEUMATIC LINIMENT
BROWN CHEMICAL CO.
ST. PAUL

(4916A)

PREVENTO WORM SYRUP
BROWN CHEMICAL CO
ST. PAUL, MINN.

(4916B)

DR. S. G. COBB
366 PRIOR AVE.
ST. PAUL, MINN.

(4924A)

[BOWLIN, P. J. & SON - See Whiskey section]

4916 BROWN CHEMICAL CO.	1899-1907

4916A . Style A5A; Aqua; H5-1/2xL1-3/4xW1;
4916B . Style unknown; Aqua

4918 CAMPBELL, A. A.	1897
4920 CAMPBELL MEDICINE CO.	1898-1905

[CLARK & FROST - See Druggist section]

4922 CLIFFORD, CHARLES	1897
4924 COBB, DR. S. G.	1890-1910

4924A . Style unknown
  (Dr. Cobb, a Homeopathist, operated a hospital
   at 2056 Inglehart St.)

4926 COLUMBIA MEDICINE CO.	1899

[CONGER BROS. - See Druggist section]

4928 COOPER REMEDY CO.	1901-1904
4930 CROOKS - FRAYER MNFG CO.	1904
4932 CROOKS, S. S. MNFG. CO.	1906-1909
4933 DEPT OF HEALTH	

4933A . 2" H Bottle

4934 DIAMOND CHEMICAL CO.	1900
4936 DICKSON CHEMICAL CO.	1912
4938 DORRIS, J. J.	1909-1912
4940 DORRIS SOVEREIGN REMEDY CO.	1905-1908
4942 DOUGLASS, GEO. M. D.	1895
4944 DUFRESNE, A. D. & Co (MNF'S of 20th Century Great French Discovery Root Medicine)	1905
4946 DUTCH CHEMICAL CO.	1895-1902
4948 DUTCH COUGH SYRUP CO.	1903
4950 EC - ZENE CO.	1912-1917

4950A . Style unknown

4952 ELLIS, MRS. M. L.	1912-1913

USE DR. GEO. P. COLLIER'S
ANTISEPTIC CORN & BUNION SHIELDS
WITH DR. COLLIER'S HEALING SALVE
AT ALL
DRUGGISTS
THEY
CURE
25¢
201 RYAN BLDG   ST. PAUL MINN.
OR AT

(4182A)

For The
HAIR
Clark & Frost's
RUM
AND
QUININE
ST. PAUL
MINN.

(4182A)

DEPT OF HEALTH
ST. PAUL, MINN.
SPUTUM BOTTLE

(4933A)

CONGER'S
WHITE PINE
COUGH COMPOUND

(4198B)

FROSTS
RUM
&
QUININE
LOTION
FOR THE
HAIR

(4310H)

FROST'S
ROSE
AMANDINE
CREAM

(4310G)

FROST'S
EXPECTORANT & COUGH BALSAM
FROST & BROWN

(4308C)

GILHOOLEY
DR. DeCOURSEY
IRISH LINIMENT
ST. PAUL, MINN.

(4980A)

(4980B)
GILHOOLEY
DR. DeCOURSEY'S
LINIMENT
ST. PAUL, MINN.

4954 FAMILY MEDICINE CO.		1905
4956 FEIERABEND, MAX		1894-1899
4958 FEMCURA MEDICINE CO.		1896
4960 FERNOLINE CHEMICAL CO.		1890
4962 FISHER CHEMICAL CO.		1899
4964 FIVE OIL MEDICINE CO.		1894
4966 FOSTER, C. A.		1909
4968 FRAYER, ABRAM		1900-1902
4970 FRAYER PHARMACAL CO.		1904

[FROST, W. A. & CO. - See Druggist section]

4972 GAUGHRAN BROS.		1905-1910
4974 GEBHARD, E. C.		1909-1910
4976 GERMAN FAMILY MEDICINES		1894-1912
4978 GIBBENS, V. L.		1909

4980 GILHOOLEY IRISH LINIMENT CO.   1908-1912
4980A . Style unknown; Aqua
4980B . Style unknown; Aqua

4982 GLEWWE, JOHN   1904-1913
4982A . Style unknown

4984 GLOBE COMPOUNDING CO.   1889-1891
4984A . Clear; H9-1/4xL2-5/8xW1-1/8
4984B . Clear; bottle fragment

4986 GOLD COIN CHEMICAL WORKS   1910

4988 GOOD, ELMER   1911

4989 GREAT MORMAN REMEDY CO.   1893-1894
4989A . Round; Clear; H11 x D3; Slug Plate

4990 GREWE, A. C. & CO.   1888-1906
4990A . Style unknown
(In 1900 Grewe advertised as Prop. of Dr. E. B.
Hallidays Blood Purifier Co.)

[GUERNSEY, A. T. & SON - See Druggist section]

(4984B)

(4984A)

GREAT MORMON
REMEDY CO LTD
St PAUL MINN

(4989A)

A.C. GREWE & CO.
SAINT PAUL, MINN.

(4990A)

CY-DO-LINE
A.T. GUERNSEY & SON
ST. PAUL

(4345B)

```
┌─────────────────────────────┐
│  HALSEY BROS.CO.            │
│  CHICAGO & ST.PAUL          │
└─────────────────────────────┘
```
(4358A)

```
┌─────────────────────────────┐
│  COCA-CALISAYA TONIC        │
│  HALSEY BROS.CO.            │
│  CHICAGO & ST.PAUL          │
└─────────────────────────────┘
```
(4358B)

HEAL DRUG CO.
ST. PAUL, MINN.

(4998A)

HURLEY BROS.
PEPSINIZED BITTERS

HURLEY BROS.
ST. PAUL, MINN.

(1258B)

HURLEY BROS.
BITTERS

HURLEY BROS.
ST. PAUL, MINN.

(1258C)

SYRUP
WILD CHERRY
COMPOUND
MANUFACTURED
BY
W.J. HOVORKA
FAMILY DRUGGIST

(4398A)

(5016A)

BLOOD & RHEUMATISM REMEDY
NO. 6088
MATT. J. JOHNSON CO.
ST. PAUL, MINN.

(5016B)

SIXTY-EIGHTY-EIGHT
(5016C)

4992 HALLIDAY'S, DR. E.B. BLOOD PURIFIER CO. 1897-1911
Samuel E. Blackford came to St. Paul in 1877, hoping to make his mark in the patent medicine business. He set up shop at 67 Wabasha Ave, below a photography studio, to manufacture and sell his product, Dr. E.B. Halliday's Blood Purifier. The Blood Purifier was advertised specifically for kidney and urinary diseases, female complaints, and general debility.

[HALSEY BROS. - See Druggist section]

4994 HARTMAN, M. E.   1897

4996 HAZLE, W. H.   1899-1904

4998 HEAL DRUG CO.   1898
4998A . 12 sides, Aqua

5000 HEAL, J. N.   1900-1906

5002 HORN, NICHOLAS   1899

[HOVORKA, W. J. - See Druggist section]

5004 HOYT MEDICINE CO.   1909-1913

5006 HURD, DR. W. J. MNFG. CO.   1894-1895

5008 HURLBUT, E. B.   1905-1906

[HURLEY BROS - See Whiskey section]

5010 HUTCHINS MEDICINE CO.   1909-1913

5012 JAPANESE MEDICAL CO.   1896-1903

5014 JAPANENE PILE CURE CO.   1896-1897

5016 JOHNSON, MATT J.   1901-1908
5016A . Style K5G; Aqua; H9 x L3 x W1-3/4
5016B . Style K5G; Aqua; H9 x L3 x W1-3/4
5016C . Style K5G; Aqua; H9 x L3 x W1-3/4
One of the nicer local patent medicines is the Matt Johnson Company "6088" bottle.

The company was named, logically enough, after Matt Johnson, its founder and president. He seems to have been a druggist in Duluth in the 1880's. In 1892 he moved his business to the other side of the bay, setting up at 627 Tower St., Superior, Wisconsin. He kept this location until 1896. Somewhere in the period prior to 1896, Mr. Johnson discovered the formula for "6088" and began selling it over the counter in his drug store. The demand was evidently heavy enough to warrant placing ads in the local papers, which brought even greater sales.

The Matthew J. Johnson company was founded in 1897 to manufacture "6088".

The main customer for "6088" was the Leithead Drug Company of Duluth, a wholesale and manufacturing concern. A Northwestern Druggist of that period reported that when the Matt Johnson Company made deliveries to Leithead they fitted their wagons out with flags and a small brass band and made something of a parade out of it.

Superior, Wisconsin, however, was an out-of-the-way spot, and as their business improved Johnson and company shopped around for a new location, finally deciding on and moving to St. Paul in June of 1901.

They evidently leased most of the building at 153 E. 6th St. with the ground floor being private and general offices, the second floor the manufacturing department and the third floor the bottling department. The basement was a storage area for whatever it was they mixed up to make "6088".

The business seems to have done well for several years, due as much to a large advertising budget as to any qualities the medicine might have had. "6088" was the only product made by the company. A second variant of the "6088" bottle is known, almost identical to the one shown, but embossed "remedy" instead of "cure". This was probably in response

(5018A)

(5025A)

(5025B—FRONT & BACK)

to the Pure Food and Drug laws and must date from after 1905. A third variant matches the St. Paul cure but is embossed, "West Superior, Wisconsin."

In 1906 the business moved to 396 Laurel Avenue, St. Paul, and their directory ads became smaller. Probably the business was beginning to slip, and by 1909 it disappeared completely. What happened to Mr. Johnson from this point on is unclear. One story is that he moved out west (Denver, it seems) and set himself up again in the patent medicine business. In any case, one collector has a paper labeled bottle which reads "New label adopted 1941. None genuine without signature. Copyrighted 1898 in U.S. and 1899 in Canada." The box reads "manufactured & distributed by Matt J. Johnson Co., Kasota, North Dakota, R. Roberts Reg't. Pharmacist."

5018 KA-DO-RA   ?
5018A . Style unknown; base embossing

5020 KELLEY CURTIS CO.   1902-1903

5022 KENDRICK, DR. CHEMICAL CO.   1905-1911
5022A . Style unknown

5024 KNAPP, W. B.   1902

5025 KOEHLER & HINRICH   1887-1916
Ferdinand Hinrichs was born in Germany, in 1860, into a family of modest means. Though his father was a lumber mill worker, and there were other mouths to feed (5 brothers), Ferdinand obtained some university education before immigrating with his family to America in 1877. The six brothers settled in Milwaukee. Ferdinand became a bookkeeper for a leather goods company until 1885, when he moved to St. Paul. That year, at age 25, he formed a wholesale grocery business with another young man, George W. Koehler, 23, of Wisconsin, as his junior partner.

Born in 1862 in Manitowoc, Wisconsin, George had been educated in the "common and high schools" of Manitowoc. He engaged in his father's merchandise business there until 1885 when he joined Hinrichs in St. Paul.

The firm, which was advertised in the city directory as "George W. Koehler and Ferdinand Hinrichs--Wholesale Dealers in Cheese, Pickled Fish, and Fancy Groceries," began modestly at the address of "St. Peter, S.W. corner of 4th."

A 1906 biographer said of the two partners, "They began on a small scale, but soon built up a large trade and employed a large number of men in both the house and as travelling salesmen upon the road."

As the grocery business prospered, the firm often changed location and added to its line of goods. From 1903 to 1910, Koehler & Hinrichs occupied their largest and grandest facility--225-265 E. 3rd St. It employed 80 people and filled a six story building and 100,000 square feet of storage and display space. Their trade extended to the East Coast, and annually the firm published an immense illustrated catalog of goods for their mail order business.

(5025D)

(5025F)

169

An observer in 1906 reported: "There are departments of fancy groceries, including the higher grades of imported and domestic canned and bottled delicacies; butcher's and packer's supplies; bar and glassware supplies; billiard & pool tables (which they manufacture on a large scale), bowling alleys; coin operated machines; hotel supplies; soft drinks; artificial flowers & palms; music boxes and talking machines, and other commodities for the wholesale trade."

It is probable that the Red Star Stomach Bitters and Ko-Hi Bitters were produced at this time as part of their bar and glassware or hotel supplies.

Hinrichs did not live to see his creation boom. Having married, in 1887, into the prominent Adolph Munch family of St. Paul, he died, well-to-do, in 1903, leaving a wife and two children residing in a substantial home that he had built.

Koehler, too, was socially prominent, married, and had two children. Highly respected in the St. Paul community, he was called, "a courteous, affable gentleman of personal charm and magnetism and of the highest business qualities."

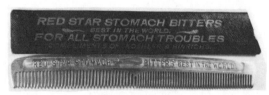

KOEHLER & HINRICHS,
Butchers' and Packers' Supplies.
CASINGS, ETC.
ENGLISH SHEEP CASINGS. | ACME OIL ENGINES.
53 & 55 WEST THIRD STREET, ST. PAUL, MINN.

KOEHLER & HINRICHS,
CHEESE, SAUSAGE, FISH.
FANCY GROCERIES.
EUROPEAN AND AMERICAN DELICACIES.
53 & 55 WEST THIRD STREET, · ST. PAUL, MINNESOTA

(5025C-FRONT)

(5025C-BACK)

5025A . Private mold; honey amber; H11-1/4xD3-1/2
5025B . Rotterdam Bitters; amber; H9xL3-1/2xW2-1/4
5025C . Comb
5025D . Mug
5025E . Mini Bitters; Amber; See photo
5025F . Fancy Shot Glass

5026 KRUSE, E. A.	1903
5028 LA FAVOR MEDICINE CO.	1912-1913
5030 LEAL, J. B.	1889-1890
5032 LIGHTNING DRUG CO.	1906
5034 MARKOE, J. C.	1907
5036 McKESSON & ROBINS	?

5036A . Style unknown; Clear;
5036B . Style unknown, Amber

McKESSON
& ROBBINS
(5036B)

McKESSON
&ROBBIN'S
(5036A)

[METZGER, ZIEN & CO - See Whiskey & Bitters sections]

5038 MICROCIDE CHEMICAL CO.	1905
5040 MINERO CHEMICAL CO.	1905
5042 MINNEHAHA SPRAY MED. CO.	1894-1897
5044 MINNESOTA PHARMACEUTICAL MNFG. CO.	1894-1913

5044A . Private mold; milk glass

5046 MINNESOTA VIAVI CO.	1896-1900
5048 M.I.S.T. CO.	1888-1890
5050 MOHN, R. M.	1894-1901
5052 MURNANE GERMICIDE CO.	1895-1896
5054 NELSON, WALTER	1894
5056 NORTHWESTERN DRUG CO.	1899-1903
5058 NORTHWESTERN MEDICINE CO.	1894-1907

5058A . Mamouth oval; amber

(5044A)

N.W. MED. CO.
BITTERS
(5058A)

171

PRUSSIAN SPAVIN CURE

(5084A)

(5094A)

THE RHEUMATOX CO.
RHEUMATOX
ST. PAUL, MINN. U.S.A.

Quaker Medical Association
Quaker Remedies
St. Paul, Minn.

(5086A)

PIERCE'S WHITE PINE & TAR BALSAM

PIERCE BROS CHEMISTS

(5080A)

DR. ROLANDER'S SWEDISH LINIMENT

(5098A)

[NOYES BROS. & CUTLER - See Household section]

5062 OLSON, H. B.	1898-1900
5064 ORIENTAL REMEDY CO.	1905
5066 PARKER, F. M. & CO.	1905-1907
5068 PARTRIDGE, A. P. & CO.	1888
5070 PASTEUR CATARRH REMEDY CO.	1897
5072 PASTEUR REMEDIES CO.	1903-1908
5074 PATTY, PROF. C. S. HERB REMEDIES	1910-1913
5076 PHILLIPS, F. F.	1897
5078 PHIPPS, GEORGE	1894-1901

5080 PIERCE BROS.   ?
5080A . Style A6C; Aqua; H7xL2-1/4xW1-1/8

5082 P. Q. MEDICINE CO.
  (A.P. Partridge Prop.)   1890-1912

5084 PRUSSIAN REMEDY CO.   1894-1912
5084A . Clear; H5-7/8xD2-1/4

5086 QUAKER MEDICAL ASSN   1894-1904
5086A . Style A6A; Clear; H5-1/2xL1-3/8xW1-3/4

5088 RADAMS MICROBE KILLER	1898-1908
5090 REED REMEDY CO.	1899-1905
5092 REEVES IRON PILLS CO.	1904-1909

5094 RHEUMATOX CO. THE   1895-1896
The Rheumatox company seens to have been a sideline for Chester L. Caldwell, a teacher at St. Paul Mechanic Arts High School. Caldwell's newspaper ads show that he had a pretty good store of medical knowledge, but this seems to have been no particular asset in the patent trade, and his company folded after 2 years.
5094A . Style A6G; Aqua; H8

5096 ROBERTS, J. J.   1901-1913

5098 ROLANDER SWEDISH REMEDY CO.   1903-1913
5098A . 12 sided; Aqua

GLYCOID
TAYLOR & MYERS PHAR. CO.
ST. PAUL, MINN.

(4760E)

COCA-CALISAYA TONIC
TAYLOR & MYERS PHARMACY CO.
109 E. 7TH STREET
ST. PAUL, MINN.

(4760F)

[SCHEIN, SAMUEL B. - See Whiskey section]

5100 SCHWEIGER, F. H.   1894

5102 SCHIFFMANN, R. CO.   1898-1913
  Mfgr. of "German Asthma Cure"

5104 SHAFER, J. W.   1903

5106 SHEPPARD, W. R.   1886-1895

5108 SIGLER, W. H. MNFG. CO.   1888-1911

5110 SILBERMAN, O & S   1886

5126 SWANSON MNFG. CO.   1903

5128 SWARTZ, G. R.   1894-1901

[TAYLOR & MEYERS - See St. Paul Druggist section]

5130 TIDBALL, F. I.   1913

5132 TWIN CITY DRUG CO.   1913

5134 UCALYPTOL CHEMICAL CO.   ?
5134A . Style unknown

5136 UNIVERSAL SUPPLY CO   1908

SIMON'S
AROMATIC STOMACH
BITTERS

SAMUEL B. SCHEIN
PROP. & MNFR.
ST. PAUL, MINN.

(1289A-FRONT & BACK)

(4771A)

[SIMON, B. - See Whiskey section]

5112 SNEDEKERS, D. R. REMEDY CO.   1903

5114 SPRAY CO.   1890

5116 SPRAY MEDICINE CO.   1889-1890

5118 ST. PAUL CHEMICAL OIL CO.   1894-1897

5120 ST. PAUL OXYGENOR CO.   1902

5122 ST. PAUL VIAVI CO.   1894-1908

5124 STEWARD, J. H.   1898-1905

5137 UPHAM, F.A. (OPTICIAN)
5137A . French square; Amber; H2-3/4 x L1 x W1

5138 UPHAM, F. A. & SON
5138A . French square; Amber; H2-3/4 x L1 x W1

5139 VIAVI CO.   1909-1913

5140 VIMEDIA CO.   1912-1913

5142 VOGUE, F. S.   1900-1902

5144 WALKER, GEORGE   1888-1889

5146 WALKER MEDICINE CO.   1887, 1894-1913

PYRO DENTIN
THE IDEAL ANTISEPTIC
UCALYPTOL CHEM. CO.
ST. PAUL, MINN.

(5134A)

UPHAM'S
EYE WATER
F. A. UPHAM & SON
ST. PAUL, MINN.

(5138A)

THE GREAT
FRENCH EYE WATER
F. A. UPHAM
ST. PAUL MINN.

(5137A)

5148 WERRICK, HENRY   1896

5150 WRIGHT MEDICINE CO., THE   1896-1897

5152 ZIEGLER, J. S.   1898

5154 Z-MEX-O-CO   ?
5154A . Private mold; Round; Clear; Shoulder
        embossing; H5-3/4 x D2-1/4; Extract Lip

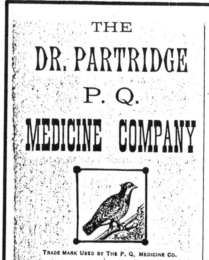

(5154A)

LATE ARRIVALS

(4828C)

9

PATENT MEDICINES

(EXCLUDING MINNEAPOLIS & ST PAUL)

Anoka

P20 GOODRICH & JENNINGS
            HOFFS GERMAN LINIMENT

Lumber, a river, and mills were the three things important to the pioneer Minnesota town of Anoka. By the 1850's Minnesota had become populated with strong, industrious men, and Herman Tichnor was one of these men. He arrived in 1850 and opened a dry goods and grocery store on the east side of the Rum River. He was the first store keeper in Anoka. He later moved to another lot and built the building which would eventually become the Goodrich and Jennings drug store.

On July 8, 1860, George Goodrich was born in Potville, Wisconsin. After attending normal school he became a teacher. Not satisfied, he moved in 1884 and settled in Anoka in 1886. He met and married Mary A. Funk that same year, and they had four children, two boys and two girls.

In 1887 Goodrich formed a partnership with a Mr. Jennings on Behive Avenue. At this location the famous Hoffs German Liniment was born and produced. The liniment was a great success and demand was almost overwhelming. Large quantities were sent to every state in the union.

Soon the firm was also operating a drug store on the corner of Nicollet and Lake in Minneapolis. By 1888 Goodrich had bought the stock of A.L. Peters and had moved into the Norell Block. Business prospered, and by 1902 he had bought the stock of H.L. Tichnor and had moved into the Tichnor Block on the main street of Anoka. By 1910 Goodrich had dropped the words "Jennings" and "German" from the brand name, calling it simply Hoff's Liniment and referring to his company as the Goodrich Drug Company, Anoka, Minnesota. In 1940 the company name changed to read Goodrich and Gamble. Today Hoff's Liniment, still original in all ingredients, is marketed nationally by Goodrich Universal Co., Inc. at 500 Robert Street, St. Paul, Minnesota.
P20A. Aqua; 12 sided; H5-1/2, H7
P20B. Clear; Round; Prescription Lip
P20C. Druggist Style

Arlington

P30 HELLEMAN   date unknown
P30A . Cobalt Blue and Clear; Common Whitehall Tatum Style bottle: H9-1/2; This rare bottle is one of the most desirable of all American cures. Still manufactured in 1935 by the Arlington Drug Company. Label says "enviable reputation" for "39 years".

Cambridge

P40 DR SONERAL   date unknown
P40A. Style A6A; Aqua; H7 x W1 x L2-1/4

Carver

P45 PARVENU MEDICINE CO   date unknown
P45A. Round; Aqua; H6 x D1; Double Roll Lip

HOFF'S
GERMAN
LINIMENT
(P20B)

HOFF'S GERMAN LINIMENT
GOODRICH & JENNINGS
ANOKA   MINN.
(P20A)

GOODRICH & JENNINGS
PRESCRIPTION DRUGGISTS
ANOKA, MINN.
(P20C)

HILLEMAN'S AMERICAN
CHICKEN CHOLERA CURE
ARLINGTON, MINN.
(P30A)

DR. SONERAL
DR. SONERAL'S
RHEUMATIC CURE
COMPANY
CAMBRIDGE, MINN.
(P40A)

PARVENU OIL
PREPARED ONLY BY THE
PARVENU MEDICINE CO.
CARVER, MINN. U.S.A.
(P45A)

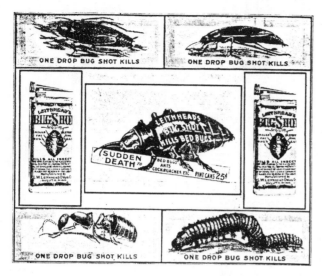

(P60C)

P90   FOSTER   date unknown
P90A. Aqua;

Mankato

P160   DR WARNERS MINNESOTA TONIC   circa 1880's
              WARNER'S MINNESOTA TONIC
   Information about this product has been hard to
find. However, a label on the bottle reads "One
wineglass full taken three times a day before
meals, will strengthen the stomach, arouse the
action of the liver & thereby cure all kinds of
dyspepsia & liver complaints. FOR INDIGESTION IT
IS UNEQUALED. A cure for all blood disorder,
consequently prevents boils, pimples, roughness of
skin and all conditions depending on bad blood. An
unfailing remedy as a tonic after fevers and any
disease that has prostrated the strength and vital
powers. As an antibillious alternative and safe
tonic under all circumstances it has no equal. As
a remedy for chronic RHEUMATISM, NEURALGIA, &
COSTIVENESS, IT EXCELS ALL. If one eats well and
digests well, he must get healthy in due time. An
agreeable and reliable tonic and stimulant under
any circumstances. Those who are weak, should
begin with small doses and increase as the strength
improves. WARNER BROTHERS originators, PROPRIETORS
& MANUFACTURES 86 S. Front Street, Mankato, Minn."

The Warner brothers started their drug business in
1869. Exactly when they first concocted their
tonic is unknown.

In 1880 druggist E. J. Segerstrom advertised that
he was manufacturing Warner's Minnesota Tonic,
Warner's Condition Powder and Warner's Asthma
Remedy from his office at 92 S. Front Street.
P160A. Amber; Square base

BERLINER MAGEN
BITTERS CO.

(P60B)

(P60A)

(P60D)

PURE NORWEGIAN
COD LIVER OIL
IMPORTED BY ALFRED SWEDBERG
DULUTH, MINN.

(P65A)

Duluth

P60   BERLINER MAGEN BITTERS CO   date unknown
      To date no research has been done on this
      company.
P60A. Amber;
P60B. Paper Label version of P60A
P60C. Dose Glass
P60D. Dose Glass

P65   SWEDBERG, ALFRED   date unknown
P65A. Rectangular; Clear; H8, Patent Lip

P70   MEDERINE REMEDY CO
P70A . Aqua; H10; Double Roll Lip; "MEDERINE"
       embossed on sides; paper label says "A BLOOD
       and CATARRH REMEDY"

(P160A)

Owatonna

P220 GOLDEN MEDICINE CO   date unknown
P220A. Aqua; Rectangular; H8-3/4; Embossed Panels;
  Double Roll Lip

Plainview

P240 LANDON & BURCHARD
  See Dr Ward's Liniment story under Winona for
information about this company.
P240A. Amber; Square Base

Sauk Centre

P300 STANDARD MEDICINE CO   date unknown
P300A. Amber

Sherburn

P320 NORGREN, C.E.   date unknown
  See Minneapolis Patent Medicine section for
additional bottles from C.E. NORGREN.
P320A. Style A5A; Aqua

St. Peter

P360A .Cobalt Blue; Druggist Style Bottle; only
  shards of this bottle have been found and the
  manufacturer is unknown.

Winona

P400 LANDON & BURCHARD
  See Dr Ward's Medicine Co story for information
about this company.
P400A . Aqua; Paper Label on the side of this bottle
reads "Wards BLOOD AND STOMACH BITTERS"

[McCONNAN & CO - See Minnesota Miscellaneous section]

P410 DR WARDS MEDICAL CO
                DR WARD'S LINIMENT
The history of Dr. Ward's Liniment begins in the
early 1850s when Richard Ward of Harrison, Ohio,
concocted an all-purpose liniment which he sold
under the names Ward's Botanical Liniment and R.
Ward's Botanical Liniment. Ward was called
"Doctor", but in reality was not a physician.

On July 16, 1856, Ward sold his formula to J. H.
Sands for $5. Sands was provided with labels from
Ward's own supply, and was given the sole right to
manufacture and sell the product in Minnesota
Territory. Sands moved to Winona, Minnesota
Territory, and the product rapidly gained wide
popularity. When the labels supplied by Ward ran
out, Sands printed new labels with the legend Dr.
Ward's Celebrated Liniment - the first use of a
trade name which was to become the subject of a
series of long and contentious lawsuits.

During the ensuing years several events led, with
almost glacial certainty, to the courts. In 1867
Richard Ward again sold the "rights" to his
liniment, selling the trade rights to Ward's
Celebrated Liniment in Minnesota, Iowa and Wisconsin
to J. R. Watkins of Plainview, Minnesota. Ward also
supplied Watkins with bottles embossed Wards's
Liniment, and agreed that he would patent the

GOLDEN LINIMENT
MANF'D BY
GOLDEN MEDICINE CO.
OWATONNA, MINN.

(P220A)

LANDON & BURCHARD
DR. WARD'S
BARB WIRE CURE
PLAINVIEW, MINN.

(P240A)

DR. WARD'S
LINIMENT MADE BY
LANDON & BURCHARD
PLAINVIEW, MINN.

(P240B)

STANDARD MEDICINE COMPANY
MURPHY'S KIDNEY &
LIVER CURE
AN EXCELLENT TONIC
SAUK CENTRE, MINN.

(P300A)

FRISCO COUGH SYRUP
C.E. NORGREN
MANUFACTURED
SHERBURN, MINN

(P320A)

POULTRY REMEDY
MFG BY
ST. PETER, MINN.

(P360A)

formula. Unfortunately for Watkins, the formula was never patented. Watkins sold the liniment using Ward's bottles and labels until the supply was exhausted, and then began to produce new bottles, and labels featuring his own name.

Watkins threatened to sue Sands for the use of the trade-name in 1868. Sands, who could not afford the expense of a trial at that time, began calling his product J. H. Sand's Celebrated Liniment.

On May 14, 1870, Watkins registered two trade-marks: Dr. Ward's Vegetable Anodyne Liniment, for use on paper labels, and Dr. Ward's Liniment, to be embossed on the side-panels of bottles.

During the following fifteen years Watkins also sold the liniment in bulk form to the firm of Landon & Burchard, also of Plainview, who sold the product labeled as Dr. Ward's Liniment, Landon & Burchard Druggists, Plainview, Minnesota. It was Watkins' own retail sales of his product, however, that led to rapid growth of the company, and to a move to larger quarters in Winona in 1885. The liniment sales in those early years established the great Watkins empire.

When Watkins left for Winona in 1885, Landon & Burchard began to manufacture and sell a similar liniment, which they called Dr. Hoffman's Vegetable Anodyne. The labels on these bottles were identical to the labels then used by Watkins, with the exception of the product and company names, giving mute testimony to the fierce competition for the lucrative liniment trade.

Then, on February 27, 1889, Landon & Burchard purchased Ward's original formula and "right to sell" from Sands, which they began to produce as Dr. Ward's Liniment, labeling the product as they had when they purchased it bulk from Watkins. A year later the firm of Batterton Bros. purchased all rights to a liniment from Richard Ward, who seemed to have no end of "rights" to sell! Battenton Bros. then sold whatever they had acquired to Watkins in 1891.

Thus, the stage was set for the first in the series of legal battles over Dr. Ward's Liniment. In 1891 Watkins sued Landon & Burchard, asking for $4,000 in damages and an order preventing their use of that or any similar trade-name. By 1893 the case was before the Minnesota Supreme Court and Landon & Burchard won the right to use the name, but also were ordered to use distinctive labels which identified their product as being manufactured and sold by themselves.

The Court found that Landon & Burchard had lawfully acquired the knowledge of an unpatented formula, and therefore could manufacture the liniment. This was, of course, the case with most "patent" medicines. The medicines were not actually patented and the manufacturers were forced to great efforts to keep their formulas secret.

As for the trade-name, the Court stated that since Landon & Burchard could legally make the liniment, they could also identify it as being from the original formula. The Court ruled that Watkins couldn't appropriate the name as a trade-mark, because it had been in wide use long before Watkins had attempted to register it, and was used as a descriptive term.

179

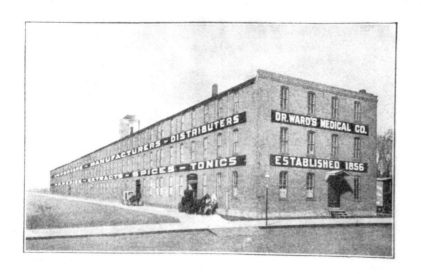

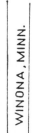

LANDON & BURCHARD

Dr.Ward's 1856 Medicines

(P400A)

WINONA, MINN.

CREAMOLA

DR. WARD'S

MEDICAL CO

WINONA

MINN.

(P410B)

1856

DR.WARD'S

MEDICAL CO.

WINONA

MINN.

(P410C)

As a result of this decision, Watkins registered another trade-mark in 1893, claiming the words Dr. Ward's with a line drawn through them horizontally. The mark was registered for use on labels and bottles.

On January 11, 1894, J. R. Watkins reorganized his company as the J. R. Watkins Medical Company, transferring all rights in the liniment to the company. The name change is one of the best ways to determine the approximate age of many Watkins and Ward's Liniment bottles.

In 1895 the J.R. Watkins Medical Company sued Landon & Burchard for perjury, fraud, and subornation of perjury, claiming that they had induced J. H. Sands to forge his bill of sale from Richard Ward, and to perjure his testimony in the earlier trial. Watkin's timing of the second suit is at least a little suspicious, since Sands had died the year before and was no longer able to defend his own good name.

Thus, after three cases which had been fought all the way to the State Supreme Court, Watkins had lost on every issue, with the small exception of the order directing Landon & Burchard to make their labels distinctive in appearance. Perhaps these futile efforts are the reason that, a short time later, Watkins changed the name of the product to the much simpler Watkins Liniment.

By 1900 Landon & Burchard had reorganized as the Dr. Ward's Medical Company, with Mr. Landon as president, and they too, had moved to Winona. They had also begun to produce Dr. Ward's Kidney Compound, a concoction of which Richard Ward had undoubtedly never heard.

J.R. WATKINS - PLAINVIEW, MN.	1867-1885
J.R. WATKINS - WINONA, MN.	1885-1894
J.R. WATKINS MEDICAL CO. - Winona, MN.	1894-1982
LANDON & BURCHARD - Plainview, MN.	1870-1900
DR. WARD'S MEDICAL CO. - Winona, MN.	1900-?

(P410A)

(P410D)

(P240A)

The 1895 lawsuit, like the prior one, did the Watkins Company little good, however. By 1897 the case had been before the State Supreme Court and Watkins had lost because it could have asserted the same claims at the first trial, and because the three year statute of limitations on such claims had expired.

And the Watkins Company's troubles were still not finished. That same year J. H. Sands Jr. began to manufacture and sell Dr. Ward's Vegetable Liniment and Dr. Ward's Vegetable Oil Liniment using the formula he had learned as a boy while helping his father.

So the J.R. Watkins Medical Company went to court again in 1900, seeking $2000 in damages and an order preventing Sands Jr. from using the Dr. Ward's name. A year later the cast was before the Minnesota Supreme Court, and once again Watkins lost. As before, the Court found that, because Sands Jr. had learned the unpatented formula in a lawful way, he had a right to use it. The same applied to the use of the "descriptive name" Dr. Ward's. And the Court went further on this occasion, saying that Watkins could not register other descriptive names such as "vegetable liniment" or "vegetable anodyne liniment."

P410A. Aqua; Sarsaparilla Style
P410B. Clear; Blake Style; Prescription Lip; H5-1/4 x W2 x L1-3/8
P410C. Style Unknown
P410D. Metal Scraper

[McCONNAN & CO - see Minnesota Miscellaneous section in Volume 1]

P420 WATKINS, J. R. MEDICINE CO
         "THE MAN WITH THE MARKET BASKET"
              J.R. Watkins Company
The man with the market basket...or something similar...was a familiar figure in 1868 when the young Joseph R. Watkins founded The J.R. Watkins Company. The son of the Reverend B.U. Watkins, of Hamilton County, Ohio, Joseph R. Watkins was born in Cincinnati, Ohio, on August 21, 1840, and moved to Minnesota with the rest of his family in 1862.

In 1868 Mr. Watkins, then 28 years old, secured from a Dr. Richard Ward of Cincinnati, Ohio, the right to manufacture and sell medicines compounded by Dr. Ward. Chief among those medicines was a

WATKINS' EXTRACTS

J.R.WATKINS MED.CO.

J.R.Watkins
PRESIDENT

WINONA, MINN. U.S.A.

(P420A)

DR.WARD'S REMEDIES

J.R.WATKINS
MEDICAL COMPANY
PROPRIETORS

TRADE MARK DR.WARD'S

WINONA, MINN.

(P420B)

J.R.WATKIN'S
PROPRIETOR
WINONA, MINN.

TRADE MARK DR.WARD'S

(P420C)

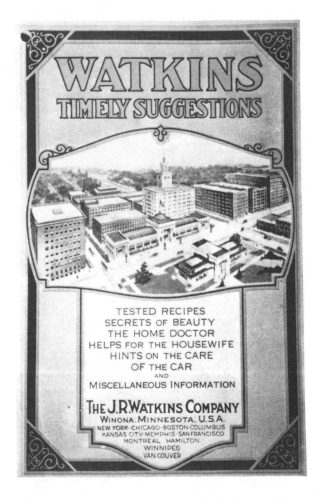

WATKINS
TIMELY SUGGESTIONS

TESTED RECIPES
SECRETS OF BEAUTY
THE HOME DOCTOR
HELPS FOR THE HOUSEWIFE
HINTS ON THE CARE
OF THE CAR
AND
MISCELLANEOUS INFORMATION

THE J.R.WATKINS COMPANY
WINONA, MINNESOTA, U.S.A.
NEW YORK·CHICAGO·BOSTON·COLUMBUS
KANSAS CITY·MEMPHIS·SAN FRANCISCO
MONTREAL HAMILTON
WINNIPEG
VAN COUVER

---

liniment which Dr. Ward had used quite successfully in his own practice. He began to make and sell Dr. Ward's Liniment in the neighborhood of Plainview, Minnesota, a town situated about 50 miles from Winona. He mixed up the ingredients in the family kitchen, bottled the product by hand in the woodshed and marketed it by the simple expedient of loading the bottled liniment into a market basket, climbing into his buggy, putting the basket under the seat and making a tour of nearby farms and villages. It was not long before the liniment became widely known in southern Minnesota and young Watkins' tours covered more and more territory. Gradually he began to spend days and later weeks on the road, selling the liniment and other items. The liniment, however, was his leader.

Even then he had formulated the selling idea that later made Watkins Liniment and Watkins products a household word in thousands of homes; the idea was simple...satisfaction or money refunded. In the case of the liniment, young Watkins had his bottles molded with a "trial mark" part way down the side. The customer who purchased a bottle was told to use the liniment down to the "trial mark." If by that time she was not satisfied she was instructed to hold the bottle until Watkins returned when he would pick it up and refund her money. Very few were ever returned.

For 17 years thereafter J.R. Watkins sold his liniment within a radius of possibly 50 to 100 miles of his home. Gradually he added other items-extracts, salves, home remedies of various kinds... and the business grew slowly. Then, in 1885, he made the move that eventually resulted in the world-wide development of the J.R. Watkins Company; he moved his little business to Winona, Minnesota, a thriving town of 15,000 or so, situated on the banks of the Mississippi River. Logging and lumber milling were the chief business enterprises in Winona at that time and the town swarmed with lumberjacks...it can safely be said that they found good use for the liniment. More important, however, was the fact that with the river steamboats making regular stops at Winona and with the Chicago, Milwaukee and St. Paul railroad coming through, facilities for expanding the business beyond the backyard stage were readily available. Watkins, then 45 years old, rented a four-room frame house, living in two of the rooms and using the other two for manufacturing purposes. As an assistant, he employed a 14 year old boy, George Smith, who started in washing bottles and later graduated to mixing liniment in large barrels. George Smith thus became the first Watkins employee

WATKINS DANDRUFF REMOVER
AND
SCALP TONIC

(P420E)

J.R.WATKINS MEDICAL CO.
WINONA, MINN.U.S.A.

(P420D)

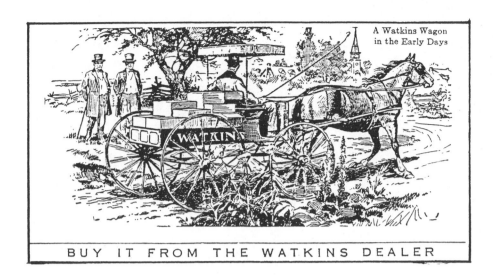

A Watkins Wagon in the Early Days

BUY IT FROM THE WATKINS DEALER

(P420H)

(P420F)

A WATKINS STORE AT YOUR DOOR

The trucks and wagons of Watkins Dealers, if lined up for parade, would make a procession ten miles long and would take three hours to pass a given point!

The Watkins Dealer

BUY IT FROM THE WATKINS DEALER

183

(P420G)

and continued with the company until 1947 when he retired after 60 years of continuous service.

In the years following 1885, the number of "wagon salesmen" featuring Watkins products began to increase steadily and the salesmen themselves began to recruit others in increasingly distant localities.

By this time Mr. Watkins began to think of the business in larger terms. A two-story factory building was erected in Winona and the "Watkins Line" made its appearance, consisting of Watkins Liniment, Watkins Improved Condition Powder, Watkins Egyptian Stick Salve, Watkins Vegetable Cathartic Pills and Watkins Petro-Carbo Salve. Specially printed labels adorned the products, bearing the picture and facsimile signature of J.R. Watkins.

In 1893 the first Watkins Branch House was established in San Francisco, California, later the unit was moved to Oakland. The second branch was located in Memphis, Tennessee in 1910 and in 1912 a third was established in Baltimore and later moved to New York and still later to Newark, New Jersey. The branches functioned mainly as distributing points. Gradually, however, manufacturing facilities were installed at all these branches.

Mr. Watkins brought a nephew into the business and in 1911, when Mr. Watkins died unexpectedly in Jamaica, Paul Watkins became president of the company. A Mr. E.L. King, Sr. also joined the firm and later married the daughter of J.R. Watkins.

About 1911 plans were made for erecting the magnificent administration building which now houses the Watkins home offices at Winona, Minnesota. In 1912 the building was erected and became a familiar view to thousands of customers the world over, through the millions of advertising pieces distributed by Watkins dealers.

In 1931 Paul Watkins died and E.L. King, Sr. became the president of the company. He had married Grace Watkins and two children were born of that marriage. E.L. King, Jr. later became president of the company and at the present his sons David and Fred are serving the company as President and Vice President. With the exception of the years 1965 to 1973 the firm has maintained the Watkins-King "family leadership."

P420A. Style Unknown
P420B. Style Unknown
P420C. Style Unknown
P420D. Style Unknown
P420E. Style Unknown
P420F. Jug
P420G. Jug

P425 PROCHOWICZ, A.   date unknown
P425A . Style Unknown

RHEUMATISM OINTMENT
PAT'D. AP'L. 17. 1888
A. PROCHOWICZ. WINONA MINN.

(P425A)

P430 WEYEHGRAM, DR. H.   date unknown
P430A. H8-1/2; Style Unknown

Dr. H. Weyehgrams

HERBAL MEDICINES

WINONA. MINN.
(P430A)

McCONNON & CO.
McCONNON'S
COUGH CURE
WINONA, MINN.
(M810B)

McCONNON & CO
DR. TOLSTOIS
LIFE PROLONGER
WINONA, MINN.
(M810D)

McCONNON & CO.
DR. TOLSTOIS
CAUCASIAN LINIMENT
WINONA, MINN.
(M810E)

Campho-Sene
COLDS-CATARRA
CAMPHO-SENE-CO
MANKATO, MINN.

(P145A)

VON ROHR'S REMEDIES
(P427A-A WINONA COMPANY)

McCONNON & CO.
DR. MALAKOFF'S
CONSUMPTION CURE
WINONA, MINN.
(M810F)

10
MINNESOTA
BITTERS

(1210N & 1210Q-4 SIZES OF APPETINE BITTERS FROM 3-1/2" TO 8" HIGH)

(P60A FRONT)

(P60A BACK)

Minnesota is blessed with a number of fine bitters. However, most of these bitters are also very rare and limited to five or less known specimens. Therefore, few collectors have the opportunity to see all the Minnesota bitters and become familiar with them. This guide attempts to list all the embossed or labeled Minnesota bitters as well as bitters for which advertisements have been seen but specimens are not known.

ALLEN'S IRON TONIC BITTERS (No specimens known)
An 1890 newspaper ad said J.P. Allen of St. Paul manufactured this bitters. This product advertised as early as 1885 and late as 1894.
AMERICAN STOMACH BITTERS (No specimens known)
A paper labeled bitters from Duluth.
APPETINE BITTERS (Embossed)
This beautiful, ornate and highly desirable bottle may also be the most common Minnesota bitters. The embossing on the side reads "GEO. BENZ & SONS APPETINE BITTERS ST. PAUL, MINN." and on the base reads "PAT. NOV 23, 1897". It's common color is amber but is also found in black amethyst. Four sizes are known, 8-1/2", 6-1/2", 4-1/4" and 3-1/2" high. This bottle is also found unembossed except for the patent information on the base. The black amethyst bottle has a plain base and the scrollwork is different than that on the amber bottles.

BENSON'S HEALTH BITTERS (Paper label only)
 Manufactured by Benson & Kendall of Winona, Minn.
 A variant label says manufactured by Chas. Benson.
BERLINER MAGEN BITTERS (Paper label only)
 A dose glass advertises this bitters as
 manufactured by J.P. Zien, Duluth, Mn. The bottle
 is amber and square.
BUEL'S BUCHONA BITTERS (No specimens known)
 An 1894 ad reads "B.B.B. the T.T.T. - The true
 temperance tonic, Buel's Buchon Bitters Co., Sole
 Proprietors & Manufacturers, Duluth, MN."
CHAMPION STAR BITTERS (No specimens known)
 The early 1870's city directories advertised this
 bitters as manufactured by H.M. Martin of
 Minneapolis. Several variations of hutch sodas are
 known from Martin who also manufactured Star Cronk
 Beer.
COLUMBIAN STOMACH BITTERS (Paper label only)
 The paper label reads "1893 the best tonic and
 appetizer... Webster Chemical Co., Saint Paul,
 Minnesota." The bottle is a square "Hostetter's"
 style, amber, 8-1/2" high.

(SIDE VIEW OF HURLEY BROS PEPSINIZED
BITTERS 1258B & EDGE VIEW OF 996C)

(1213F)

DIGESTINE
BITTERS
P.J. BOWLIN & SON
SOLE PROPRIETORS
ST. PAUL MINN.
(1214A)

DIGESTINE
BITTERS
(1213G)

(3728A)

CURRAN'S HERB BITTERS PEPSINISED (Embossed)
 This rectangular, green bottle has ribbed and
 beveled edges. Embossing on the other side reads
 "THE NAPA VALLEY WINE CO. MINNEAPOLIS, MINN.".
 This company operated from 1888 to 1913.
CURRAN'S HERB BITTERS PEPSINISED (Embossed)
 This bottle is the identical shape as the bottle
 put out by the Napa Valley Wine company except that
 it is amber in color and the embossing on the other
 side reads "HURLEY BROS. ST. PAUL, MINN.".
DAKOTA BITTERS (No specimens known)
 The Minneapolis City Directory advertised this
 bitters as manufactured by C.A. Mann from 1882 to
 1884.
DIGESTINE BITTERS (Embossed)
 This spectacular bottle rivals the Appetine Bitters
 for the title of most desirable Minnesota bitters.
 The remaining front panel embossing reads "P.J.
 BOWLIN LIQUOR COMPANY SOLE PROPRIETORS ST PAUL
 MINN".
 A second variant of this bottle has the words
 changed to "P.J. BOWLIN & SONS SOLE PROPRIETORS ST
 PAUL MINN". A third variant is a 3-1/4" high
 miniature embossed simply "Digestine Bitters."
 Bowlin started in the St. Paul liquor business in
 1869 and incorporated with his sons in 1897.

186

(1269B) (1268C)

DR DUNLOP'S ANCHOR BITTERS (Embossed)
This amber rectangular bottle was produced by the "ARCTIC MANUFACTURING CO. MINNEAPOLIS" (note misspelling on bottle) about 1881-1883.

DR BOPP'S HAMBURGER STOMACH BITTER (marked stoneware jug) The wording on the jug reads "METZGER ZIEN & CO DISTILLERS ST. PAUL MINN. Sole Agents For The U.S. for Dr. Bopp's Hamburger Stomach Bitters".

DR F. J. HORTENBACH LIFE BITTERS (Paper label only)
Label also reads "Sole PROP. TWIN CITIES MINN". The city directories listed Frank Hortenbach as a medicine manufacturer from 1897-1899, bitters manufacturer from 1900-1911.

DR FRENCH BITTERS (No specimens known)
The 1882 St. Paul city directory advertised Merell, Sahlgaard & Thwing as the manufacturers of this product.

DOCTOR GREGORY'S SCOTCH BITTERS (Embossed)
As early as 1869 a newspaper advertised this bitters for sale in Minneapolis. The city directories provide the following listing of manufacturers for the product.

    Young, Patterson & Co. (Mpls) 1875-1880
    Nichol's Medicine Co. (St. Paul) 1896-1905
    Spink & Co. (Mpls) 1880-1896

Unembossed versions of this bitters with paper labels for Spink & Co., and Nichol's Medicine Co. are known.

DR WARD'S BLOOD AND STOMACH BITTERS (Paper label only)
Label reads "Mfg only by Dr. Ward's Medical Co., Winona".

HURLEY BROS.
PEPSINIZED BITTERS
HURLEY BROS.
ST. PAUL, MINN.

(1258B)

HURLEY BROS.
BITTERS
HURLEY BROS.
ST. PAUL, MINN.

(1258C)

CURRAN'S HERB BITTERS
PEPSINIZED
HURLEY BROS.
ST. PAUL, MINN.

(1258D)

FORCE STOMACH BITTERS (No specimens known)
A 1902 newspaper advertised this product as manufactured by KOEHLER & HEINRICH.

GRIGG'S AROMATIC BITTERS (No specimens known)
An 1869 St. Paul Pioneer newspaper ad stated "NOYES BROS GENERAL AGENTS FOR THE NORTHWEST".

HARVEST BITTERS (No specimens known)
An 1874 ad says this bitters was made by Dr. F.B. HINKLEY of Sheldon, Minn.

HURLEY BROS BITTERS (Embossed)
An amber colored bottle similar in shape to Currans Herb Bitters and Hurley Bros Pepsinized Bitters.

HURLEY BROS PEPSINIZED BITTERS (Embossed)
This amber bottle is similar in shape to the Currans Herb Bitters. Embossing on the other side reads "HURLEY BROS ST. PAUL MINN."

JENNER (No specimens known)
The Minneapolis City Directory listed Bernhardt Jenner as a "bitters manufacturer in the 1890's".

KENSUFAN STOMACH BITTER (No specimens known)
KENNEDY, STUFFEL & ANDREWS, a Minneapolis wholesale drug company, advertised this product in 1904-1905.

(3996E)

187

(5025B-FRONT)

(5025B-BACK & 5025E)

(M810A)

KO-HI BITTERS (Embossed)
   An unusually shaped amber colored bottle. The embossing on the back reads KOEHLER & HINRICHS ST. PAUL. Two variants of the bottle are known, full size and 3-1/2" sample size.

LOCK HORN BITTERS (No specimens known)
   Advertisement for this product was found on a Globe Wine Co. Minneapolis corkscrew.

MCCONNON'S STOMACH BITTERS (Embossed)
   An amber colored rectangular bottle. The remaining embossing reads "MCCONNON & COMPANY WINONA MINN."

NIX BITTERS (No specimens known)
   An 1874 ad says this bitters was made by B.N. OHLHOUSE of Rushford, Minn.

N.W. MED CO. BITTERS (Embossed)
   The paper label on this bottle reads "PCL BITTERS" (maybe "CPL BITTERS"?). The product was manufactured by the Northwestern Medicine Company of St. Paul 1894-1907.

OLD BETTS BITTERS (No specimens known)
   Advertised as manufactured in St. Paul, by A. Hirschman.

OLD KENTUCKY BITTERS (No specimens known)
   Advertised in 1905 as manufactured by Rea Bros. & Co. of Minneapolis, Louisville, and New York.

OMEGA BITTERS (Paper label only)
   Manufactured by BUEGER & MATSCHINGER of St. Paul.

ORIENTAL HERB BITTERS (Paper label only)
   Manufactured by L.S. LOEB & CO. Duluth, Mn.

P.C.L. BITTERS (See N.W. MED Co. Bitters)

RED STAR STOMACH BITTERS (Embossed)
   A fancy, amber colored, cylindrical bottle produced by KOEHLER & HINRICHS of St. Paul.

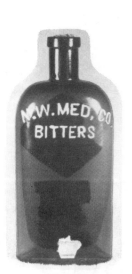

(5058A)

(LABEL ON BACK OF 5058A)

(5025A)

(1204B)

SIMON'S AROMATIC STOMACH BITTERS (Embossed)
   Back embossing reads "SAMUEL B. SCHEIN PROP & MNFR
   ST PAUL MINN." B. Simon of St. Paul manufactured
   this bitters from 1898-1910. Samuel B. Schein
   manufactured the product from 1910-1913.
SOUTHWARD'S PERUVIAN BITTERS (No specimens known)
   An 1870 newspaper ad says this product was
   manufactured by E. SOUTHWARD, a Minneapolis
   druggist.
ST AUGUSTINE BITTERS (Embossed)
   Remaining embossing reads "ABERLE- WESTHEIMER CO
   SOLE PROPRIETORS ST. PAUL MINN". This liquor
   dealership was in business from 1897-1904. About a
   dozen of these bottles were found (most broken) in
   the Irene, South Dakota dump.
SWISS ALPINE HERB STOMACH BITTERS (No specimens known)
   A 1902-1903 directory ad attributed this bitters to
   N. Jaax at 1101 Main St. N.E., Mpls., Mn.

(1289A-BACK)

(1289A-FRONT)

(3788A)

"Standard of
Excellence."

Old
Kentucky
Bitters

ESTABLISHED 1857

Endorsed by physi-
cians and the general
public. The genuine
made only by Rea
Bros & Co. To the
trade, $7.50 per dozen
large size or 2 dozen
small size.

Distributors for

Pure Old Trimble Co. Ky. Hand Made Rye Whiskey
Shipped either from their ware house or from the
Greenwood Distillery, Milton, Trimble Co., Ky. Price
per case of 1 dozen short quarts $8.50; pints, $8.75; half
pints $9.00. Per gallon, $2.50.

REA BROS. & CO.,
Wholesale Druggists. Manufacturing Chemists.
MINNEAPOLIS.   LOUISVILLE.   NEW YORK

VAN BIBBER BITTERS (Paper label only)
   The label says manufactured by DANIEL ABERLE & SONS
   ST. PAUL, which dates it to after 1904.
VEGETABLE TONIC BITTERS (Marked stoneware jug)
   The wording on this jug reads "VEGETABLE TONIC
   BITTERS DIME REMEDY CO. MINNEAPOLIS". An extremely
   rare product that could be the prize in anybody's
   collection.
WILD CHERRY BITTERS (Paper label only)
   The label says this product was manufactured by Max
   Adler of Minneapolis.
WOLD'S TONIC BITTERS (No specimens known)
   Manufactured by O.O. WOLD, a St. Paul druggist.

(LABEL ON 1201F)

INDEX

BUTLER, M.J., 121
BYRNES, WILLIAM J., 83

CABLE & JUDD, 83
CABLE, F.M., 83
CALDWELL, CHESTER L., 172
CALIFORNIA CHEMICAL CO., 153
CALIFORNIA WINE DEPOT, 33-38
CALIFORNIA WINE HOUSE, 18,48,57,73
CALLAHAN, STEPHAN, 73
CAMDON TONIC CO., MADAM, 153
CAMILLA BRANDY (BOWLIN), 57
CAMP NELSON BOURBON, 56,57
CAMPBELL BROS., 122
CAMPBELL BROS. & ST. CLAIR, 122
CAMPBELL MEDICINE CO., 166
CAMPBELL, A.A., 121,166
CAMPBELL, D.R., 122
CAMPBELL, J.E., 122
CANNON DIGESTIVE JUICE, 153
CANNON, C.H. & CO., 122
CAPITAL DRUG CO, 122
CAPITAL PHARMACY - SEE ZIMMERMANN
CAPPELL, JOHN F., 122
CARDINAL REMEDY CO., 153
CARLSON, C.E. LITTLE FALLS, 70
CARLSON, FRANK A., 72
CARON, ARRESTIDE, 83
CARROTHERS, W.H., 122
CASE - SEE RUSSEL & CASE
CASE, J.W., 83
CASINO, THE, 19
CASWELL'S BLOOD CLEANER, 164
CATARACT DRUG STORE (SEE BENNER, WEBSTER)
CAVANAUGH, C.A., 83
CENTRAL DRUG CO., 83
CENTRAL DRUG STORE, 122
CENTRAL PHARMACY, 122
CENTRAL WINE CO., 19,24
CHADBOURNE & JOFFOSS, 83
CHAMBERLAIN - SEE TUPPER & CHAMBERLAIN
CHAMPION STAR BITTERS, 186
CHAMPLIN - SEE ALLEN & CHAMPLIN
CHAPIN & HARTFIELD, 122
CHARENDON DRUG CO., 122
CHASE - SEE ALLEN & CHASE
CHENEY, I.L., 153
CHERRY, D.S., 83
CHIEF MOUNTAIN ASH, 153
CHILDS, E., 83
CHILSTROM - SEE PATTERSON & CHILSTROM
CHILSTROM & CO., 83
CHILSTROM DRUG CO., 83
CHILSTROM, C.E., 83
CHILSTROM, MATILDA, 83
CHURCHILL & SCHELDRUP, 83
CHURCHILL, G.S., 83

CIRKLER, C.H., 83,154,82,114
CITY DRUG STORE, 122
CITY DRUG STORE - SEE MELENDY & LYMAN
CITY HALL PHARMACY, 84
CLARK & FROST, 122,166
CLARK & HARRIS, 84
CLARKE, A.H., 84
CLASON, J.J., 154
CLAYTON & CO., M.A., 154
CLEVENGER, WM., 154
CLIFFORD, CHARLES, 166
CLOUGH, C.F., 122
CLOUGH, L.H., 154
CLUB, THE, 73
COAN, M.E., 122
COATES, JOHN, 69
COBB, DR. S.G., 166
COBB, WM. S., 84
COCA-CALISAYA TONIC, 168,173
COFFIN, W.A., 84
COLBERG & PAEHLER, 122
COLBRATH & RUSSELL, 84,100
COLBRATH & THOMPSON, 84
COLBRATH, W.C., 84
COLBRATH, W.N., 84
COLE, A.L., 84
COLE, DANFORTH, 154
COLLIER - SEE HIPPLER & COLLIER
COLLIER, W.K., 122
COLLINS, F.H., 84
COLTON & CO., 84
COLUMBIA MEDICINE CO., 166
COLUMBIA STOMACH BITTERS, 186
COLUMBIA WINE HOUSE, 57
COMB, RICHARD F., 122
COMMERCIAL, THE - SEE EISCHLAGER
COMO DRUG CO., 84
COMSTOCK, A.W., 84
CONDIT - SEE LAMBIE & CONDIT
CONDIT & LAMBIE, 84,130
CONDIT, A.D., 122
CONGER, BROS., 123,166
CONGER, F.A., 122
CONGERS WHITE PINE COUGH COMPOUND, 166
CONTINENTAL CATERING, 14
COOK - SEE NOBLE & COOK
COOK & NOBLE, 123
COOK, MRS. CLARA, 84
COOPER - SEE WEINHOLD BROS.
COOPER REMEDY, 166
COPP - SEE BELDEN & COPP
COREY, C.A., 84
CORNELL, M.C., 84
COURTNEY PHARMACY, 124
COWIN, G.A., 84
CRANDALL & BAKER, 124
CRASPER - SEE SHUMPIK & CRASPER
CREAMERY BUFFET, 19
CRESCENT BRAND (SMITH), 34
CRESCENT DRUG STORE - SEE L.A. BROWN

CROCKER - SEE FEELEY & CROCKER
CROCKER & THOMPSON, 84,154
CROCKER, GEORGE, 84
CROCUS HILLS PHARMACY, 124
CROOKS - FRAYER MFG. CO., 166
CROOKS, S.S. MFG. CO., 166
CROSBY DRUG CO., 85
CROSMAN & PLUMMER, 85
CROSMAN, C.F., 85
CROW, C.E., 85
CROW, JAMES, 85
CROWELL, A.B., 85
CROWELL, F.W., 85
CROWN SAMPLE ROOM - SEE M.D. SVENSON
CUBAN MEDICINE CO., 154
CURIO OLD RYE (ZIEN), 69
CURRAN'S HERB BITTERS PEPSINISED, 29,159,186
CUTRATE DRUG STORE - SEE HUGHES
CY-DO-LINE, 167

DAHL, HANS, 124
DAKOTA BITTERS, 186
DALE STREET PHARMACY, 124
DAMM - SEE JENNINGS & DAMM
DAMM, L.F., 85
DAMM, OLAF, 20,50
DANEK & SHUMPIK, 85
DANEK'S PHARMACY, 85
DANEK, J.F., 85
DANEK, JOHN, 154
DANIELSON'S DRUG CO., 85
DANIELSON, F.J., 85
DAVENPORT & SCHOELL, 124
DAVENPORT, GEORGE C., 124
DAVIDSON - SEE PROCTOR & DAVIDSON
DAVIDSON, F.P., 124
DAVIDSON, J.P., 154
DAVIS & BIGELOW, 85
DAVIS, J.M., 20,50
DAVIS, J.T., 72
DAVIS, S.S., 85
DAY - SEE GRIFFIN & DAY
DAY & CO., 85
DAY & JENKS, 124
DAY, J.H. & CO., 124
DAY, JOHN H., 85
DAYOLHEASALE, CHIEF, 154
DAYTONS BLUFF PHARMACY, 124
DE RAICHE DRUG CO., 85
DE RAICHE, EMIL D., 85
DE RAICHE, MONS, 86
DE VOE & BUTLER, 86
DE VOE BROS., 86
DE VOE, CHARLES M., 86
DEAD SHOT REMEDY CO., 154
DEAN, A.P., 85
DEER PARK DISTILLERY CO., 58
DENEK - SEE KADLEC & DENEK
DENNELL, E.L., 21
DENTORIS, 154
DEPT OF HEALTH, 166

DERMOLA, 155
DETTLOFF, F.E., 124
DEUTSCHER RATHSKELLER, 48
DEVELDA DRUG CO., 176
DEVILLIERS, A.W., 72
DEVILLIERS, C.H., 72
DIAMOND CHEMICAL CO., 166
DIBB, T.J., 124
DICKMAN BROS., 124
DICKMAN, G.A., 124
DICKMAN, H.W., 124
DICKSON CHEMICAL CO., 166
DIEMERT, W.H., 71
DIEMERT & MURPHY, 71
DIETZ, JOHN, 73
DIGESTINE BITTERS, 56,166,186
DILLIN DRUG CO., 86
DIME REMEDY CO., 154,189
DINSMORE, W.E., 86
DINWOOD & WYLLIE, 124
DOCTOR GREGORY'S SCOTCH BITTERS, 185
DOCTORS SPECIAL (BENZ), 53
DONAHUE, J.C., 21
DONALDSON'S L.S., 86
DONALDSON'S PHARMACY, 86
DONALDSON'S WM. & CO., 86
DORAN, J.E., 154
DORIS, J.J., 124,166
DORRIS SOVEREIGN REMEDY CO., 166
DORRIS, J.J., 166,124
DORSEY - SEE ALLEN & DORSEY
DOUGLAS, R.H., 124
DOUGLASS & SON, 86
DOUGLASS, A.C., 86
DOUGLASS, ANNA, 86
DOUGLASS, GEO. M.D., 166
DOUGLASS, L.W., 86
DOUGLASS, M.E., 86
DOUGLASS, M.R., 86
DOW & SKINNER, 86
DOW, J. NEIL, 86
DR BOPP'S HAMBURGER STOMACH BITTER, 61,187
DR DECOURSEY IRISH LINIMENT, 167
DR DUNLOP'S ANCHOR BITTERS, 151,186
DR F.J. HORTENBACH LIFE BITTERS, 187
DR FRENCH BITTERS, 187
DR GREGORIES SCOTCH BITTER, 3,162,187
DR HOOPER'S PENETRATING OIL, 157
DR JOYS BAR COUGH ELIXIR, 160
DR KOEHL'S GERMAN THROAT & LUNG BALSAM, 155,164
DR. MALAKOFF, 184
DR ROLANDER'S SWEDISH LINIMENT, 172
DR SONERAL'S RHEUMATIC CURE, 175
DR WARD'S BLOOD AND STOMACH BITTERS, 187
DR WARD'S LINIMENT, 178
DR WARD'S MEDICAL CO., 181
DR WARNER'S MINNESOTA TONIC, 177

DR WEYEHGRAM, H., 184
DRECHSLER, F.X., 124
DREIS & MESSING, 124
DREIS & MITSCH, 86,124
DREIS, P.J., 124
DRULLARD, MRS. M.B., 86
DRULLARD, SOLOMON, 86
DRYER, 21
DUBE, E.P., 86
DUFAUD WINE & LIQUOR CO., 22
DUFRESNE, A.D. & CO., 166
DUKES, J.B., 154
DULUTH CITY WHISKEY (SMITH), 69
DUPONT, J.G., 86
DUPONT, J.W., 22,86
DURHAM, G.H., 154
DUTCH CHEMICAL CO., 166
DUTCH COUGH SYRUP CO., 166
DVORACEK, J.F., 86
DWYER, R.H., 87
DYE, A.M., 86

EAGLE DRUG CO., 87
EAGLE DRUG STORE, 125
EATON & CO., R.D., 154
EATON CHEMICAL CO., 154
EBERHARD & WASSER, 87
EC - ZENE CO., 166
ECKSTEIN, E.J., 87
ECLIPSE DRUG CO., 125
EDWARDS, D.E., 155
EDWARDS, E.H., 125
EGBERT, H.G., 125
EGGERT, FRED, 58
EHRENHOLM & TURNER, 87
EHRENHOLM, C.A., 87
ELECTRIC LINE DRUG STORE - SEE BIGELOW
EISLER, ADOLPH, 22
ELK'S DELIGHT RYE, 68
ELLIOTT, C.H. & BRENNAN, F.E., 23
ELLIS, D.W., 87
ELLIS, MRS. M.L., 166
ELMQUIST DRUG CO., 125
ELMQUIST, ALDOR, 125
ELMQUIST, J.G., 125
ELSCHLAGER & HASER, 23
EMERSON AVE. DRUG STORE, 87
EMMERT, L.Z., 125
EMPRESS DRUG STORE, 125
ENDICOTT PHARMACY, 125
ENGELKA - SEE NELSON & ENGELKA
ENGELKE - SEE BORATH & ENGELKE
ENGELS, EUGENE, 70
ENGLUND, D.C., 87, 125
ENTRUP & SELLS, 125
ENTRUP, L.F., 125
EPSTEIN, L. & CO., 58
ERDEL, THOMAS, 71
ERICSON - SEE GLADER & ERICSON
ERICKSON - SEE JOHNSON & ERICKSON
ERKEL - SEE BREDE & ERKEL
ERKEL, A.G., 87
ERNST, MRS. J.A., 155
ERNST, O.A., 125
ESCH, JACOB, 58

ESTERLEY, T.W., 87
ESTERLY MEDICINE MFG. CO., 155,164
ETTER - SEE VAWTER & ETTER
EUREKA DRUG STORE, 87
EVANS - SEE SCHUNEMAN & EVANS
EVENSON, C.H., 125
EWING, W.B., 125
EXCELSIOR DRUG CO., 87
EXPO PHARMACY, 125

FABER & BROWN, 125
FABER, F.W., 125
FABER, F.W. & CO., 125
FAMILY DRUG STORE, 87, 112
FAMILY LIQUOR STORE (DIEMERT), 71
FAMILY LIQUOR STORE (ROBITSHEK), 32
FAMILY MEDICINE CO., 167
FARBER, A., 125
FARWELL - SEE NOBEL & FARWELL
FEDERAL LIQUOR STORE, 50
FEELY, MARY & CROCKER, FRED, 155
FREIERABEND, MAX, 167
FEILZER, JOHN A., 23
FEMCURA MEDICINE CO., 167
FERNOLINE CHEMICAL CO., 167
FERTE, C.E., 87
FERTE, JOSEPH E., 125
FIDELITY WHISKEY, 74
FIELD, SCHLICK & CO., 125
FIEN, U.D., 69
FIESELER, K.L., 125
FINCHES GOLDEN WEDDING RYE, 51
FINEMAN, JULIUS, 18, 23
FINK, B., 67
FINK, MORRIS, 7,58
FISCHER, C.F., 87
FISCHER, E.T., 164
FISCHER, R.E., 155
FISHER CHEMICAL CO., 167
FISHER, W.F., 125
FISHER, W.N., 87
FIVE OF HEARTS SALOON - SEE WALIN
FIVE OIL MEDICINE CO., 167
FJELLMAN - SEE OLSON & FJELLMAN
FJELLMAN, CHAS., 23
FJELLMAN, JOHN, 23
FLANAGAN, W.T., 125
FLIESBURG & GOLDNER, 87
FLOUR CITY RYE WHISKEY (WEIL), 46
FLYING CLOUD WHISKEY (SMITH), 69
FOELL, J.J., 87
FOELL, JACOB, 87
FOLTY, G.F., 125
FORCE STOMACH BITTERS, 187
FORD, JAMES, 23
FORD, T.F., 155
FOREST HEIGHTS DRUG STORE, 87, 114

FORNWALT & CO., 87
FORNWALT, M.L., 87
FORTIER, MRS. N.C., 155
FOSTER, 177
FOSTER, C.A., 167
FOURTH AVENUE PHARMACY, 87
FRANK, D.F., 88
FRAYER PHARMACAL CO., 167
FRAYER, ABRAM, 167
FRECH, HERMAN, 24
FREDERICKSON, ALFRED, 24
FREIDLAND, MATHIAS, 88
FREIDLANDER - SEE MATHIS & FRIEDLANDER
FREIDLANDER, SAMUEL, 88
FRENCH - SEE NOBEL & FRENCH
FREY, G.R., 125
FRIEDMANN, F.C., 125
FRISCO COUGH SYRUP, 159
FROST & AKERS, 126
FROST & BROWN, 126
FROST & CO., B.C., 88
FROST & CO., 126
FROST, W.A. & CO., 126,167
FROST'S EXPECTORANT & COUGH BALSAM, 167
FROST'S ROSE AMANDINE CREAM, 167
FROST'S RUM & QUININE LOTION, 167
FRY, CHRISTIAN, 126
FUCH, E.J., 126
FUCHS, ANTHONY, 126
FUCHS, ANTHONY & SON, 126
FULLER & MERRILL, 88
FULLERTON, B.B. - SEE MINNEAPOLIS PHARMACY

GALE, C.F., 88
GALUSHE & SCHULZE, 88
GAMBLE & LUDWIG, 88
GAMBLE, J.S., 88
GARDINER, THOMAS, 88
GARFIELD PHARMACY, 88
GAUGHRAN BROS., 167
GEBHARD, E.C., 167
GEISENHEYNER, WM. O. & CO., 127
GEISERT, T.B., 127
GEISSEL - SEE HALL GEISSEL
GEM DRUG STORE - SEE HUHN
GENTSCH - SEE HAGAN & GENTSCH
GERICKE, J.T. DRUG CO., 126
GERMAN BEER HALL - SEE J.A. FEILZER
GERMAN FAMILY MEDICINES, 167
GERMAN MEDICINE CO., 155
GERMANIA BREWING ASSN., 14
GERMANIA DRUG STORE - SEE GROTEFEND
GETTY - SEE MCMASTERS & GETTY
GETTY'S ARCADE PHARMACY, 127
GETTY, W.S., 127
GIBBENS, V.L., 167

GIBBS - SEE BERNARD & GIBBS
GIBSON (SIMON), 65
GIBSON WHISKEY (PERKINS), 62
GIFFORD - SEE PEABODY & GIFFORD
GIFFORD - SEE REGAN & GIFFORD
GIFFORD, HENRY, 127
GILHOOLEY IRISH LINIMENT CO., 167
GILMORE, J.P., 88
GILMORE, J.R., 88
GIRBACH, G.F., 155
GJESDAHL, SVEN, 88
GLADER, & ERICSON, 24
GLADER, P.M., 7,24
GLEWWE, JOHN, 167
GLOBE COMPOUNDING CO., 167
GLOBE WINE CO., 24,187
GLUCK, CHARLES, 24
GLUCK, F.P. & CO., 24
GLYCOID, 173
GOES, JOHN, 88
GOLD COIL CHEMICAL WORKS, 167
GOLD MINE JUG HOUSE, 71
GOLD MINE, THE, 72
GOLDBERG - KEILBRON CO., 127
GOLDEN LINK (ABERLE), 51
GOLDEN MEDICINE CO., 178
GOLDEN OIL RHEUMATIC LINIMENT, 166
GOLDEN RULE, 127
GOLDEN WEDDING (BROWN), 16
GOLDEN WEDDING RYE (ABERLE), 51
GOLDMAN, ISAAC, 24
GOLDMAN, LOUIS, 49
GOLDMAN, M.R., 24
GOLDNER - SEE FLIESBURG & GOLDNER
GOLDNER, J.E., 88
GONNIEA, G.D.W., 127
GOOD, ELMER, 167
GOODRICH, GEORGE, 175
GOODRICH & JENNINGS, 88,175,176
GOODSELL, W.R., 88
GOODWIN & CO., THURSTON, 155
GOPHER, 158
GOPHER DRUG STORE, 88
GOPHER RYE (BROWN), 17
GORDON - SEE JENKS & GORDON
GORMLEY & CO., 88
GORMLEY & MORAN, 88
GORMLEY, JOHN 88
GOTHMANN - SEE BASTYR & GOTHMANN
GOTWALD, G.A., 127
GOULD - SEE LINCOLN & GOULD
GOULD & SON, J. FRANK, 88
GOULD, J. FRANK, 88
GOWDEY & OBERT, 88
GRABEN & CO., OTTO H., 89
GRABEN DRUG CO., 127
GRABEN, O.H., 127
GRANBERG, MARTIN, 155

GRAND AVE. PHARMACY CO.,
127
GRATTON, TIMOTHY, 156
GRAVES BROS., 24
GRAVES, G.H., 89
GRAY - SEE GREELEY & GRAY
GRAY & CO., T.K.,
89,156,78
GRAY & HOFFLIN, 90,156
GRAY BROS. (J.D. & T.K.),
89
GRAY, ORRIN, 156
GRAY, THOMAS K., 89
GREAT FRENCH EYE WATER,
173
GREAT MORMAN REMEDY CO.,
167
GREAT NORTHERN BOTTLING
CO., 8
GREELEY & GRAY, 90
GREEN BRIER (BROWN), 16
GREEN, C.G., 24
GREWE, A.C. & CO., 167
GRIESEL BROS., 73
GRIFFIN & DAY, 90
GRIFFIN, TRUMAN, 90
GRIGGS AROMATIC BITTERS,
187
GRINNELL, ANDREW J., 90
GRISWOLD & CO., 127
GROOCOCK, SAMUEL & SONS,
90
GROSS, LOUIS, 28
GROTEFEND, AUGUST H.F.,
90
GRUENTER, AUGUST, 59
GRUWELL - SEE HILL &
GRUWELL
GUARANTY MORPHINE CURE
CO., 156
GUERNSEY, A.T., 127
GUERNSEY, A.T. & SON,
127,167
GUIDE TO MINNESOTA
BITTERS,
GUIWITS & JONES, 90
GUIWITS, F.M., 90
GWEN - SEE BISHOP & GWEN

HAASE DRUG CO., 127
HADDEN & MOWAT, 90
HAGAN & GENTSCH, 127
HAGGENMILLER, CHARLES, 59
HAINERT DRUG CO., 90
HAINERT, F.H., 90,127
HAISH, C.F., 90
HALL & GEISSEL, 128
HALL & KRAFT, 128
HALL, A.T., 127
HALL, ANDREW & CO., 25
HALL, W.W., 128
HALLIDAY'S,   DR.   E.B.
BLOOD PURIFIER CO., 168
HAWTHORNE, E.P., 91
HAYNER DISTILLING
COMPANY, 59
HAYNES, S.C., 91
HAZEL GROVE BOURBON
(BOWLIN), 57
HAZEL MFG. CO., 128
HAZLE, W.H., 168
HEAL DRUG CO., 156,168
HEAL, J.N., 168
HEBERHART, C.E., 128
HEDDERLY, A.H. & CO., 91

HEDDERLY, EDWIN, 91
HEDDERLY, G.W., 91
HEEDELS, AVTON, 91
HEIBERG, E.B., 91
HEIMANN & CO., L.C., 91
HEINZEL, HENRY, 128
HEITZMAN, FRANK, 128
HELLEMAN, 175
HELLER, B., 25
HELLER, C.T., 128
HENDRICKS, W.E., 128
HENDRICKSON, F.C., 156
HENING, J.C., 128
HENNEPIN AVENUE PHARMACY,
91
HENNEPIN PHARMACY, 91
HENRICHS - SEE SWEET &
HENRICHS
HERBERT & CO., 128
HERBERT BROS., 128
HERRICK, FRANK H., 91
HERRMANN & HAUGAN, 91
HERRMANN, A.B., 91
HERZ, A., 59,67
HESSELBERG, EYVIND, 91
HICKMAN, F.M., 91
HICKS - SEE ROSE & HICKS
HICKS & CO., WM. K., 91
HICKS, WM. K., 91
HIGGENS, ASKE, CO., 71
HIGGINS, GEORGE E., 91
HIGH SCHOOL DRUG STORE,
92
HIGHLAND PARK DRUG STORE,
91,109
HIGHOUSE, J.C., 128
HIGMAN, L.F., 156
HILL, A & GRUWELL, C., 92
HILLEMAN'S AMERICAN
CHICKEN   CHOLERA   CURE,
175
HILLSDALE DISTILLERY CO.,
59
HINKLEY, DR. F.B., 187
HINKLEY, J.W., 92
HINRICH - SEE KOEHLER &
HINRICH
HIPPLER & COLLIER, 128
HIRCHMAN & CO., 59
HIRSCHMAN, A., 187
HIRSCHNER, V.A., 128
HOFF & HARRIS, 25
HOFFARTH, JOS., 74
HOFFLIN - SEE GRAY &
HOFFLIN
HOFFLIN & GRAY, 92
HOFFLIN - THOMPSON DRUG
CO., 92
HOFFLIN, J.R., 156
HOFFLIN, JOSEPH R., 92
HOFFLIN, JOSEPH R. & CO.,
92
HOFFLINS DRUG STORE, 92
HOFFMAN - SEE BEBB &
HOFFMAN
HOFFMAN - SEE SPORRONG &
HOFFMAN
HOFFMAN, C.A., 25
HOFFS GERMAN LINIMENT,
175,176
HOLCOMB & MAGNUSON, 129
HOLCOMB, F.A., 129
HOLLINGWORTH, F.S., 74
HOLLISTER DISTILLING, 60
HOLMES BROS., 93
HOLMGREN DRUG CO., 93

HOLSTEIN & MILLER, 70
HOLZSCHUH, JOHN J., 93
HOMEOPATHIC PHARMACY -
SEE STARK
HOMEOPATHIC PHARMACY -
SEE GARDINER
HOOKWITH & WEED, 25
HOOPER & MATTSON, 93
HORN & KISTLER, 93
HORN, NICHOLAS, 168
HORN, S.J., 93
HORRIGAN & MCCOLL, 129
HORTENBACH, F.J.,
156,185,187
HOSKINS, A., 93
HOSKINS, C.A., 129
HOUSE OF ST. CROIX, 60
HOVORKA, W.J., 129,168
HOWARD CHEMICAL CO., 156
HOWARD, GEORGE M., 93
HOYT MEDICINE CO., 168
HUB, THE, 73
HUFFMAN HANSEN DRUG CO.,
156
HUGHES & SWEET, 93
HUGHES, L.G., 156
HUGHES, WALTER J., 93
HUHN & CO., GEORGE E., 93
HUHN, C.H., 93
HUHN, GEORGE E., 93
HULBERG, A.O., 93
HUMBOLT'S 1880 RYE
(BOWLIN), 56,57
HUNT, P.C., 93
HURD, DR. W.J. MNFG. CO.,
168
HURD, G.E., 93
HURLBUT, E.B., 168
HURLEY BROS., 60,168,185
HURLEY BROS. BITTERS,
185,187
HUTCHINS MEDICINE CO.,
168
HYGENOL CO., 156

INDIAN HAIR BALSAM - SEE
WM. CLEVENGER
INTERNATIONAL BEER HALL,
25,27
INTERNATIONAL FOOD CO.,
157
INTERNATIONAL STOCK FOOD
CO. (M.W. SAVAGE), 153
ITALIA DRUG CO., 129
IVES & CO., G.A., 93

JAAX, HUBERT, 25
JAAX, N., 187
JACK SILVER BOURBON
(BENZ), 54
JACOBS, MRS. MARY, 157
JACOBSEN, JACOB, 93
JAGGER - SEE TICHNOR &
JAGGER
JAMES, J.P.R., 157
JANIKULA, PAUL, 26
JANSEN MEDICINE CO., DR.,
157
JAPANENE PILE CURE CO.,
168
JAPANESE MEDICAL CO., 168
JELINEK, J.P. & CO., 129
JENKS - SEE DAY & JENKS
JENKS & BIRD, 129
JENKS & GORDON, 129

JENKS, J.R., 94,129
JENNER, 187
JENNER, B-ESSENCE OF
LIFE, 157
JENNER, BERNHARD, 157,187
JENNINGS & DAMM, 94
JENSEN, H.P., 129
JOCKEY CLUB RYE
(MICHAUD), 61
JOHNSON - SEE THOMPSON &
JOHNSON
JOHNSON & CO., P., 94
JOHNSON & ERICKSON, 94
JOHNSON & HARRAH, 94
JOHNSON, CHAS., 26
JOHNSON, H. MARTIN DRUG
CO., 129
JOHNSON, MATT J., 168
JOHNSTON - SEE SAVORY &
JOHNSTON
JOHNSTREET WINE & BRANDY
CO., 68
JONES - SEE GUIWITS &
JONES
JONES PHARMACY, O.V., 94
JONES, HENRY, 94
JOSEPH, J.P., 94
JUDD - SEE CABLE & JUDD

KA-DO-RA, 169
KADLEC & DENEK, 94
KAMI-KU-RI MEDICINE CO.,
157
KAMPFF & CO., GEORGE, 94
KARRAS DRUG CO., 130
KAY, E.M., 94
KEABER, H.P., 157
KELLAN, A.B., 130
KELLEY CURTIS CO., 169
KELLOGG - SEE BOND &
KELLOGG
KELLY & STEINMETZ, 26
KELLY & THOMPSON, 94
KELLY, JAMES L., 26,48
KEMPE, J. & CO., 72
KENDRICK, DR. CHEMICAL
CO., 169
KENNEDY, SUFFEL &
ANDREWS, 157,187
KENNY, R.A., 157
KENSUFAN STOMACH BITTER,
187
KENTUCKY CLUB, 72
KENWOOD PHARMACY, 94
KENYON, E.S. & CO., 130
KENYON, T.N., 157
KEPIER, E.E., 130
KERKER & SON, F.X., 94
KERKER, F.X., 94
KERSTEN, H.T., 94
KEYES - SEE SPINK & KEYES
KILGORE, WILLIAM, 94
KIMBALL - SEE SMITH &
KIMBALL
KING & CO., WILLIAM D.,
94
KING & PATTERSON, 94
KING, E.L., 184
KINPORTS, JOHN H., 94
KIRKPATRICK & BOURQUIN,
157
KISSEL, DANIEL C., 130
KISTLER - SEE HORN &
KISTLER
KISTLER - SEE SWEET &
KISTLER

KISTLER, C.M., 94
KJELGREN, MAURITZ, 26
KLASSY & SEIBEL, 26
KLEIN, ISRAEL & PAUNTZ, IGNATZ, 26
KLENERT BROS., 94
KLINE - SEE PATTERSON & KLINE
KLINE & BURGER, 94
KLINE, A.J., 94,157
KLINGSPORN, THEORDORE, 94
KLUNGS MFG. CO., 157
KNAPP - SEE SCOFIELD & KNAPP
KNAPP & CO., 157
KNAPP, W.B., 169
KNICKERBOCKER DRUG C., 130
KNOWLTON'S LINIMENT, 162
KNOX BROS., 94
KNOX DRUG CO., 130
KNUDSEN, JAS., 130
KO-HI BITTERS, 169,188
KO-HI-NOR, 169
KOCH, L.W., 95
KOEHLER & HINRICH, 169,185,187
KOLL, J.L., 158
KONDON MFG. CO., 158
KOZLOWSKI & WIRKUS, 95
KRAFT - SEE HALL & KRAFT
KREGEL, W.C., 130
KRENT - SEE BRENCK & KRENT
KREYCHIE, J.L., 130
KRUCKEBERG, H.C., 95
KRUSE, E.A., 170
K.S.&A. (KENNEDY, SUFFEL & ANDREWS), 95
KUHL, B. & CO., 60
KULT, FREDERICK, 130
KURTH, A.F., 130

LA FAVOR MEDICINE CO., 170
LADNER BROS., 72
LAKE STREET DRUG CO., 95
LAKE STREET PHARMACY, 95
LAKE, W.E., 95
LAMB, MRS. L.M., 158
LAMBERT - SEE NORGREN & LAMBERT
LAMBERT, EDWARD, 95
LAMBERT, GEORGE M., 130
LAMBIE, 130
LAMBIE & BACON, 130
LAMBIE & BETHUNE, 130
LAMBIE & CO., BETHUNE, 96
LAMBIE & CONDIT, 84,130
LANDON & BURCHARD, 178,181
LANDSFELDT MEDICAL SKIN TONIC, 158
LANDSFELDT MEDICAL WASH CO., 158
LANE & SUMMERS, 95
LANE, RUFUS, H., 95
LANES DRUG STORE, 95
LANTZ & SON, HENRY, 95
LANTZ, HENRY, 95
LAPAUL, G.F., 95,158
LAPENOTIERE & CO., 96
LAPENOTIERE, E.M., 95
LARRABEE, B.H. PHARMACY, 96
LARRABEE, R.C., 96

LARSON, A.E., 96
LASHER - SEE ARNOLD & LASHER
LASHER - SEE SCOTT & LASHER
LASHER, C.W., 96
LATZ, F.W., 96
LATZ, H. & F.E., 96
LATZ, HENRY E., 96
LAVORIS CHEMICAL CO., 158
LAWS & STEIN, 96
LAWS DRUG CO., 96
LAWS, YNGVAR, 96
LAWSON, A.A., 130
LEAL, J.B., 170
LEE, J.D., 158
LEE, OLOF, 130
LEE, WM., 130
LEHMANN, J.A., 130
LEHMANN, J.H., 130
LEIGH, C.E., 96
LEITHHEAD DRUG CO., 176
LENIHAN, MALACHY, 27
LEONARD & CO., W.H., 96
LEONARD, W.H., 96
LESTERBROOK RYE (HELLER), 25
LEVY, B.L., 96
LEVY, HENRY, 130
LEWIS, G.H., 158
LEXINGTON DRUG STORE, 96
LIBBY - SEE SPRAGUE & LIBBY
LIBBY, CHARLES H., 130
LIDDELL, M.B., 130
LIEBIG'S CORN CURE, 156
LIFE BITTERS, 187
LIFE WONDER CO., 158
LIGHTNING CORN ERADICATOR, 156
LIGHTNING DRUG CO., 170
LIGHTNING OIL CO., 146,158
LILJA, GUSTAV, 96
LILLIS, M.A. & CO., 130
LILLYBECK, P.L., 130
LINCOLN & GOULD, 96
LINCOLN, L.T., 96
LINDBERG, C.V., 132
LINDEN HILLS DRUG STORE, 96
LINDSAY & POMEROY, 96
LINDSTROM, FRANK, 27
LINKER, J.L., 27,49
LINKERS OLD RESERVE, 27
LION DRUG STORE, 96 114,132,141
LION PHARMACY, 96
LIQUID CAMPHOLINE, 156
LITTON, EDWARD E., 96
LITTON, EDWARD E. & CO., 96
LIVINGSTONE, ANDREW, 97
LOCK HORN BITTERS, 24,188
LODGORD, OLE, 27
LOEB, L.S. & CO., 187
LOEW, WM. E., 132
LONDON DRUG CO., 132
LONERGAN'S DRUG STORE, 97
LOUGHLIN & CO., H.R., 97
LOW PRICE LIQUOR STORE, 60
LOWERY HILL DRUG STORE, 97
LOY - SEE WOOSTER & LOY
LUCAS, A.C., 158

LUDINGTON, T.E., 132
LUDINGTON, THOMAS E., 97
LUDWIG - SEE GAMBLE & LUDWIG
LUDWIG, 48
LUEDERS & CO., 132
LUEDERS, G.H., 132
LUEDERS, L.H., 132
LUEDERS, MRS. SUSAN, 132
LUND - SEE NORDEEN & LUND
LUND, J.G., 97
LUNDBERG - SEE SAMPSON & LUNDBERG
LUNDBERG, ANDREW, 27
LUNELL & SEARLE, 132
LUNKENHEIMER, P.T., 132
LUTZ - SEE STUART & LUTZ
LUTZ, PETER C., 132
LYFE'S ONE-DER CO., 158
LYMAN - SEE MELENDY & LYMAN
LYMAN & TUCKER, 97
LYMAN & WILLIAMS, 97
LYMAN BROS., 97
LYING & CO., K., 97
LYONS - SEE SCHIFFMANN & LYONS
LYONS & HAWLEY, 132
LYONS & TICKNOR, 132
LYONS, ADAM, 132

MACALESTER PHARMACY, 132
MACRAY DRUG CO., 132
MADSON, HANS & CO., 132
MAEDER, CARL, 27
MAGNETIC PAIN KILLER CO., 158
MAGNUSON - SEE HOLCOMB & MAGNUSON
MAGNUSON DRUG CO., 133
MAGNUSON PHARMACY, 133
MAGNUSON, E.C., 132
MAGNUSON, F.A., 132
MAGNUSON, H., 4,27,50
MAILER & CO., 97
MAJERUS BROS., 97
MALTESE OLD TOM GIN (BENZ), 53
MANN, C.A., 185
MANSUR DRUG CO., 133
MANUFACTURING PHARMACIST CO., 158
MANWARING, J.J., 133
MARCHBANK, WM., 97
MARELIUS & BECKER, 133
MARELIUS, C.R., 133
MARELIUS, MRS. A.C., 133
MARK, JOSEPH, 133
MARK, P., 97
MARK, P.M., 96,97
MARKOE, J.C., 170
MARSDEN, C.B., 133
MARSH, ALANSON H., 97
MARSHALL & CO., 97
MARTI, GEORGE, 133
MARTI, JOHN, 133
MARTIN, H.M. & CO., 185
MARTIN, J.B., 97
MARTTY & SON, 97
MARTTY, SAMUEL, 97
MARYLAND AAA RYE (HURLEY), 60
MARYLAND OLD RYE (METZGER), 61
MASONIC TEMPLE PHARMACY, 93,97

MATHIS & FRIEDLANDER, 98
MATHIS, W.D., 98
MATSCHINGER - SEE BUEGER & MATSCHINGER
MATTHEW, D.J., 133
MATTHEWS, C.M., 98
MATTSON - SEE HOOPER & MATTSON
MAURER, LOUIS, 27
MAXWELL, H.A., 133
MCCALL DRUG CO., 98
MCCALL DRUG CO., IN., 98
MCCLUSKEY, F.A., 158
MCCOLL - SEE HORRIGAN & MCCOLL
MCCOLL, HENRY, 133
MCCONNAN & CO., 178
MCCONNAN & CO., 181,188
MCCONNON'S STOMACH BITTERS, 188
MCCURDY, G.H., 158
MCDONALD PHARMACY, 133
MCKESSON ROBINS, 170
MCLAUGHLIN, A., 133
MCMAHON, H.C., 98
MCMASTERS & GETTY, 133
MCMASTERS, S. RUSSELL, 133
MCMILLAN, T.J., 99
MCNEAR - SEE SCHRODER & MCNEAR
MEACHEM, JOHN M., 98
MEDERINE REMEDY CO., 177
MEDICATED VAPOR CO., 158
MEIER, ERNEST, 98
MELBROOK (ABERLE), 51
MELENDY & LYMAN, 84,98,122
MELGORD & ORBECK, 27
MELGORD, JOHN, 27
MENGELKOCH, H. & CO., 27
MENGELKOCH, JACOB, 28
MENTHO-JELL CO., 176
MERCHANTS PHARMACY, 133
MERRIAN PARK PHARMACY, 133
MERRILL - SEE FULLER & MERRILL
MERWIN DRUG CO., 98
MESSING - SEE DREIS & MESSING
METROPOLITAN DRUG STORE, 98
METROPOLITAN PHARMACY, 98,113
METZGER MEDICINE CO., 158
METZGER, LEWIS, 61,68,187
METZGER, ZIEN, 61,170,187
MEUERER - SEE SANDBERG & MEUERER
MEURER, J.J., 99,158
MEWHIRTER, H.D., 99
MICHAUD BROS., 61
MICROCIDE CHEMICAL CO., 170
MIDDENTS, P.H., 133
MIDDLETON & CO., J.E., 158
MIERKE, E.A., 133
MIKOLAS, ALBERT, 8
MILL SPRINGS RYE (KUHL), 57
MILLER & CO., A.H., 99
MILLER BROS., 28
MILLER, W.H., 99,133
MILLER, WILLIAM H. & SON, 133

MILNE, H.J., 99,133
MINERO CHEMICAL CO., 170
MINNEAPOLIS DRUG CO., 158
MINNEAPOLIS DRY GOODS CO., 99
MINNEAPOLIS MEDICINE CO., 159
MINNEAPOLIS PHARMACY, 99
MINNEAPOLIS PHARMACY, 99,159
MINNEAPOLIS VIAVI CO., 159
MINNEHAHA DRUG CO., 99
MINNEHAHA SPRAY MED. CO., 170
MINNESOTA CLUB, 59,60,61,68
MINNESOTA MEDICAL CO., 159
MINNESOTA OIL OF LIFE CO., 159
MINNESOTA PHARMACEUTICAL MNFG. CO., 170,171
MINNESOTA STATE VETERINARIAN REMEDY CO., 159
MINNESOTA TRANSFER DRUG CO., 133
MINNESOTA VIAVI CO., 159,170
MINNESOTA VIMEDIA CO., 159
MINNETONKA PURE RYE, 24
MISSISSIPPI PHARMACY, 134
M.I.S.T. CO., 170
MITSCH - SEE DREIS & MITSCH
MITSCH, GEO. J. & CO., 134
MODEL DRUG STORE - SEE DRULLARD
MOHL, FRED, 134
MOHN, R.M., 170
MOHR, GEO. H., 61
MONAHAN, J.A., 99
MONAHAN, T.H., 99
MONARCH MEDICINE CO., 159
MONFORT & CO., 61
MONITOR LINIMENT, 155
MONONGAHELA RYE (ZIEN), 69
MOODY, J.H., 99
MOORE & CO., JOSEPH B., 99
MOORE & MUNGER, 99
MORAN - SEE GORMLEY & MORAN
MORAN, J.T., 99
MOREY, A.L., 99,134
MORGAN - SEE ROSE & MORGAN
MORGAN DRUG CO., 99
MORGAN, F.M., 134
MORRISON, FRANK, 134
MORTON, W.H., 134
MOSCOTTE SALOON (SODINI), 38
MOSS & DAVIS, 20,28
MOSS, ALBERT, 20
MOSS BROS., 20,28
MOSS, CHARLES, 20
MOSS, JESSE, 20
MOTOR LINE DRUG STORE - SEE BIGELOW

MOUNTAIN PANTHER, CHIEF, 159
MOWAT - SEE HADDEN & MOWAT
MUELLER, C., 99
MULLER, E.J., 134
MUNCH, F.A., 134
MUNGER - SEE MOORE & MUNGER
MUNNS, J.F., 99
MURNANE GERMICIDE CO., 170
MURPHY, F.P., 28
MURPHY'S KIDNEY & LIVER CURE, 178
MURRISON & CO., JAMES, 99
MURRISON, JAMES, 159
MUSSETTER - SEE WAMPLER & MUSSETTER
MUSSETTER, L. & W.A., 134
MUSSETTER, LATHROP, 134
MUSSETTER, W.A., 134

NAGEL, F.J., 99
NAPA VALLEY WINE CO., 28,29,185
NATIONAL HERB CO., 159
NATURE'S LIVER RENOVATOR, 167
NATURE'S LUNG ELIXIR, 167
NEFF & ROSENQUIST, 134
NELSON - SEE ARNEBERG & NELSON
NELSON & BOHLIG, 7,29
NELSON & CO., E., 100
NELSON & ENGELKA, 134
NELSON, A.C., 29
NELSON, ERICK, 29
NELSON, G.W., 100,134
NELSON, J.T., 159
NELSON, J.W., 134
NELSON, MRS. JENNIE, 134
NELSON, N.P., 100
NELSON, NELS, 28,29,47,100
NELSON, O.H., 100
NELSON, WALTER, 134,170
NERVOSUS, 174
NEW STORE PHARMACY, THE, 100
NEWELL & CO., EL. L., 100
NEWELL, E.L. & CO., 134
NICHOLLS BALSAM, 161
NICHOLS, B.H., 100
NICHOLS MEDICINE CO., 185
NICOLLET DRUG STORE, 87,100,105
NICOLLET HOUSE DRUG STORE, 111
NIERENHAUSEN, J.N., 29,48
NIX BITTERS, 188
NOAH'S ARK, THE STORY, 8
NOBLE & FARWELL, 134
NOBLE & FRENCH, 100,134
NOBLE, W.W., 134
NOBLES & COOK, 134
NONPAREIL RYE (PERKINS), 62
NORA PHARMACY, 100
NORDEN CLUB RYE (SANDELL), 64
NORDEEN & LUND, 29
NORGREN & LAMBERT, 100
NORGREN MEDICINE CO., 100,159

NORGREN, C.E., 178
NORGREN, G.P., 100
NORTH STAR LIQUOR CO., 39
NORTH STAR LUNG & THROAT BALSAM, 159,162
NORTH STAR WINE CO., 30
NORTHERN VIMEDIA CO., 160
NORTHFIELD BOTTLING WORKS, 30
NORTHWESTERN DRUG CO., 134,170
NORTHWESTERN MEDICINE CO., 170
NORTHWESTERN MEDICINE CO., 187
NORTHWESTERN WINE CO., 160
NOTHAKEL, MATHIAS, 31
NOVELTY DRUG STORE, 100
NOYES BROS. & CUTLER, 134,172
N.W. MED CO. BITTERS, 188
NYE, ALEXANDER M., 100
NYE, WALLACE G., 100

O'DONNELL & CO., 30
O'HERN, WM. F., 30
OAK LAKE DRUG STORE, 100
OAK PARK DRUG STORE, 81,100
OAK STREET DRUG STORE, 100
OAK STREET PHARMACY, 100
OBERG, CARL E., 100
OBERT - SEE GOWDEY & OBERT
OGG BROS., 100
OGG, J.J., 100
OHDE, L.A., 135
OHLHOUSE, B.N., 187
OLANDER, M.L., 100
OLD BETTS BITTERS, 188
OLD BLUE RIBBON (BENZ), 52-55
OLD DAYS (BENZ), 52-55
OLD KENTUCKY BITTERS, 188,189
OLD KING COLE, 50
OLD MONOGRAM RYE (BROWN), 16
OLD RED STILL BOURBON (PERKINS), 62
OLD SHIELDS, 73
OLD ST. CROIX RYE, 60
OLD SUGAR LOAF RYE, 74
OLD TAYLOR (BROWN), 16
OLD WILSON PURE RYE, 24
OLD YUCCA RYE (THEOBALD), 65
OLIMB, I.E., 30
OLIVER & SHIPMAN, 100
OLIVER AVENUE DRUG STORE, 100
OLIVER, J.E., 100
OLIVER, J.M., 100
OLSON - SEE THOMPSON & OLSON
OLSON & CO., S.E., 100
OLSON & FJELLMAN, 30
OLSON & RYBERG, 30
OLSON, A.H., 135
OLSON, F.L., 30
OLSON, H.B., 172
OMEGA BITTERS, 188
OPERA HOUSE DRUG CO., 100

ORBECK, EDWARD, 31
ORIENTAL DRUG STORE, 101
ORIENTAL HERB BITTERS, 188
ORIENTAL REMEDY CO., 172
OSWALD, HENRY, 31
OSWALD, J.C., 31,50
OTTO, E.A., 135
OUSDAHL, EVEN, 101
OVERLOCK BROS., 101
OWL DRUG STORE, 81,101
OZOFORM CO., 160
OZONET, 146

PABODY & WHITAKER, C.S., 101
PAEGEL, GEORGE R., 135
PAEHLER - SEE COLBERG & PAEHLER
PALMER - SEE BAKKEN & PALMER
PAN-AMERICAN RYE, 18
PANORAMA DRUG STORE, 101
PARDOE & CO., C.M., 101
PARDOE, C.M., 101
PARKER & PROCTOR, 101
PARKER & WESTBY, 135
PARKER BROS., 101
PARKER, F.M., 135,172
PARKER, F.M. & CO., 135
PARKER, J.W., 101
PARMENTER, H.M., 160
PARRANT, PIERRE "PIGS EYE", 7
PARSON, O.M., 101
PARTRIDGE, A.P. & CO., 172
PASTEUR CATARRH REMEDY CO., 172
PASTEUR REMEDIES CO., 172
PARVENU MEDICINE CO., 175
PATTEE, IRVIN, 101
PATTERSON - SEE KING & PATTERSON
PATTERSON & CHILSTROM, 101
PATTERSON & KLINE, 101
PATTY, C.S., 160,172
PATTY, PROF. C.S. HERB REMEDIES, 172
PAULLE, JOSEPH, 28
PAUNTZ - SEE KLEIN & PAUNTZ
PAYNE, G.A., 101
PEABODY & GIFFORD, 101
PEABODY, LYONS & CO., 62
PEABODY, O.M., 101
PECK & RANDALL, 101
PECK, C.C., 101
PEDERSON MERCANTILE CO., 71
PEERLESS CO., 160
PELTZER, H.M., 101
PENNINGTON, HENRY, 101
PEOPLES DRUG CO., 135
PERKINS AMERICAN HERBS, 160
PERKINS, W.L., 62
PERSALL, A.H., 101
PERSIAN TOILET CO., 160
PERSON - SEE ROMAN & PERSON
PERSON, OSCAR, 31
PETERSEN - SEE RUDD & PETERSEN

UNITED STATES DISPENSARY CO., 163
UNIVERSAL STOCK CABINET CO., 163
UNIVERSAL SUPPLY CO., 173
UNIVERSITY DRUG STORE, 110
UPHAM, F.A. & SON, 173
UPHAM, F.A., 173
UPHAM'S EYE WATER, 173
U.S. CABINET RYE (SMITH), 38

VALLHALA - SEE CHAS. JOHNSON
VALLHALA - SEE C.A. HOFFMAN
VAN BIBBER BITTERS, 189
VAN DUYNE, F. & CO., 140
VAN GIESON, M.M., 163
VANGIESON, EFFIE, 110
VANGIESON, MARCELLUS M., 110
VAN NEST - SEE BABENDRIER & VAN NEST
VAN'S QUICK CURE, 163
VAUGHAN, E.A., 140
VAWTER & ROSE, 140
VAWTER, ROSE & ETTER, 140
VEDELER, JOACHIM, 110
VEGETABLE TONIC BITTERS, 189
VENVE, CHARLES & CO., 140
VERNON, MRS. E.M., 140
VERNON, P.C., 140
VEYRAC, J.M., 163
VIAVI CO., 173
VIMEDIA CO., 173
VIVIDUS CO., 163
VOEGELI BROS., 78,82,110,163
VOEGELI BROS. DRUG CO., 110
VOEGELI BROS. DRUG CO. (INC.), 110
VOGUE, F.S., 110,173
VOLK REMEDY CO., 164
VON ROHR'S REMEDIES, 184

WA HOO REMEDY CO., 164
WABASHA DRUG STORE, 140
WAGNER, ANTON, 140
WAIDT, PAUL, 42
WALIN, CHAS., 42
WALKER MEDICINE CO., 173
WALKER, GEORGE, 173
WALLA VALLEY WINE HOUSE, 42
WALLEN, A.J., 110
WALLS, JRS. G., 164
WALTHERS, DR. E., 140
WAMPLER & CO., 111
WAMPLER & MUSSETTER, 140
WAMPLER, A.J., 111,140
WANG, OLAUS, 43
WANOUS, J.A., 111
WARDS MEDICAL CO., DR., 178,181
WARDE, A.G., 164
WARK - SEE BIRD & WARK
WARMELIN, GUSTAV, 43
WARNER'S MINNESOTA TONIC, 177
WASHBURN BROS., 111

WASHBURN, M.E., 111
WASHINGTON LOTION, 154
WASHINGTON SCHOOL DRUG STORE, 84,111,154
WASSER, 111
WATERBURY, E.M., 111
WATHNE, OSCAR, 140
WATKINS, CHARLES, 111
WATKINS, J.R. PLAINVIEW, MN, 178,181
WATKINS, J.R. - WINONA, MN, 181
WATKINS, J.R. MEDICAL CO., 177,178,181
WAY, J.R., 140
WEBB, J.W., 140
WEBBER, B.E., 111
WEBSTER & CHURCHILL, 111,164
WEBSTER CHEMICAL CO., 185
WECHSLER, HYMAN, 140
WEIL & GARDNER, 45
WEIL, BENJAMIN, 43
WEIL, CHARLES, 43
WEIL, HERMANN, 43
WEIL, ISAAC, 43
WEIL, ISAAC & SONS, 45
WEIL, ISAAC & SONS, INC., 45
WEIL, JONAS, 45
WEIL, WILLIAMS, 45
WEILER, NIC & SON, 66
WEINHOLD BROS., 112
WEINHOLD BROS., 164
WEINHOLD BROS. & COOPER, 113
WEINHOLD DRUG CO., 112
WEINHOLD, F.C., 113
WEINHOLD, E.H., 113
WEITER, F.W., 141
WELLER, J.H., 113
WELLS, J.C., 141
WELZ-MANGLER & CO., 66
WENDT, S.M., 113
WENNER, HERMANN
WERRICK, HENRY, 174
WEST END DRUG STORE, 113
WEST END PHARMACY, 113,141
WEST HOTEL DRUG STORE, 113

WEST SIDE PHARMACY, 141
WEST, C.E., 113
WESTBY - SEE PARKER & WESTBY
WESTBY, SEVER, 141
WESTERN AVENUE PHARMACY, 113
WESTERN CONSOLIDATED DISTILLING CO., 47
WESTHEIMER, FERDINAND & SONS, 52,66
WET GOODS STORE, 147
WEYEHGRAM, DR. H., 184
WHEELER'S SARSAPARILLA, 164
WHITAKER - SEE PABODY & WHITAKER
WHITAKER - SEE SAVORY & WHITAKER
WHITAKER & HESLER, 113
WHITCOMB, S.O., 113
WHITE HOUSE DEPARTMENT STORE, 141
WHITE ROSE RYE (BOWLIN), 56,57
WICKS, W.G., 141
WILKES, A.P., 113,141
WILLIAMS - SEE LYMAN & WILLIAMS
WILLIAMS & STAPLETON, 141
WILLIAMS DRUG CO., 113
WILLIAMS, J.M., 113
WILLIAMS, J.W., 113
WILLIAMS, R.E., 114
WILLIAMS, R.S., 164
WILLIAMS, U.G., 114
WILLMERT, G.A. DRUG CO., 141
WILSON BROS., 114
WILSON, E.B., 114
WILSON, E.Y., 114
WILSON, S.J., 114
WINCOTT, R.T., 141
WINCOTT, R.T. & CO., 141
WINSLOW, N.A., 114
WIRKUS - SEE KOZLOWSKI & WIRKUS
WISHARD & HILL, 114
WITTE, B.J. & CO., 141
WITTICH & GLEASON, 114
WITTICH, M.H., 114
WOERNER, CAROLINE, 141

WOLD - SEE SCHELDRUP & WOLD
WOLD'S TONIC BITTERS, 189
WOLD, O.O., 187
WOLD, OSCAR O., 141
WOLFF, ADOLPH, 47
WOLFRUM, G.A., 141
WOLFRUM, MRS. CHARLES, 114
WOLFRUM, MRS. EMILY, 114
WOLFT, W.H., 141
WOOLSEY - PRINCELL CO., 141
WOOLSEY, A.L., 141
WOOSTER - SEE BUNDY & WOOSTER
WOOSTER & LOY, 114
WORKMAN, H.A., 114
WORKMANN & PRIEDEMANN, 114,141
WORKMANN, H.A., 141
WORLD MEDICAL CO., 164
WRIGHT MEDICINE CO., 164,174
WYETH, JNO & BRO. (INC.), 142
WYLLIE - SEE DINWOOD & WYLLIE

YERXA, F.R. & CO., 142
YOST, FRANK, 142
YOST, FRANK C., 114
YOUND & TUCKER, 142
YOUNG-PATTERSON & CO., 114,185

Z-MEX-O-CO., 174
ZIEGLER, J.S., 174
ZIEN, J.P., 185
ZIMMERMANN, B. & E., 142
ZIMMERMANN, E. & CO., 142
ZIMMERMANN, EMIL, 142

DERIVING HIS SUPPORT FROM LITERATURE.
THE NORTH STAR LUNG & THROAT BALSAM. IS A SURE CURE FOR COUGHS & COLDS.

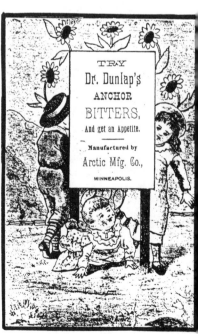

TRY Dr. Dunlap's ANCHOR BITTERS, And get an Appetite. Manufactured by Arctic Mfg. Co., MINNEAPOLIS.

BIBLIOGRAPHY

The following is a partial listing of some of the many books and newspapers used in the preparation of this book:

AMERICAN-GERMAN REVIEW (newspaper),   Dec 1960
ANTIQUE JOURNAL (magazine),   April 1974
BOTTLE MAKERS & THEIR MARKS, by Julian Toulouse, 1971
HISTORY OF GOODHUE COUNTY, by Wood Alley & Co., 1878
HISTORY OF HENNEPIN COUNTY, by Col. J.H. Stevens, 1896
HISTORY OF MINNEAPOLIS, by Isaac Atwater,   1893
HISTORY OF RAMSEY COUNTY & CITY OF ST. PAUL, 1881
HISTORY OF THE BREWING INDUSTRY, by John T. Arnold
ILLUSTRATED HISTORICAL ATLAS OF MINNESOTA,
    by A.T. Andreas   1874
LITTLE SKETCHES OF BIG PEOPLE,
    by R.L. Polk & Co.   1907
MINNEAPOLIS ILLUSTRATED   1889
MINNEAPOLIS INDUSTRIAL EXPOSITION BOOKLET   1886
MINNEAPOLIS - ITS RESOURCES & INDUSTRIES   1902

Miscellaneous resources of the Hill Reference
    Library, The Minneapolis Public Library,
    The St. Paul Public Library, and the
    Minnesota Historical Society
Miscellaneous MINNEAPOLIS & ST. PAUL Newspapers,
                                        1865-1930
MY MINNEAPOLIS, by Carl G.O. Hansen   1956
NORTHWESTERN DRUGGIST JOURNALS   1890-1920
ONE HUNDRED YEARS OF BREWING, A SUPPLEMENT
    TO THE WESTERN BREWER   1903
PAST & PRESENT OF ST. PAUL, MINN,
    by W. B. Hennessy   1906
PROGRESSIVE MEN OF MINNESOTA, by M.B. Shutter 1897
UP & DOWN THE WORLD OR PADDLE YOUR OWN CANOE,
    by A.M. Smith
WINONA AND ITS ENVIRONS ON THE MISSISSIPPI IN
    THE ANCIENT & MODERN DAYS, by L.H. Bunnell 1897

ABOUT THE AUTHOR

RON FELDHAUS IS A 39 YEAR OLD REGISTERED PROFESSIONAL ELECTRICAL ENGINEER ENGAGED IN THE DESIGN OF BUILDING ELECTRICAL SYSTEMS. HE IS A GRADUATE OF THE SOUTH DAKOTA SCHOOL OF MINES AND TECHNOLOGY IN RAPID CITY. RON WAS FIRST EXPOSED TO BOTTLE COLLECTING WHILE EXPLORING THE ABANDONED GOLD MINING CAMPS IN THE BLACK HILLS. HIS MAIN BOTTLE COLLECTING PASSION IS DAKOTA TERRITORY BOTTLES. VERNIE FELDHAUS, RON'S BEST FRIEND AND WIFE, ACTIVELY SUPPORTS HIS HOBBY. VERNIE ALSO ENJOYS ATTENDING BOTTLE CONVENTIONS AND COLLECTS DARK GREEN PERFUMES. RON AND VERNIE'S SON ALSO COLLECTS BOTTLES. THEIR TWIN DAUGHTERS ENGAGE IN THE NORMAL ACTIVITIES OF TEENAGERS, WHICH DO NOT INCLUDE COLLECTING.

AN INVITATION

Many contributors to this book belong to at least one of the two antique bottle collecting clubs in the Twin Cities area. This is your invitation to join and enjoy the hobby. Whether you thrill at the discovery of an old jug or bottle lying half buried in the dirt or seek your treasures at antique shows and shops, you will find an uncommon, very special camaraderie within one or both of these organizations.

Minnesota's First Antique Bottle Club, Inc. was founded in 1967. It is the smaller of the two local clubs, consisting of about 20 members. Meetings are held in members' homes on the first Thursday of each month, September through June. An educational program relating to some aspect of the hobby is usually featured. An extensive reference library is available to members. The club also publishes a monthly newsletter and co-sponsors an annual bottle, stoneware, and advertising show and sale each spring. Dues are $10.00 per year. Correspondence may be sent to 5001 Queen Avenue North, Minneapolis, MN 55430. Phone inquiries may be directed to 612-920-4205.

North Star Historical bottle Association, Inc. was founded in 1970. The club roster contains approximately 50 members. Meetings are held at the YMCA at 4100 28th Avenue South, in Minneapolis (across from Roosevelt High School) on the third Sunday evening of each month, September through June. Monthly activities include a business meeting, a show-and-tell session which usually features one to two dozen old bottles, and an educational program. An award-winning monthly newsletter and access to a club library are included in the $10.00 annual membership fee. North Star is also the second sponsor of the annual bottle, stoneware, and advertising show and sale. Please send correspondence to 3308 32nd Avenue South, Minneapolis, MN 55406. Phone inquiries may be directed to 612-920-4205.

It should be noted that collecting antique bottles is far from just a local activity. Both local clubs belong to the Federation of Historical Bottle Clubs, a national organization with over 100 member clubs throughout the nation. The Federation exists to promote the antique bottle collecting hobby and sponsors numerous activities to this end. Annual conventions are held in conjunction with bottle shows across the country, and a large national exposition featuring 300 to 400 tables of antique bottles and related collectibles is held every four years. The Federation also operates the National Bottle Museum in Ballston Spa, New York, just three miles from Saratoga. The museum is housed in a three-story Victorian mansion and features many fine displays of antique glass.

If collecting and learning about old bottles is a passion, or if you are just mildly curious about the old jar in the basement, please consider this an invitation to join a local bottle club. The hobby welcomes you.